THE WAVE IN THE MIND

The

WAVE
in the MIND

TALKS AND ESSAYS ON
THE WRITER, THE READER,
AND THE IMAGINATION

Ursula K. Le Guin

SHAMBHALA *Boston* 2004

Shambhala Publications, Inc.
Horticultural Hall
300 Massachusetts Avenue
Boston, Massachusetts 02115
www.shambhala.com

9 8 7 6 5 4 3 2

Printed in the United States of America

∞ This edition is printed on acid-free paper that meets the
American National Standards Institute z39.48 Standard.

Distributed in the United States by Random House, Inc.,
and in Canada by Random House of Canada Ltd

Library of Congress Cataloging-in-Publication Data
Le Guin, Ursula K., 1929–
  The wave in the mind: talks and essays on the writer, the
reader, and the imagination/Ursula K. Le Guin—1st ed.
    p. cm
ISBN 1-59030-006-8 (alk. paper)
  1. Le Guin, Ursula K., 1929–   2. Le Guin, Ursula K.,
1929—Authorship. 3. Science fiction—Authorship.
4. Science fiction—History and criticism. I. Title.
PS3562.E42 W38 2004
813'.54—DC21
200301931

In loving memory of Virginia Kidd

As for the *mot juste,* you are quite wrong. Style is a very simple matter: it is all *rhythm.* Once you get that, you can't use the wrong words. But on the other hand here am I sitting after half the morning, crammed with ideas, and visions, and so on, and can't dislodge them, for lack of the right rhythm. Now this is very profound, what rhythm is, and goes far deeper than words. A sight, an emotion, creates this wave in the mind, long before it makes words to fit it; and in writing (such is my present belief) one has to recapture this, and set this working (which has nothing apparently to do with words) and then, as it breaks and tumbles in the mind, it makes words to fit it. But no doubt I shall think differently next year.

—Virginia Woolf
writing to Vita Sackville-West,
16 March 1926

CONTENTS

DISCUSSIONS AND OPINIONS

ON WRITING

PERSONAL MATTERS

INTRODUCING MYSELF

Written in the early nineties as a performance piece, performed a couple of times, and slightly updated for this volume.

I am a man. Now you may think I've made some kind of silly mistake about gender, or maybe that I'm trying to fool you, because my first name ends in *a*, and I own three bras, and I've been pregnant five times, and other things like that that you might have noticed, little details. But details don't matter. If we have anything to learn from politicians it's that details don't matter. I am a man, and I want you to believe and accept this as a fact, just as I did for many years.

You see, when I was growing up at the time of the Wars of the Medes and Persians and when I went to college just after the Hundred Years War and when I was bringing up my children during the Korean, Cold, and Vietnam Wars, there were no women. Women are a very recent invention. I predate the invention of women by decades. Well, if you insist on pedantic accuracy, women have been invented several times in widely varying localities, but the inventors just didn't know how to sell the product. Their distribution techniques were rudimentary and their market research was nil, and so of course the concept just didn't get off the ground. Even with a genius behind it an invention has to find its market, and it seemed like for a long time the idea of women just didn't make it to the bottom line. Models like the Austen and the Brontë were too complicated, and people just laughed at the Suffragette, and the Woolf was way too far ahead of its time.

So when I was born, there actually were only men. People were men. They all had one pronoun, his pronoun; so that's who I am. I am the generic he, as in, "If anybody needs an abortion he will have to go to another state," or "A writer knows which side his bread is buttered on." That's me, the writer, him. I am a man.

Not maybe a first-rate man. I'm perfectly willing to admit that I may be in fact a kind of second-rate or imitation man, a Pretend-a-Him. As a him, I am to a genuine male him as a microwaved fish stick is to a whole grilled Chinook salmon. I mean, after all, can I inseminate? Can I belong to the Bohemian Club? Can I run General Motors? Theoretically I can, but you know where theory gets us. Not to the top of General Motors, and on the day when a Radcliffe woman is president of Harvard University you wake me up and tell me, will you? Only you won't have to, because there aren't any more Radcliffe women; they were found to be unnecessary and abolished. And then, I can't write my name with pee in the snow, or it would be awfully laborious if I did. I can't shoot my wife and children and some neighbors and then myself. Oh to tell you the truth I can't even drive. I never got my license. I chickened out. I take the bus. That is terrible. I admit it, I am actually a very poor imitation or substitute man, and you could see it when I tried to wear those army surplus clothes with ammunition pockets that were trendy and I looked like a hen in a pillowcase. I am shaped wrong. People are supposed to be lean. You can't be too thin, everybody says so, especially anorexics. People are supposed to be lean and taut, because that's how men generally are, lean and taut, or anyhow that's how a lot of men start out and some of them even stay that way. And men are people, people are men, that has been well established, and so people, real people, the right kind of people, are lean. But I'm really lousy at being people, because I'm not lean at all but sort of podgy, with actual fat places. I am untaut. And then, people are supposed to be tough. Tough is good. But I've never been tough. I'm sort of soft and actually sort of tender. Like a good steak. Or like Chinook salmon, which isn't lean and tough but very rich and tender.

But then salmon aren't people, or anyhow we have been told that they aren't, in recent years. We have been told that there is only one kind of people and they are men. And I think it is very important that we all believe that. It certainly is important to the men.

What it comes down to, I guess, is that I am just not manly. Like Ernest Hemingway was manly. The beard and the guns and the wives and the little short sentences. I do try. I have this sort of beardoid thing that keeps trying to grow, nine or ten hairs on my chin, sometimes even more; but what do I do with the hairs? I tweak them out. Would a man do that? Men don't tweak. Men shave. Anyhow white men shave, being hairy, and I have even less choice about being white or not than I do about being a man or not. I am white whether I like being white or not. The doctors can do nothing for me. But I do my best not to be white, I guess, under the circumstances, since I don't shave. I tweak. But it doesn't mean anything because I don't really have a real beard that amounts to anything. And I don't have a gun and I don't have even one wife and my sentences tend to go on and on and on, with all this syntax in them. Ernest Hemingway would have died rather than have syntax. Or semicolons. I use a whole lot of half-assed semicolons; there was one of them just now; that was a semicolon after "semicolons," and another one after "now."

And another thing. Ernest Hemingway would have died rather than get old. And he did. He shot himself. A short sentence. Anything rather than a long sentence, a life sentence. Death sentences are short and very, very manly. Life sentences aren't. They go on and on, all full of syntax and qualifying clauses and confusing references and getting old. And that brings up the real proof of what a mess I have made of being a man: I am not even young. Just about the time they finally started inventing women, I started getting old. And I went right on doing it. Shamelessly. I have allowed myself to get old and haven't done one single thing about it, with a gun or anything.

What I mean is, if I had any real self-respect wouldn't I at least have had a face-lift or some liposuction? Although liposuction sounds to me like what they do a lot of on TV when they are young or youngish, though not when they are old, and when one of them is a man and the other a woman, though not under any other circumstances. What they do is, this young or youngish man and woman take hold of each other and slide their hands around on each other and then they perform liposuction. You are supposed to watch them while they do it. They move their heads around and flatten out their mouth and nose on the other person's mouth and nose and open their mouths in different ways, and you are supposed to feel sort of hot or wet or something as you watch. What I feel is like I'm watching two people doing liposuction, and *this* is why they finally invented women? Surely not.

As a matter of fact I think sex is even more boring as a spectator sport than all the other spectator sports, even baseball. If I am required to watch a sport instead of doing it, I'll take show jumping. The horses are really good-looking. The people who ride them are mostly these sort of nazis, but like all nazis they are only as powerful and successful as the horse they are riding, and it is after all the horse who decides whether to jump that five-barred gate or stop short and let the nazi fall off over its neck. Only usually the horse doesn't remember it has the option. Horses aren't awfully bright. But in any case, show jumping and sex have a good deal in common, though you usually can only get show jumping on American TV if you can pick up a Canadian channel, which is not true of sex. Given the option, though I often forget that I have an option, I certainly would *watch* show jumping and *do* sex. Never the other way round. But I'm too old now for show jumping, and as for sex, who knows? I do; you don't.

Of course golden oldies are supposed to jump from bed to bed these days just like the horses jumping the five-barred gates, bounce, bounce, bounce, but a good deal of this super sex at seventy business seems to be theory again, like the woman CEO of General Motors and the woman president of Harvard. Theory is invented mostly to reassure people in their forties, that is men, who are worried. That is why we had Karl Marx, and why we still have economists, though we seem to have lost Karl Marx. As such, theory is dandy. As for practice, or praxis as the Marxists used to call it apparently because they liked *x*'s, you wait till you are sixty or seventy and then you can tell me about your sexual practice, or praxis, if you want to, though I make no promises that I will listen, and if I do listen I will probably be extremely bored and start looking for some show jumping on the TV. In any case you are not going to hear anything from me about my sexual practice or praxis, then, now, or ever.

But all that aside, here I am, old, when I wrote this I was sixty years old, "a sixty-year-old smiling public man," as Yeats said, but then, he *was* a man. And now I am over seventy. And it's all my own fault. I get born before they invent women, and I live all these decades trying so hard to be a good man that I forget all about staying young, and so I didn't. And my tenses get all mixed up. I just am young and then all of a sudden I was sixty and maybe eighty, and what next?

Not a whole lot.

I keep thinking there must have been something that a real man could have done about it. Something short of guns, but more effective than Oil of Olay. But I failed. I did nothing. I absolutely failed to stay young. And then I look back on all my strenuous efforts, because I really did try, I tried hard to be a man, to be a good man, and I see how I failed at that. I am at best a bad man. An imitation phony second-rate him with a ten-hair beard and semicolons. And I wonder what was the use. Sometimes I think I might just as well give the whole thing up. Sometimes I think I might just as well exercise my option, stop short in front of the five-barred gate, and let the nazi fall off onto his head. If I'm no good at pretending to be a man and no good at being young, I might just as well start pretending that I am an old woman. I am not sure that anybody has invented old women yet; but it might be worth trying.

BEING TAKEN FOR GRANITE

Sometimes I am taken for granite. Everybody is taken for granite sometimes but I am not in a mood for being fair to everybody. I am in a mood for being fair to me. I am taken for granite quite often, and this troubles and distresses me, because I am not granite. I am not sure what I am but I know it isn't granite. I have known some granite types, we all do: characters of stone, upright, immovable, unchangeable, opinions the general size shape and pliability of the Rocky Mountains, you have to quarry five years to chip out one little stony smile. That's fine, that's admirable, but it has nothing to do with me. Upright is fine, but downright is where I am, or downwrong.

I am not granite and should not be taken for it. I am not flint or diamond or any of that great hard stuff. If I am stone, I am some kind of shoddy crumbly stuff like sandstone or serpentine, or maybe schist. Or not even stone but clay, or not even clay but mud. And I wish that those who take me for granite would once in a while treat me like mud.

Being mud is really different from being granite and should be treated differently. Mud lies around being wet and heavy and oozy and generative. Mud is underfoot. People make footprints in mud. As mud I accept feet. I accept weight. I try to be supportive, I like to be obliging. Those who take me for granite say this is not so but they haven't been looking where they put their feet. That's why the house is all dirty and tracked up.

Granite does not accept footprints. It refuses them. Granite makes pinnacles, and then people rope themselves together and put pins on their shoes and climb the pinnacles at great trouble, expense, and risk, and maybe they experience a great thrill, but the granite does not. Nothing whatever results and nothing whatever is changed.

Huge heavy things come and stand on granite and the granite just stays there and doesn't react and doesn't give way and doesn't adapt and doesn't oblige and when the huge heavy things walk away the granite is there just the same as it was before, just exactly the same, admirably. To change granite you have to blow it up.

But when people walk on me you can see exactly where they put their feet, and when huge heavy things come and stand on me I yield and react and respond and give way and adapt and accept. No explosives are called for. No admiration is called for. I have my own nature and am true to it just as much as granite or even diamond is, but it is not a hard nature, or upstanding, or gemlike. You can't chip it. It's deeply impressionable. It's squashy.

Maybe the people who rope themselves together and the huge heavy things resent such adaptable and uncertain footing because it makes them feel insecure. Maybe they fear they might be sucked in and swallowed. But I am not interested in sucking and am not hungry. I am just mud. I yield. I do try to oblige. And so when the people and the huge heavy things walk away they are not changed, except their feet are muddy, but I am changed. I am still here and still mud, but all full of footprints and deep, deep holes and tracks and traces and changes. I have been changed. You change me. Do not take me for granite.

INDIAN UNCLES

By Ursula Kroeber Le Guin

From a talk given for the Emeriti Lectures at the Department of Anthropology of the University of California at Berkeley, November 4, 1991. I rewrote the piece for a celebration of the hundredth anniversary of the department, November 16, 2001.

Because I was talking to people who knew my background (some of them perhaps better than I did) and all the people I mentioned, I did no explaining; therefore a few explanations are in order:

Alfred L. Kroeber, my father, founded that department in 1901, and taught in it till he retired in 1947. He married Theodora Kracaw Brown, my mother, in 1925. We lived in Berkeley near the campus.

In 1911 a "wild" Indian appeared in a small northern California town. He spoke a language the remaining local Indians did not know, and had evidently lived his entire life in hiding, with the remnant of his people, from the whites. A linguist from the university, T. T. Waterman, was able to talk a little with him, and brought him down to the museum of anthropology, then in San Francisco. He lived there from then on, learning the ways of the new world he had entered and teaching the ways of his own lost world to the scientists and to visitors to the museum. His people did not name themselves to others, so he was called Ishi, which means "man" in his own Yahi language. I relate below how my mother became Ishi's biographer. Her books about him are Ishi in Two Worlds and Ishi, Last of His Tribe. His story is, I think, essential reading to anyone who thinks they know, or wants to learn, how the West was won, and who Americans are.

Many, many people have asked me, eager and expectant, "Wasn't it wonderful to know Ishi?"

And I'm floored every time. All I can do is disappoint them by explaining that Ishi died thirteen years before I was born. I can't remember even hearing his name until the late fifties, when a biography of him became first a subject of family conversation and then the consuming object of my mother's work and thought for several years.

But my father, in my recollection, didn't talk about Ishi. He talked very little about the past; he didn't reminisce. As a man twenty years older than his wife, a father of grandfather age, he may well have determined never to be a garrulous old bore bleating about the good old days. But also by temperament he didn't live in the past, but in the present, in the moment, right up to his death at eighty-four. I wish he had reminisced more, because he had done so many interesting things in interesting places, and was a fine storyteller. But getting his own past out of him was like pulling hen's teeth. Once he did describe to us what he did during the 1906 Fire in San Francisco (it's in my mother's biography of him), and while he was in the remembering vein I asked him what he *felt* during the earthquake and after. He worked on his pipe for a while, lighting matches and making neat little piles of them, and then he said, "Exhilaration."

I don't mean to suggest that he was one of those yup-nope men. He was a highly conversable person, but he was too interested in what was happening now to look back much. I longed to know something about his first wife, Henrietta Rothschild, of San Francisco, but I didn't know how to ask and he didn't know how to answer, or there was too much old grief buried there and he wasn't going to dig it up and display it. There is a modesty of grief, and he was a modest man.

That may also be why he didn't talk about Ishi. So much old grief, old pain, still sharp. Not the cheap guilt trips the psychodramatisers pull out of their cheap hats: emotionally stunted scientist exploiting noble savage—Dr. Treves and the Elephant Man, Dr. Kroeber and

Ishi—that is not what happened. It has happened, as we all know, and as he knew. But not in this case. Perhaps just the opposite.

The idea that objective observation can be performed only by an observer totally free of subjectivity involves an ideal of inhuman purity which we now recognise as being, fortunately, unattainable. But the dilemma of the subjective practitioner of objectivity persists, and presents itself to anthropologists in its most acute and painful form: the relationship between observer and observed when both of them are human. Novelists, people who write about people, have the same moral problem, the problem of exploitation, but we rarely face it in so stark a form. I'm awed at the courage of any scientist who admits it in all its intractability.

Looking at it from my naive, outsider's standpoint, it seems to me that most of the Boasians had a pretty strict take on it. I know my father distrusted whites—amateurs or professionals—who claimed emotional or spiritual identification with Indians. He saw such claims as sentimental and co-optative. To him the term *going native* was one of disapproval. His friendships with Indians were that: friendships. Beginning in collaborative work, based on personal liking and respect, they involved neither patronisation nor co-optation.

With Ishi, a man almost unimaginably vulnerable in his tragic solitude, dependent by necessity, yet strong, generous, clear-minded, and affectionate, an extraordinary person in every way, this relationship of friendship must have been unusually complex and intense.

My father was consciously, consistently loyal to the ideal of objective science, but it was the passions of personal grief and personal loyalty that dictated his message from New York trying to prevent the autopsy of Ishi's body—"Tell them as far as I am concerned science can go to hell. We propose to stand by our friends."

His message came too late. A contemporary anthropologist has said that if he felt so strongly about the matter, why didn't he get on an airplane and come West and see about it? One would think that an anthropologist might be aware that in 1916 there was a certain lack of airplanes to get on. A telegram was the only means he had to try to prevent the desecration.

I know little of the circumstances of the subsequent grotesque division of the body, which reminds me of the way kings and emperors were buried in bits, the head in Vienna, the heart in Habsburg, other pieces in other parts of the empire. Saints the same—an arm here, a finger there, a toe in a reliquary. . . . It would appear that to the European, dismembering a body and keeping bits of it around is a sign of respect. This is definitely a strain on our American cultural relativism. I leave it to you anthropologists to work it out.

Kroeber accepted defeat and got on with the work to be done. I do not think his silence was indifference but the muteness of undesired complicity and the dumbness of the bereaved. He had lost his friend. He had lost a person whom he loved and was responsible for, and lost him to the same sickness that had killed his wife a few years earlier, tuberculosis, the "White Sickness." Over and over he had worked with individuals who were among the last of their people. One way or another his people and their white sicknesses had destroyed them. He was silent because neither he nor his science had a vocabulary for his knowledge. And if he couldn't find the right words, he wouldn't use the wrong ones.

Not long after Ishi's death, my father took leave from anthropology, was psychoanalyzed, and practiced analysis for some years. But I don't think Freud had quite the words he needed, either. The scope of his work and writing widened with the years, but at the very end of his life he returned to Californian ethnology, using his long-accumulated expertise to support Californian tribes in their suit against the U.S. government for restoration and reparation of their lands, spending months of testimony and cross-examination in a federal courtroom. My brother Ted, who drove him to many of these sessions, recalls the judge's attempts to give the old man a break now and then, and Alfred's patient but urgent determination to get the job done.

He wrote as little about Ishi as possible. When asked about Ishi, he answered. When it was suggested he should write a biography of Ishi, he declined. Robert Heizer took the excellent expedient of offering the task to my mother, who had never known Ishi, never been his friend, was not an anthropologist, was not a man, and could be trusted to find the right words if anybody could.

I was in the Lowie Museum here with Alfred Kroeber's little great-granddaughter, ten years ago, and she showed me the headphones at the Ishi exhibit, where you can hear Ishi telling a story. I put them on and heard his voice for the first time. I broke into tears. For a moment. It seems the only appropriate response.

⟳

Some of you may have hoped to hear more about the family or about my father's colleagues and students, who were certainly a large element in our family life. I am afraid I share Alfred's incapacity for reminiscence. I am much better at making things up than at remembering them. The two Indian friends of my father's that I can say something about, because as a child I did really relate to them, are the Papago Juan Dolores and the Yurok Robert Spott. But here I run into the moral problem we storytellers share with you anthropologists: the exploitation of real people. People should not *use* other people. My memories of these two Native American friends are hedged with caution and thorned with fear. What, after all, did I or do I understand about them? When I knew them, what did I know about them, about their political or their individual situation? Nothing. Not their people's history, not their personal history, not their contributions to anthropology—nothing.

I was a little kid, youngest of the family. We always went up to the Napa Valley in June as soon as school was out. My parents had bought a forty-acre ranch there for two thousand dollars. We settled in and set up the packed-dirt croquet court, and Juan—a killer croquet player—always got there in time for his birthday.

I was amazed to learn that Juan Dolores, a grown-up, actually didn't know what day he was born on. Birthdays were important. Mine and my brothers' and my parents' were celebrated with cake and ice cream and candles and ribbons and presents, and it was a matter of great moment that one was now seven. How could it *not matter* to a person? In pondering this first discovery of the difference between Western time and Indian time, I was perhaps composting the soil from which the cultural relativism of my fictions would grow and flourish. But Juan (we kids called him Wahn, we didn't know Spanish Hwahn)— Juan had to have a birth date in order to fill out the papers for his social security or his pension from the university or something; bureaucrats, like me, believe in birthdays. So he and my father chose him a birthday. Now, that was nifty, sitting around and deciding when you wanted to be born. They picked St. John's Eve, Midsummer Night. And thereafter, Juan's birthday was celebrated with cake, candles, and all the rest: a festival of this small tribe, celebrated soon after their annual migration sixty miles to the north, marking both the summer solstice and the ritual visit of the Papago.

The Papago stayed for a month or longer. The top front bedroom of the old house in the Valley is still called Juan's Room by the elders of the tribe. During those visits he and my father may have worked together. I paid no attention to that. All I remember about Juan's visits is using him. The use of grown-ups by children is one of the numerous exceptions to my absolute rule that people should not use other people. Weaker people, of course, get to use stronger ones; they have to. But the limits of use are best set by the strong, not by the weak. Juan was not very good at setting limits, at least when it came to children. He let us get away with murder. We got him to make a drum for us, and as I recall we insisted that it be a Plains Indian drum, because that was a *real* Indian drum, no matter that he was a real non–Plains Indian. In any case he made a marvelous drum, and we beat on it for years.

We picked up phrases like "Lo! the poor Indian!" and, from some magazine article, a title, "The Vanishing Red Man." With what is called the cruelty of children, we used these phrases; we called Juan Lo, the Vanishing Papago. Hello, Lo! You haven't vanished yet! I think he thought it was funny too; I think if he hadn't, we'd have known it, and shut up. I hope so. We weren't cruel, we were ignorant, foolish. Children are ignorant and foolish. But they learn. If they are given a chance to learn.

There's a lot of poison oak in those hills, and we were all covered with calamine lotion all the time. Juan boasted that Indians never got poison oak. My brothers challenged him—Indians don't *ever* get poison oak? Never? Prove it! Dare you!—Juan went down on a hundred-degree day into a twelve-foot thicket of poison oak by the creek and cut it all down with a machete. We have a tiny Kodak picture: a sea of poison oak, one small, bald, dark head just visible in it, shining with sweat. He got tired, but he didn't get poison oak. Decades later when I read in Sarah Winnemucca's autobiography how she nearly died as a child from her first exposure, I modified Juan's claim: *some* Indians never get poison oak. It may have been that he was determined not to.

He was, I think, a strong, determined man; the intellectual work he did is proof of it; which makes his endless patience with us kids even more beautiful. This memory is not my own but of my mother's telling: Juan's first summer visit, long before he had a birthday, was the summer I learned to walk, 1931 I suppose. This infant would stagger over to Juan and say "Go-go?" And whatever he was doing, writing or reading or talking or working, Juan would excuse himself and gravely accompany me across the yard and up the driveway on a great journey of a hundred yards or so, I holding on to him firmly by one finger. Now that part I do seem to remember; perhaps it's just my mother's vivid telling; but I know which finger it was, the first of his left hand, a strong, thick, dark finger that entirely and warmly filled my hand.

In the forties when he was living in Oakland, Juan was mugged, robbed, and badly beaten. When he came for a visit at our Berkeley house after he got out of the hospital, I was afraid to come downstairs. I had heard that "his head was broken," and imagined horrors. I finally was ordered down, and said hello, and sneaked a look. He wasn't horrible. He was tired, and old, and sad. I was too ashamed and shy to show him my affection. I didn't know I loved him. Children brought up in great security, tribal or familial, aren't very aware of love, as I suppose fish aren't very aware of water. That's the way it ought to be, love as air, love as the human element. But I see Juan now, a gentle, intellectual man, living in exile and poverty, licensed by bigotry to be a prey of bullies—the world was full of such people in the 1940s. It is full of such people now. I wish I had had the sense to take his hand.

⸾

The first time Robert Spott came to stay with us in the Valley, his major problem must have been getting enough to eat. My memory of Yurok table manners is that if anybody speaks during a meal, everybody puts down their fork or soupspoon or whatever, swallows, and stops eating till the conversation is done. Only when speech is over does eating resume. Such a custom might arise among a rather formal people who had plenty to eat and plenty of time to eat it in. (With that idea in mind, as a novelist, I once invented some people living on an Ice Age planet where food, warmth, and leisure were often hard to come by: to them it was extremely bad manners to speak at all during a meal. Eat now, talk later—first things first. This is probably far too logical for a real custom.) And I may well have misunderstood or misremembered; my brother Karl's recollection of correct Yurok table manners is that having taken a bite, one puts one's spoon or hand down on the table until quite done chewing; and that also, when the host stops eating, the guest stops. In any case, there was Robert, and us four kids and Aunt Betsy and my parents and probably some other odd relatives or ethnologists or refugees around the dinner table, and we were a talkative and discursive and argumentative lot, with the kids encouraged to take a responsible part in the conversation. So every time anybody said anything, which was constantly, poor Robert laid down his fork, swallowed, and looked up with courteous and undivided attention, while we gobbled and babbled on. And as my father ate with extreme, neat rapidity, Robert must have had to stop eating before he had had anything much to eat at all. I believe he learned eventually to imitate our uncouthness.

I often felt uncouth around Robert Spott. He had tremendous personal dignity and authority. I believed for years that he was a—what my linguistic nephew informs me is now pronounced shawman, but which I continue to pronounce shayman, since my father did, and it doesn't sound so New Agey. My brother Ted's memory, more enlightened than mine by six years, is that Robert's mother was the shaman, and that she and perhaps other women of his people trained him, not specifically as a shaman or doctor but in the knowledge of tribal and religious customs. They demanded this learning of him, a heavy and lifelong commitment, because there was no other fit candidate and the knowledge would die with them if he did not accept it. I have it in my head that Robert accepted the burden only with reluctance. Ted tells me that Robert served as an advocate for his people in Sacramento, taking on the then seemingly hopeless struggle to preserve Yurok culture and values against white contempt and exploitation—a task that might daunt anyone. At the time, I understood nothing of that grim political work, and may have romanticised it by mythologising Robert as an unwilling shaman. A girl does tend to spin romances about a handsome, stately, stern, dark man who doesn't say much.

Robert was grave, serious; we took no liberties with him. Was it a cultural or a temperamental difference, or both, that Juan Dolores was long-suffering with us brats, and Robert Spott was aloof and instructive? I can still blush when I remember myself rather unusually holding the table, chattering away breakneck, telling some event of the day, and being abruptly silenced by Robert. I had far exceeded the conversational limit proper to a well-bred Yurok girl, which I imagine may be a word or two. Robert laid down his fork and swallowed, and when I paused for breath, he spoke to the adults on a subject of interest to adults. My culture told me that it is rude to interrupt people, and I was resentful; but I shut up. Children have to be stupid, or to have been culturally stupidised, not to recognise genuine authority. My resentment was an attempt to justify my embarrassment. Robert had introduced me to a very Yurok moral sentiment, shame. Not guilt, there was nothing to be guilty about; just shame. You blush resentfully, you hold your tongue, and you figure it out. I have Robert to thank in part for my deep respect for shame as a social instrument. Guilt I believe to be counterproductive, but shame can be immensely useful; if, for example, any member of Congress was acquainted in any form with shame—well, never mind.

Both Juan and Robert are associated in my mind with the moving of great rocks. Blue boulders of serpentine, dug from the reddish dirt above the road. The menfolk and my great-aunt Betsy built a drylaid wall of them. The end rock nearest the house, a beautiful blue-green monster, is still called by all members of the tribe Juan's Rock, though some of them may not know why. He selected it and directed and labored in the levering and rolling of it from above the driveway down to its present place. No one got killed or even maimed, though the women worried and lamented in the kitchen, and I was told two thousand times to *keep uphill* from that rock.

Then, or before that—there was definitely some competition between the two men, some matter of my rock is bigger than your rock—Robert built us a marvelous outdoor fireplace. It is both technically and in fact a sacred place. It is built as a Yurok meditation shelter is built, and so oriented; but the fire burns where the meditator would sit, and so he completed the half circle of the shelter with a half circle of flat stones for people to sit on around the fire. And there my people have sat for seventy years, to eat, and tell stories, and watch the summer stars.

There is a photograph of my father and Robert, one listening, the other telling, with lifted hand and faraway gaze. They are sitting on those fireplace stones. Robert and Alfred talked together sometimes in English sometimes in Yurok. It was perhaps unusual for the daughter of a first-generation German immigrant from New York to hear him talking Yurok, but I didn't know that. I didn't know anything. I thought everybody spoke Yurok. But I knew where the center of the world was.

MY LIBRARIES

A talk given in 1997 at a celebration of the renovation of Portland's Multnomah County Library.

A library is a focal point, a sacred place to a community; and its sacredness is its accessibility, its publicness. It's everybody's place. I remember certain libraries, vividly and joyfully, as *my* libraries—elements of the best of my life.

The first one I knew well was in Saint Helena, California, then a small, peaceful, mostly Italian town. The library was a little Carnegie, white stucco, cool and sleepy on the fiery August afternoons when my mother would leave my brother and me there while she shopped at Giugni's and Tosetti's. Karl and I went through the children's room like word-seeking missiles. After we had read everything, including all thirteen volumes of the adventures of a fat boy detective, we had to be allowed to go into the Adult Side. That was hard for the librarians. They felt they were hurling us little kids into a room full of sex, death, and weird grown-ups like Heathcliff and the Joads; and in fact, they were. We were intensely grateful.

The only trouble with the Saint Helena library was you could only take five books out at a time and we only went into town once a week. So we checked out really solid books, I mean five hundred pages of small print in two columns, like *The Count of Monte Cristo*. Short books were no good—two days' orgy and then starve the rest of the week—nothing but the farmhouse bookcase, and we could recite every-thing in it by the time we were ten. I imagine we were the only people in the Napa Valley who regularly hit each other on the head with quarter-staves while shouting, "Varlet! Have at thee!"—"Why, fat knave, think'st thou to cross this bridge?" Karl usually got to be Robin Hood because he was older, but at least I never had to be Maid Marian.

Next in my life was the branch of the Berkeley Library near Garfield Junior High, where my dearest memory is of my friend Shirley leading me to the N shelf and saying, "There's this writer called E. Nes-bit and you HAVE to read the one called *Five Children and It,*" and boy, was she right. By eighth grade I sort of oozed over into the adult room. The librarians pretended not to notice. But when I arrived at the adult checkout carrying a thick, obscure biography of Lord Dunsany like a holy relic, I remember the librarian's expression. It was very much like the expression of the U.S. customs inspector in Seattle, years later, when he opened my suitcase and found a Stilton cheese—not a decent whole cheese, but a ruin, a mouldy rind, a smelly remnant, which our friend Barbara in Berkshire had affectionately but unwisely sent to my husband. The customs man said, "What *is* it?"

"Well, it's an English cheese," I said.

He was a tall, black man with a deep voice. He shut the suitcase and said, "Lady, if you want it, you can have it."

And the librarian let me have Lord Dunsany, too.

After that came the Berkeley Public Library itself, which is bless-edly placed just a block or two from Berkeley Public High School. I loved the one as deeply as I hated the other. In one I was an exile in the Siberia of adolescent social mores. In the other I was home free. With-out the library I wouldn't have survived the school, not in my right mind, anyhow. But then, adolescents are all crazy.

I discovered that the foreign books were up on the third floor and nobody ever went there, so I moved in. I lived there, crouched in a spi-derwebby window, with *Cyrano de Bergerac,* in French. I didn't know enough French yet to read *Cyrano,* but that didn't stop me. That's when I learned you can read a language you don't know if you love it enough. You can do anything if you love it enough. I cried a lot up there, over Cyrano and other people. I discovered *Jean-Christophe,* and cried over him; and Baudelaire, and cried over him—only a fifteen-year-old can truly appreciate *The Flowers of Evil,* I think. Sometimes I raided the lower, English-speaking regions of the library and brought back writers such as Ernest Dowson—"I have been faithful to thee, Cynara! in my fashion"—and cried some more. Ah, those were good years for crying, and a library is a good place to cry in. Quietly.

Next in my life was Radcliffe's small, endearing college library, and then—when they decided I could be permitted to enter it, even though I was a freshman, and what was far worse, a freshwoman—Widener Library at Harvard.

I will tell you my private definition of freedom. Freedom is stack privileges at Widener Library.

I remember the first time I came outside from those endless, incredible stacks I could barely walk because I was carrying about twenty-five books, but I was flying. I turned around and looked up the broad steps of the building, and I thought, That's heaven. That's the heaven for me. All the words in the world, and all for me to read. Free at last, Lord, free at last!

I hope you'll understand that I am not quoting those great words lightly. I do mean it. Knowledge sets us free, art sets us free. A great library is freedom.

So then, after a mad but brief Parisian affair with the Bibliothèque Nationale, I arrived in Portland. Our first years here we had two little babies, and I was at home with them. The great treat for me, the holiday I wanted, the event I looked forward to all week or month, was to get a sitter and come downtown with Charles and go to the Library. At night, of course; no way to do it in the daytime. A couple of hours, till the Library closed at nine. Plunging into the ocean of words, roaming in the broad fields of the mind, climbing the mountains of the imagination. Just like the kid in the Carnegie or the student in Widener, that was my freedom, that was my joy. And it still is.

That joy must not be sold. It must not be "privatised," made into another privilege for the privileged. A public library is a public trust.

And that freedom must not be compromised. It must be available to all who need it, and that's everyone, when they need it, and that's always.

MY ISLAND

Written for Islands *magazine.*

Invited to write about a favorite island, at first I couldn't think of a real one—only the unattained or the imaginary. Islands are by definition separated from the ordinary world, not part of it. Isolate . . .

So I thought first of the Farallons, those foggy rocks sometimes visible from San Francisco's Cliff House, dimly seen way out in the grey sea. When I was a child they were my image of the loneliest place, the farthest west you could go. And they have such a beautiful name. *Los farallones* means cliffs, crags; a lovely word, and in English it gathers echoes—far away and all alone. . . . But that's all I know about the Farallons, where I will never go.

So then I thought about islands I'd found in my own mind, the ones I called Earthsea, a whole archipelago occupied by wizards, housewives, dragons, and other fascinating people. I know those islands well; I have written books about them. I gave them fine names, Gont and Roke and Havnor, Selidor and Osskil and The Hands. I never expected to see Earthsea in the real world, but I did, once. I was on a ship that sailed right round the British Isles, up to the Orkneys and the Hebrides, out to Lewis and Harris, to Skye and down the western coast past Scotland and past Wales . . . and there they were, my islands, scattered before us in a golden sea, fantastic, unearthly, surely full of dragons: the Scillies. Another lovely name. Why are you gig-gling? Because I saw the Scilly Isles!

But a real island, not a dream or a name or a glimpse?—I couldn't think of one I could write about. Until I remembered that not all is-lands are in the sea.

Big oceangoing freighters sail past it every day, sometimes cruise ships, often sailboats, but my island is some eighty miles inland. A faint lift and ebb of the tides is still in the water that flows past it, but it's not salt water. Sauvie Island lies just downstream from where Port-land's river, the Willamette, enters the immense Columbia.

Sauvie is one of the biggest river islands in the country: fifteen miles long and three or four wide. Along the grey beaches of its outer side runs the broad, powerful current of the Columbia. On the inner side, a slow-flowing slough lets fishermen's rowboats drift along be-tween the marshes, the clusters of houseboats, the landing stages of old farms. Canals intersect the island, irrigating the farms. Shallow lakes deepen and dry up with the seasons.

In the old days before the dikes were built, before the upriver Co-lumbia was dammed and dammed again, Sauvie Island flooded every year. It was all dairy farms then. The farmers rounded up the cattle when the water rose and drove them onto the few bits of high ground (still called "islands" within the island). There they waited out the flood, some of them mooing and some of them chewing tobacco, I imagine. Then they came back down to the rich, silty pastures. They sent their milk and butter by boat to Portland, just upstream. There was no bridge from the mainland to Sauvie Island until 1950.

There used to be an old man who rowed his boat round the whole island, from farm to farm—every farm had a boat ramp—selling trin-kets and buttons and thread and candy: a kind of one-man, two-oared dime store for the islanders. Hearing about those old days, you get the feeling it wasn't the islanders who wanted the bridge. They were quite content. It was the mainlanders who longed to get across the water.

But, racked by the huge trucks we use now, the bridge is threatening to break down, and the farmers of the island are getting a bit desperate, worrying that they won't be able to get their produce to the Portland markets.

Long before the pioneers, Sauvie was a home and a trading center for the peoples of the river, those marvelous canoe makers for whom the Columbia was not a barrier but a highway. Lewis and Clark called it Wappato Island for the food staple that still grows there, an underwater root with tall lance-shaped leaves. But epidemics brought by early white explorers devastated the Columbia River peoples, and a fur trader wrote of the island people in 1835 that "there is nothing to attest that they ever existed except . . . their graves." When the Oregon Trail led homesteaders to the island, they found it desolate. And it still keeps a deep quietness, which sometimes becomes uncanny.

These days, the downstream half of the island is a wildlife preserve—a dreamy silence of marshy woods, huge old oaks, vast flocks of ducks, geese, and trumpeter swans feeding and flying—until hunting season, when it gets noisy for a while. The upstream half is still farmed. I know no place in America that looks so *gardened,* the way old farmlands in England look; the care and thought with which it's planted and tended and cherished make it beautiful. But behind the thriving nurseries, berry farms, and pumpkin patches rise the great blue hills above the Columbia, still forested, still half wild. Turn around, and to the northeast see snow-crowned mountains: Hood, Adams, St. Helens looming low since her eruption, and farther north, Rainier. Then all at once, like a mirage, a huge Japanese freighter carrying cars floats quietly by between the pumpkins and the mountains.

Sauvie is only half an hour's drive from downtown Portland, a city of three-quarters of a million people. The highway to it passes the busy Port of Portland and an industrial district of warehouses, storage tanks, railway sidings, factories; then suddenly there's a turn to the little two-lane bridge, and you're deep in the country. Though it is so close, so easy to get to, and so many Portlanders love to go "over to

Sauvie's" to pick strawberries, raspberries, marionberries, blueberries in the summer, buy squash and onions in the autumn, play on the beaches, swim in the river, fish in the slough, hunt or hike the woodland trails, or bird-watch and picnic under the oaks—even so, it remains rural and peaceful, as if it were a piece of the past, timeless between its rivers.

How long can it keep that quietness? So far, it has defended itself against such fatal intrusions as a huge garbage dump and a Japanese-owned golf course for millionaires. So far, no ticky-tacky developments, no McMansions have been allowed on the farmlands or the fish and game preserve. But land-use laws are so easily tossed aside, silence is so easily broken. How long can an island in an ever-deepening sea of humanity remain far away and all alone?

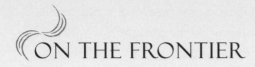

ON THE FRONTIER

This brief meditation, written in 1996 for the journal Frontiers, *where it appeared as "Which Side Am I On, Anyway?" has been rewritten for this book.*

THE FRONTIER

A frontier has two sides. It is an interface, a threshold, a liminal site, with all the danger and promise of liminality.

The front side, the yang side, the side that calls itself the frontier, that's where you boldly go where no one has gone before, rushing forward like a stormfront, like a battlefront. Nothing before you is real. It is empty space. My favorite quotation from the great frontiersman Julius Caesar: "It was not certain that Britannia existed, until I went there." It does not exist, it is empty, and therefore full of dream and promise, the seven shining cities. And so you go there. Seeking gold, seeking land, annexing all before you, you expand your world.

The other side of the frontier, the yin side: that's where you live. You always lived there. It's all around you, it's always been. It is the real world, the true and certain world, full of reality.

And it is where they come. You were not certain they existed, until they came.

Coming from another world, they take yours from you, changing it, draining it, shrinking it into a property, a commodity. And as your world is meaningless to them until they change it into theirs, so as you live among them and adopt their meanings, you are in danger of losing your own meaning to yourself.

In the wake of the North American frontier is where my father the anthropologist did his fieldwork, among the wrecks of cultures, the ruins of languages, the broken or almost-broken continuities and communities, the shards of an infinite diversity smashed by a monoculture. A postfrontiersman, a white immigrant's son learning Indian cultures and languages in the first half of the twentieth century, he tried to save meaning. To learn and tell the stories that might otherwise be lost. The only means he had to do so was by translating, recording in his foreign language: the language of science, the language of the conqueror. An act of imperialism. An act of human solidarity.

My mother continued his work with her history of a survivor of the frontier, the native Californian Ishi. I admire her book as deeply as I admire its subject, but have always regretted the subtitle, *A Biography of the Last Wild Indian in North America*, for it contradicts the sense and spirit of the story she tells. Ishi was not wild. He did not come out of the wilderness, but out of a culture and tradition far more deeply rooted and soundly established than that of the frontiersmen who slaughtered his people to get their land. He did not live in a wilderness but in a dearly familiar world he and his people knew hill by hill, river by river, stone by stone. Who made those golden hills a wilderness of blood and mourning and ignorance?

If there are frontiers between the civilised and the barbaric, between the meaningful and the unmeaning, they are not lines on a map nor are they regions of the earth. They are boundaries of the mind alone.

My Frontiers

Innate or acquired, a delight in learning unfamiliar (foreign, alien, "wild") significances and an unwillingness to limit value or significance to a single side of the frontier have shaped my writing.

North Americans have looked at their future as they looked at their Western lands: as an empty place (animals, Indians, aliens don't count) to be "conquered," "tamed," filled up with themselves and their doings: a meaningless blank on which to write their names. This is the same future one finds in much science fiction, but not in mine. In mine the future is already full; it is much older and larger than our present; and we are the aliens in it.

My fantasies explore the use of power as art and its misuse as domination; they play back and forth along the mysterious frontier between what we think is real and what we think is imaginary, exploring the borderlands.

Capitalism, which ceases to exist if it is not expanding its empire, establishes an ever-moving frontier, and its yang conquistadors forever pursue El Dorado. You cannot be too rich, they cry. My realistic fictions are mostly about people on the yin side of capitalism: housewives, waitresses, librarians, keepers of dismal little motels. The people who live, you might say, on the rez, in the broken world the conquistadors leave behind.

Living in a world that is valued only as gain, an ever-expanding world-as-frontier that has no worth of its own, no fullness of its own, you live in danger of losing your own worth to yourself. That's when you begin to listen to the voices from the other side, and to ask questions of failure and the dark.

I am a granddaughter of the American frontier. My mother's family moved and bought and farmed and failed and moved on, from Missouri to Wyoming to Colorado to Oregon to California and back. We followed yang; we found yin. I am grateful. My heritage is the wild oats the Spanish sowed on the hills of California, the cheatgrass the ranchers left in the counties of Harney and Malheur. Those are the crops my people planted, and I have reaped. There is my straw-spun gold.

READINGS

ALL HAPPY FAMILIES

At one of those times when I wanted to be writing a story but didn't have one to write, I got to thinking again about the opening words of Anna Karenina, *which are so often quoted as if they were true, and decided the time had come to write down my thoughts, since I had nothing better to do. They were published, after a while, in the* Michigan Quarterly Review.

I used to be too respectful to disagree with Tolstoy, but after I got into my sixties my faculty of respect atrophied. Besides, at some point in the last forty years I began to question Tolstoy's respect for his wife. Anybody can make a mistake in marriage, of course. But I have an impression that no matter whom he married Tolstoy would have respected her only in certain respects, though he expected her to respect him in all respects. In this respect, I disapprove of Tolstoy; which makes it easier to disagree with him in the first place, and in the second place, to say so.

There has been a long gap between the first and second places—years. But there was a period of as many years even before the first place, before I achieved the point of disagreement, the ability to disapprove. During all those years, from when I was fourteen or so and first read him, till I was in my forties, I was, as it were, married to Tolstoy, his loyal wife. Though fortunately not expected to copy his manuscripts six times over by hand, I read and reread his books with joy and zeal. I respected him without ever asking if or wondering whether he, as it were, respected me. When E. M. Forster, in an essay on Tolstoy, told me that he didn't, I replied, He has that right!

And if E. M. Forster had asked, What gives him that right? I would have answered simply, genius.

But E. M. Forster didn't ask; which is just as well, since he probably would have asked what I meant by genius.

I think what I meant by genius was that I thought Tolstoy actually knew what he was talking about—unlike the rest of us.

However, at some point, around forty or so, I began to wonder if he really knew what he was talking about any better than anybody else, or if what he knew better than anybody else was *how* to talk about it. The two things are easily confused.

So then, quietly, in my private mind, surrounded by the soft, supportive mutterings of feminists, I began to ask rude questions of Tolstoy. In public I remained a loyal and loving wife, entirely respectful of his opinions as well as his art. But the unspoken questions were there, the silent disagreement. And the unspoken, as we know, tends to strengthen, to mature and grow richer over the years, like an undrunk wine. Of course it may just go to Freudian vinegar. Some thoughts and feelings go to vinegar very quickly, and must be poured out at once. Some go on fermenting in the bottle, and burst out in an explosion of murderous glass shards. But a good, robust, well-corked feeling only gets deeper and more complicated, down in the cellar. The thing is knowing when to uncork it.

It's ready. I'm ready. The great first sentence of the first chapter of the great book—not the greatest book, but perhaps the second greatest—is, yes, we can say it in unison: "All happy families are alike; unhappy families are each unhappy in their own way." Translations vary, but not significantly.

People quote that sentence so often that it must satisfy them; but it does not, it never quite did, satisfy me. And twenty years ago or so,

I began admitting my dissatisfaction to myself. These happy families he speaks of so confidently in order to dismiss them as all alike—where are they? Were they very much commoner in the nineteenth century? Did he know numerous happy families among the Russian nobility, or middle class, or peasantry, all of them alike? This seems so unlikely that I wondered if perhaps he knew a few happy families, which is not impossible; but that those few were all alike seems deeply, very deeply implausible. Was his own family happy, either the one he grew up in or the one he fathered? Did he know one family, one single family, that could, over a substantial period of time, as a whole and in each of its component members, honestly be called happy? If he did he knew one more than most of us do.

I'm not just showing off my sexagenarian cynicism, proud though I may be of it. I admit that a family can be happy, in the sense that almost all the members of it are in good health, good spirits, and good temper with one another, for quite a long time—a week, a month, even longer. And if we go into the comparative mode, then certainly some families are far happier than others, on the whole and for years on end—because there are so many extremely unhappy families. Many people I have talked with about such matters were in one way or another unhappy as children; and perhaps most people, though they stay deeply attached to their relatives and recall joyous times with them, would not describe their family as happy. "We had some real good times," they say.

I grew up in a family that on the whole seems to have been happier than most families; and yet I find it false—an intolerable cheapening of reality—simply to describe it as happy. The enormous cost and complexity of that "happiness," its dependence upon a whole substructure of sacrifices, repressions, suppressions, choices made or forgone, chances taken or lost, balancings of greater and lesser evils—the tears, the fears, the migraines, the injustices, the censorships, the quarrels, the lies, the angers, the cruelties it involved—is all that to be swept away, brushed under the carpet by the brisk broom of a silly phrase, "a happy family"?

And why? In order to imply that happiness is easy, shallow, ordinary; a common thing not worth writing a novel about? Whereas unhappiness is complex, deep, difficult to attain, unusual; unique indeed; and so a worthy subject for a great, a unique novelist?

Surely that is a silly idea. But silly or not, it has been imposingly influential among novelists and critics for decades. Many a novelist would wither in shame if the reviewers caught him writing about happy people, families like other families, people like other people; and indeed many critics are keenly on the watch for happiness in novels in order to dismiss it as banal, sentimental, or (in other words) for women.

How the whole thing got gendered, I don't know, but it did. The gendering supposes that male readers have strong, tough, reality-craving natures, while feeble female readers crave constant reassurance in the form of little warm blobs of happiness—fuzzy bunnies.

This is true of some women. Some women have never experienced any glimpse of happiness in their whole life better than a stuffed fuzzy bunny and so they surround themselves with stuffed fuzzy bunnies, fictional or actual. In this they may be luckier than most men, who aren't allowed stuffed fuzzy bunnies, only girls in bunny suits. In any case, who can blame them, the men or the women? Not me. Anybody who has been privileged to know real, solid, nonfuzzy happiness, and then lets some novelist or critic buffalo them into believing that they shouldn't read about it because it's commoner than unhappiness, inferior to unhappiness, less interesting than unhappiness,—where does my syntax lead me? Into judgmentalism. I shall extricate myself in silence.

The falseness of Tolstoy's famous sentence is nowhere shown more clearly than in Tolstoy's novels, including the one it's the first sentence of. Dolly's family, which is the unhappy one we are promised, is in my opinion a moderately, that is to say a realistically happy one. Dolly and her children are kind and contented, often merry together, and the husband and wife definitely have their moments, for all his stupid skirt-chasing. In the greater novel, the Rostovs when we meet them might well be described as a happy family—rich, healthy, generous, kind, full of passions and counterpassions, full of vitality, energy, and love. But the Rostovs are not "like" anybody; they are idiosyncratic, unpredictable, incomparable. And, like most human beings, they can't hang on to their happiness. The old Count wastes his children's heritage and the Countess worries herself sick; Moscow burns; Natasha falls in love with a cold fish, nearly runs away with a cretin, marries and turns into a mindless brood sow; Petya is killed pointlessly in the war at sixteen. Jolly good fun! Fuzzy bunnies everywhere!

Tolstoy knew what happiness is—how rare, how imperilled, how hard-won. Not only that, he had the ability to describe happiness, a rare gift, which gives his novels much of their extraordinary beauty. Why he denied his knowledge in the famous sentence, I don't know. He did a good deal of lying and denying, perhaps more than many lesser novelists do. He had more to lie about; and his cruel theoretical Christianity led him into all kinds of denials of what in his fiction he saw and showed to be true. So maybe he was just showing off. It sounded good. It made a great first sentence.

My next essay will be about whether or not I want to be told to call a stranger Ishmael.

THINGS NOT ACTUALLY PRESENT

On *The Book of Fantasy* and J. L. Borges

In 1988 Xanadu Press published The Book of Fantasy, *a translation of the* Antologia de la literatura fantástica, *which Jorge Luis Borges, Adolfo Bioy Casares, and Silvina Ocampo first published in Buenos Aires in 1940. Asked to contribute a foreword to the English edition, I did so with pleasure. I have revised it so that I could include it in this collection, wanting to render some small homage to Borges.*

There are two books that I look on as esteemed and cherished great-aunts or grandmothers, wise and mild though sometimes rather dark of counsel, to be turned to when my judgment hesitates. One of these books provides facts, of a peculiar sort. The other does not. The *I Ching* or *Book of Changes* is the visionary elder who has outlived fact, the ancestor so old she speaks a different tongue. Her counsel is sometimes appallingly clear, sometimes very obscure indeed. "The little fox crossing the river wets its tail," she says, smiling faintly, or, "A dragon appears in the field," or, "Biting upon dried gristly meat." One retires to ponder long over such advice.

The other Auntie is younger, and speaks English. Indeed she speaks more English than anybody else. She offers fewer dragons and much more dried gristly meat. And yet *A New English Dictionary on Historical Principles,* or the OED as she is known to her family, is also a Book of Changes. Most wonderful in its transmutations, it is not the

Book of Sand, yet is inexhaustible; not an Aleph, yet all we have said and can ever say is in it, if we can but find it.

"Auntie!" I say, magnifying glass in hand, because my edition, the Compact Auntie, is compressed into two volumes of print no larger than grains of sand, "Auntie! Please tell me about fantasy, because I want to talk about a Book of Fantasy, but I am not sure what I am talking about."

"Fantasy, or Phantasy," Auntie replies, clearing her throat, "is from the Greek *phantasia*, lit. 'a making visible.'" She explains that *phantasia* is related to the verbs *phantasein*, "to make visible," or in Late Greek, "to imagine, have visions," and *phainein*, "to show." And she summarises the earliest meanings of the word *fantasy* in English: an appearance, a phantom, the mental process of sensuous perception, the faculty of imagination, a false notion, a caprice, a whim.

Then, though she eschews the casting of yarrow stalks or coins polished with sweet oil, being after all an Englishwoman, she begins to tell the Changes—the mutations of a word moving through the minds of people moving through the centuries. She shows how *fantasy*, which to the Schoolmen of the late Middle Ages meant "the mental apprehension of an object of perception," that is, the mind's very act of linking itself to the phenomenal world, came in time to signify just the reverse: an hallucination, or a phantasm, or the habit of deluding oneself. And then the word, doubling back on its tracks like a hare, came to mean the imagination itself, "the process, the faculty, or the result of forming mental representations of things not actually present." Though seemingly very close to the Scholastic use of the word, this definition of *fantasy* leads in quite the opposite direction, often going so far as to imply that the imagination is extravagant, or visionary, or merely fanciful.

So the word *fantasy* remains ambiguous, standing between the false, the foolish, the delusory, the shallows of the mind, and the mind's deep connection with the real. On this threshold it sometimes faces one way, masked and costumed, frivolous, an escapist; then it turns, and we glimpse as it turns the face of an angel, bright truthful messenger, arisen Urizen.

Since the compilation of my *Oxford English Dictionary,* the tracks of the word have been complicated still further by the comings and goings of psychologists. Their technical uses of *fantasy* and *phantasy* have influenced our sense and use of the word; and they have also given us the handy verb "to fantasise." If you are fantasising, you may be daydreaming, or you might be using your imagination therapeutically as a means of discovering reasons Reason does not know, discovering yourself to yourself.

But Auntie does not acknowledge the existence of that verb. Into her Supplement (through the tradesmen's door) she admits only *fantasist,* and defines the upstart, politely but with a faint curl of the lip, as "one who 'weaves' fantasies." She illustrates the word with quotations from Oscar Wilde and H. G. Wells. Evidently she means that fantasists are writers, but is not quite willing to admit it.

Indeed, in the early twentieth century, the days of victorious Realism, fantasists were often apologetic about what they did, offering it as mere word weaving—fancywork—a sort of bobble-fringing to *real* literature, or passing it off as being "for children" and therefore beneath the notice of critics, professors, and dictionary makers.

Writers of fantasy are often less modest now that what they do is recognised as literature, or at least as a genre of literature, or at least as a subliterary genre, or at least as a commercial product. For fantasies are rife and many-colored on the bookshelves. The head of the fabled unicorn is laid upon the lap of Mammon, and the offering is acceptable to Mammon. Fantasy has, in fact, become quite a business.

But when one night in Buenos Aires in 1937 three friends sat talking together about fantastic literature, it was not yet a business.

Nor was it even known as fantastic literature when one night in a villa in Geneva in 1818 three friends sat talking together and telling ghost stories. They were Mary Shelley, her husband Percy, and Lord Byron—and Claire Clairmont was probably with them, and the strange young Dr. Polidori—and they told awful tales, and Mary was frightened. "We will each," cried Byron, "write a ghost story!" So Mary went away and thought about it, fruitlessly, until a few nights later she had a nightmare in which a "pale student" used strange arts and machineries to arouse from unlife the "hideous phantasm of a man."

And so, alone of the friends, she wrote her ghost story, *Frankenstein, or The Modern Prometheus,* which is the first great modern fantasy. There are no ghosts in it; but fantasy, as the OED observed, is more than ghoulie-mongering.

Because ghosts haunt one corner of the vast domain of fantastic literature, both oral and written, people familiar with that corner of it call the whole thing ghost stories, or horror stories; just as others call it Fairyland after the part of it they love best or despise most, and others call it science fiction, and others call it stuff and nonsense. But the nameless being given life by Frankenstein's or Mary Shelley's arts and machineries is neither ghost nor fairy; science fictional he may be; stuff and nonsense he is not. He is a creature of fantasy, archetypal, deathless. Once raised he will not sleep again, for his pain will not let him sleep, the unanswered moral questions that woke with him will not let him rest in peace.

When there began to be money in the fantasy business, plenty of money was made out of him in Hollywood, but even that did not kill him.

Very likely his story was mentioned on that night in 1937 in Buenos Aires when Silvina Ocampo and her friends Borges and Bioy Casares fell to talking, so Casares tells us, "about fantastic literature . . . discussing the stories which seemed best to us. One of us suggested that if we put together the fragments of the same type we had listed in our notebooks, we would have a good book."

So that, charmingly, is how *The Book of Fantasy* came to be: three friends talking. No plans, no definitions, no business, except the intention of "having a good book."

In the making of such a book by such makers, certain definitions were implied by the exclusion of certain stories, and by inclusion other definitions were ignored; so, perhaps for the first time, horror story and ghost story and fairy tale and science fiction all came together between the same covers. Thirty years later the anthologists enlarged the collection considerably for a new edition, and Borges suggested further inclusions to the editors of the first English-language edition shortly before his death.

It is an idiosyncratic selection, completely eclectic; in fact it is a wild mishmash. Some of the stories will be familiar to most readers, others are exotic and peculiar. A piece we might think we know almost too well, such as "The Cask of Amontillado," regains its essential strangeness when read among works and fragments from the Orient and South America and distant centuries, by Kafka, Swedenborg, Yeats, Cortazar, Akutagawa, Niu Chiao, James Joyce. . . . The inclusion of a good many late-nineteenth- and early-twentieth-century writers, especially British ones, reflects, I imagine, particularly the taste of Borges, himself a member and perpetuator of the international tradition of fantasy that included Kipling and Wells.

Perhaps I should not say "tradition," since it has no name as such and little recognition in critical circles, and is distinguished in college English departments mainly by being ignored. But I believe there is a company of fantasists that Borges belonged to even as he transcended it, and that he honored even as he transformed it. As he included these writers in the *Book of Fantasy*, we may see it as a notebook of sources and affiliations and elective affinities for him and his fellow editors, and for their generation of Latin American writers, which preceded the ones we call magical realists.

By saying that fantasy is for children (which some of it is) and dismissing it as commercial and formulaic (which some of it is), critics feel justified in ignoring it all. Yet looking at such writers as Italo Calvino, Gabriel García Márquez, Philip K. Dick, Salman Rushdie, José Saramago, it is possible to believe that our narrative fiction has for years been going, slowly and vaguely and massively, not in the wash and slap of fad and fashion but as a deep current, in one direction—towards re-joining the "ocean of story," fantasy.

Fantasy is, after all, the oldest kind of narrative fiction, and the most universal.

Fiction as we currently think of it, the novel and short story as they have existed since the eighteenth century, offers one of the very best means of understanding people different from oneself, short of experi-ence. Fiction is often really much more useful than lived experience; it takes much less time, costs nothing (from the library), and comes in a manageable, orderly form. You can understand it. Experience just steamrollers over you and you begin to see what happened only years and years later, if ever. Fiction is much better than reality at providing useful factual, psychological, and moral understanding.

But realistic fiction is culture-specific. If it's your culture, your decade, fine; but if the story takes place in another century or another country, reading it with understanding involves an act of displacement, of translation, which many readers are unable or unwilling to make. The lifeways, the language, the morals and mores, the unspoken as-sumptions, all the details of ordinary life that are the substance and strength of realistic fiction, may be obscure, uninterpretable to the reader of another time and place. So writers who want their story to be understood not only by their contemporary compatriots but also by people of other lands and times, may seek a way of telling it that is more universally comprehensible; and fantasy is such a way.

Fantasies are often set in ordinary life, but the material of fantasy is a more permanent, universal reality than the social customs realism deals with. The substance of fantasy is psychic stuff, human constants: situations and imageries we recognise without having to learn or know anything at all about New York now, or London in 1850, or China three thousand years ago.

A dragon appears in the field. . . .

American readers and writers of fiction may yearn for the pure ve-racity of Jewett or Dreiser, as the English may look back with longing to the fine solidities of Arnold Bennett; but the societies in and for which those novelists wrote were limited and homogeneous enough to be described in a language that could seriously pretend to describe, in Trollope's phrase, "the way we live now." The limits of that language—shared assumptions of class, culture, education, ethics—both focus and shrink the scope of the fiction. Society in the decades around the second millennium, global, multilingual, enormously irrational, undergoing incessant radical change, is not describable in a language that assumes continuity and a common experience of life. And so writers have turned to the global, intuitional language of fantasy to describe, as accurately as they can, the way "we" live "now."

So it is in so much contemporary fiction that the most revealing and accurate descriptions of our daily life are shot through with strangeness, or displaced in time, or set upon imaginary worlds, or dissolved into the phantasmagoria of drugs or of psychosis, or rise from the mundane suddenly into the visionary and as simply descend from it again.

So it may be that the central ethical dilemma of our age, the use or nonuse of annihilating power, was posed most cogently in fictional terms by the purest of fantasists. Tolkien began *The Lord of the Rings* in 1937 and finished it about ten years later. During those years, Frodo withheld his hand from the Ring of Power, but the nations did not.

So it is that Italo Calvino's *Invisible Cities* may serve as a better guidebook to our world than any Michelin or Fodor's.

So it is that the magical realists of South America, and their counterparts in India and elsewhere, are valued for their revelatory and entire truthfulness to the history of their lands and people.

And so it is that Jorge Luis Borges, a writer in a marginal country, a marginal continent, who chose to identify himself with a marginal tradition, not the mainstream of modernist realism that flowed so full in his youth and maturity, remains a writer central to our literature.

His own poems and stories, his images of reflections, libraries, labyrinths, forking paths, his books of tigers, of rivers, of sand, of mysteries, of changes, are everywhere honored, because they are beautiful; because they are nourishing; and because they fulfill the most ancient, urgent function of words (even as the *I Ching* and the *Oxford English Dictionary* do): to form for us "mental representations of things not actually present," so that we can form a judgment of what world we live in and where we might be going in it, what we can celebrate, what we must fear.

CREADING YOUNG, READING OLD

MARK TWAIN'S *Diaries of Adam and Eve*

This piece was written as a preface to the Diaries of Adam and Eve *in the Oxford edition of the complete works of Mark Twain, 1996, edited by Shelley Fisher Fishkin. It appears here substantially as it did there (minus two paragraphs about the illustrations reproduced in the Oxford edition).*

Every tribe has its myths, and the younger members of the tribe generally get them wrong. My tribal myth of the great Berkeley Fire of 1923 went this way: when my mother's mother-in-law, who lived near the top of Cedar Street, saw the flames sweeping over the hill straight towards the house, she put her Complete Works of Mark Twain in Twenty-Five Volumes into her Model A and went away from that place.

Because I was going to put that story in print, I made the mistake of checking it first with my brother Ted. In a slow, mild sort of way, Ted took it all to pieces. He said, well, Lena Brown never had a Model A. As a matter of fact, she didn't drive. The way I remember the story, he said, some fraternity boys came up the hill and got her piano out just before the fire reached that hill. And a bearskin rug, and some other things. But I don't remember, he said, that anything was said about the Complete Works of Mark Twain.

He and I agreed, however, that fraternity boys who would choose to rescue a piano and a bear rug from a house about to be engulfed by a fiery inferno might well have also selected the Works of Mark Twain.

And the peculiarity of their selection may be illuminated by the fact that the piano ended up in the fraternity house. But after the fire or during it, Lena Brown somehow rescued the bear rug and the Complete Works from her rescuers; because Ted remembers the bear; and I certainly, vividly remember the Complete Works.

I also remain convinced that she was very fond of them, that she *would have* rescued them rather than her clothes and silver and checkbook. And maybe she really did. At any rate, when she died she left them to the family, and my brothers and I grew up with them, a full shelf of lightweight, middle-sized books in slightly pebbly and rather ratty red bindings. They are no longer, alas, in the family, but I have tracked down the edition in a library. As soon as I saw the row of red books I said Yes! with the startled joy one would feel at seeing an adult one had loved as a child, alive and looking just as he did fifty years ago. Our set was, to the best of my knowledge, the 1917 Authorized Uniform Edition, published by Harper & Brothers, and copyright by the Mark Twain Company.

The only other complete works I recall around the house was my great-aunt Betsy's Dickens. I was proud of both sets. Complete works and uniform editions are something you don't often see any more except in big libraries, but ordinary people used to own them and be proud of them. They have a majesty about them. Physically they are imposing, the uniform row of bindings, the gold-stamped titles; but the true majesty of a complete works is spiritual. It is a great mental edifice, a house of many mansions, into which a reader can enter at any of the doors, or a young reader can climb in the windows, and wander about, experiencing magnanimity.

My great-aunt was very firm about not letting us get into Dickens yet. She said nobody under eighteen had any business reading Dickens. We would merely misunderstand him and so spoil the pleasure we would otherwise take in him the rest of our lives. She was right, and I am grateful. At sixteen, I whined till she let me read *David Copperfield*, but she warned me about Steerforth, lest I fall in love with him as she had done, and break my heart. When Betsy died she left me her Dickens. We had him re-bound, for he had got a bit shabby traveling around the West with her for fifty or sixty years. When I take a book from that set I think how, wherever she went, she had this immense refuge and resource with her, reliable as not much else in her life was.

Except for Dickens, nobody told us not to read anything, and I burrowed headlong into every book on the shelves. If it was a story, I read it. And there stood that whole row of pebbly red books, all full of stories.

Obviously I got to *Tom Sawyer* very soon, and *Huck Finn;* and my next-older brother, Karl, showed me the sequels, which we judged pretty inferior, critical brats that we were. After *The Prince and the Pauper,* I got into *Life on the Mississippi,* and *Roughing It*—my prime favorite for years—and the stories, and the whole Complete Works in fact, one red book after another, snap, munch, gulp, snap, munch, gulp.

I didn't much like the *Connecticut Yankee.* The meaning of the book went right over my head. I just thought the hero was a pigheaded, loudmouthed show-off. But a little thing like not liking a book didn't keep me from reading it. Not then. It was like Brussels sprouts. Nobody could like them, but they existed, they were food, you ate them. Eating and reading were a central, essential part of life. Eating and reading can't all be Huck and corn on the cob, some of it has to be Brussels sprouts and the Yankee. And there were plenty of good bits in the *Yankee.* The only one of the row of red books I ever stuck at was *Joan of Arc.* I just couldn't swallow her. She wouldn't go down. And I believe our set was lacking the *Christian Science* volume, because I don't remember even having a go at that. If it had been there, I would have chewed at it, the way kids do, the way Eskimo housewives soften walrus hide, though I might not have been able to swallow it either.

My memory is that it was Karl who discovered Adam's and Eve's Diaries and told me to read them. I have always followed Karl's advice in reading, even after he became an English professor, because he never led me astray before he was a professor. I never would have got into *Tom Brown's School Days* for instance, if he hadn't told me you can skip the first sixty pages, and it must have been Karl who told me to stick with *Candide* till I got to the person with one buttock, who would make it all worthwhile. So I found the right pebbly red book and read both the Diaries. I loved them instantly and permanently.

And yet when I reread them this year, it was the first time for about fifty years. Not having the Complete Works with me throughout life, I have over the years reread only my favorites of the books, picked up here and there, and the stories contained in various collections. And none of those collections contained the Diaries.

This five-decade gap in time makes it irresistible to try to compare my reading of the Diaries as a child with my reading of them now.

The first thing to be said is that, when I reread them, there did not seem to have been any gap at all. What's fifty years? Well, when it comes to some of the books one read at five or at fifteen, it's an abyss. Many books I loved and learned from have fallen into it. I absolutely cannot read *The Swiss Family Robinson* and am amazed that I ever did—talk about chewing walrus hide!—but the Diaries give me a curious feeling of constancy, almost of immortality: because they haven't changed at all. They are just as fresh and surprising as when I read them first. Nor am I sure that my reading of them is very different from what it was back then.

I will try to follow that then-and-now response through three aspects of the Diaries: humor, gender, and religion.

⟜

Though it seems that children and adults have different senses of humor, they overlap so much I wonder if people don't just use the same apparatus differently at different ages. At about the age I first came on the Diaries, ten or eleven, I was reading the stories of James Thurber with sober, pious attention. I knew they were funny, that grown-ups laughed aloud reading them, but they didn't make me laugh. They were wonderful, mysterious tales of human behavior, like all the folk-tales and stories in which people did the amazing, terrifying, inexplicable things that grown-ups do. The various night wanderings of the Thurber family in "The Night the Bed Fell Down" were no more and no less strange to me than the behavior of the Reed family in the first chapter of *Jane Eyre*. Both were fascinating descriptions of life—eye-witness accounts, guidebooks to the world awaiting me. I was much too interested to laugh.

When I did laugh at Thurber was when he played with words. The man who came with the reeves and the cook who was alarmed by the doom-shaped thing on top of the refrigerator were a source of pure delight to me, then as now. The accessibility of Mark Twain's humor to a child surely has much to do with the way he plays with language, the deadpan absurdities, the marvelous choices of word. The first time I ever read the story about the blue jay trying to fill the cabin with acorns, I nearly died. I lay on the floor gasping and writhing with joy. Even now I feel a peaceful cheer come over me when I think of that blue jay. And it's all in the way he tells it, as they say. The story is the way the story is told.

Adam's Diary is funny, when it is funny, because of the way Adam writes it.

This made her sorry for the creatures which live in there, which she calls fish, for she continues to fasten names on to things that don't need them and don't come when they are called by them, which is a matter of no consequence to her, as she is such a numskull anyway; so she got a lot of them out and brought them in last night and put them in my bed to keep warm, but I have noticed them now and then all day, and I don't see that they are any happier there than they were before, only quieter.

Now that is a pure Mark Twain tour de force sentence, covering an immense amount of territory in an effortless, aimless ramble that seems to be heading nowhere in particular and ends up with breath-taking accuracy at the gold mine. Any sensible child would find that funny, perhaps not following all its divagations but delighted by the swing of it, by the word *numskull*, by the idea of putting fish in the bed; and as that child grew older and reread it, its reward would only grow; and if that grown-up child had to write an essay on the piece and therefore earnestly studied and pored over this sentence, she would end up in unmitigated admiration of its vocabulary, syntax, pacing, sense, and rhythm, above all the beautiful timing of the last two words; and she would, and she does, still find it funny.

Twain's humor is indestructible. Trying to make a study of the rhythms of prose last year, I analysed a paragraph from "The Jumping Frog"—laboring over it, dissecting it, counting beats, grouping phrases, reducing it to a mere drum-score—and even after all that mauling, every time I read it, it was as fresh-flowing and lively and amusing as ever, or more so. The prose itself is indestructible. It is all of a piece. It is a living person speaking. Mark Twain put his voice on paper with a fidelity and vitality that makes electronic recordings seem crude and quaint.

I wonder if this is why we trust him, even though he lets us down so often. Lapses such as the silly stuff about Niagara in Adam's Diary—evidently worked in to make it suit a publication about the Falls—would make me distrust most writers. But Mark Twain's purity is unmistakable and incorruptible, which is why the lapses stick out so, and yet are forgivable. I have heard a great pianist who made a great many mistakes in playing; the mistakes were of no account because the music was true. Though Mark Twain forces his humor sometimes, always his own voice comes back, comes through; and his own voice is one of hyperbole and absurdity and wild invention and absolute accuracy and truth.

So all in all my response to the humor of the Diaries is very much what it was fifty years ago. This is partly because a good deal of the humor is perfectly childish. I mean that as praise. There is no meanness in it, no nudging and winking, nothing snide. Now, as then, I find

Adam very funny, but so obtuse I often want to kick him rather than laugh at him. Eve isn't quite as funny, but I don't get as cross with her, so it's easier to laugh.

ↄ

I read the Diaries before I had any personal interest, as you might say, in gender. I had noticed that there were males and females and had learned from a useful Germanic book how babies occurred, but the whole thing was entirely remote and theoretical, about as immediately interesting to me as the Keynesian theory of economics. "Latency," one of Freud's fine imaginative inventions, was more successful than most; children used to have years of freedom before they had to start working their hormones into the kind of lascivious lather that is now expected of ten-year-olds. Anyhow, in the 1940s gender was not a subject of discussion. Men were men (running things or in uniform, mostly), women were women (housekeeping or in factories, mostly), and that was that. Except for a few subversives like Virginia Woolf nobody publicly questioned the institutions and assumptions of male primacy. It was the century's low point architecturally in the Construction of Gender, reduced in those years to something about as spacious and comfortable as a broom closet.

But the Diaries date from the turn of the nineteenth century, a time of revolutionary inquiry into gender roles, the first age of feminism, the period of the woman suffrage movement and of the "New Woman"— who was precisely the robust and joyously competent Eve that Mark Twain gives us.

I see now in the Diaries, along with a tenderness and a profound delicacy of feeling about women, a certain advocacy. Mark Twain is always on the side of the underdog; and though he believed it was and must be a man's world, he knew that women were the underdogs in it. This fine sense of justice is what gives both the Diaries their moral complexity.

There was an element of discomfort in them for me as a child, and

I think it lies just here, in that complexity and a certain degree of self-contradiction.

It is not Adam's superiority of brains or brawn that gives him his absolute advantage over Eve, but his blockish stupidity. He does not notice, does not listen, is uninterested, indifferent, dumb. He will not relate to her; she must relate herself—in words and actions—to him, and relate him to the rest of Eden. He is entirely satisfied with himself as he is; she must adapt her ways to him. He is immovably fixed at the center of his own attention. To live with him she must agree to be peripheral to him, contingent, secondary.

The degree of social and psychological truth in this picture of life in Eden is pretty considerable. Milton thought it was a fine arrangement; it appears Mark Twain didn't, since he shows us at the end of both Diaries that although Eve has not changed much, she has changed Adam profoundly. She always was awake. He slowly, finally wakes up, and does her, and therefore himself, justice. But isn't it too late, for her?

All this I think I followed pretty well, and was fascinated and somewhat troubled by, though I could not have discussed it, when I read the Diaries as a child. Children have a seemingly innate passion for justice; they don't have to be taught it. They have to have it beaten out of them, in fact, to end up as properly prejudiced adults.

Mark Twain and I both grew up in a society that cherished a visionary ideal of gender by pairs: the breadwinning, self-reliant husband and the home-dwelling, dependent wife. He the oak, she the ivy; power his, grace hers. He works and earns; she "doesn't work," but keeps his house, bears and brings up his children, and furnishes him the aesthetic and often the spiritual comforts of life. Now at this latter end of the century, the religio-political conservative's vision of what men and women do and should do is still close to that picture, though even more remote from most people's experience than it was fifty or a hundred years ago. Do Twain's Adam and Eve essentially fit this powerful stereotype, or do they vary it significantly?

I think the variations are significant, even if the text fudges them in the end. Mark Twain is not supporting a gender ideal, but investigating what he sees as real differences between women and men, some of them fitting into that ideal, some in conflict with it.

Eve is the intellectual in Eden, Adam the redneck. She is wildly curious and wants to learn everything, to name everything. Adam has no curiosity about anything, certain that he knows all he needs to know. She wants to talk, he wants to grunt. She is sociable, he is solitary. She prides herself on being scientific, though she settles for her own pet theory without testing it; her method is purely intuitive and rational, without a shadow of empiricism. He thinks she ought to test her ideas, but is too lazy to do it himself. He goes over Niagara Falls in a barrel, he doesn't say why; apparently because a man does such things. Far more imaginative and influenced by the imagination than he, she does dangerous things only when she doesn't know they're dangerous. She rides tigers and talks to the serpent. She is rebellious, adventurous, and independent; he does not question authority. She is the innocent troublemaker. Her loving anarchism ruins his mindless, self-sufficient, authoritarian Eden—and saves him from it.

Does it save her?

This spirited, intelligent, anarchic Eve reminds me of H. G. Wells's Ann Veronica, an exemplary New Woman of 1909. Yet Ann Veronica's courage and curiosity finally lead her not to independence but to wifehood, seen as the proper and sufficient fulfillment of feminine being. We are ominously close to the Natasha Syndrome, the collapse of a vivid woman character into a brood sow as soon as she marries and has children. Once she has won Adam over, once the children come, does Eve stop asking and thinking and singing and naming and venturing? We don't know. Tolstoy gives us a horrible glimpse of Natasha married; Wells tries to convince us Ann Veronica is going to be just fine; but Mark Twain tells us nothing about what Eve becomes. She falls silent. Not a good sign. After the Fall we have only Adam's voice, puzzling mightily over what kind of animal Cain is. Eve tells us only that she would love Adam even if he beat her—a very bad sign.

And, forty years later, she says, "He is strong, I am weak, I am not so necessary to him as he is to me—life without him would not be life; how could I endure it?"

I don't know whether I am supposed to believe her, or can believe her. It doesn't sound like the woman I knew. Eve, weak? Rubbish! Adam's usefulness as a helpmeet is problematical, a man who, when she tells him they'll have to work for their living, decides "She will be useful. I will superintend"—a man who thinks his son is a kangaroo. Eve did need him in order to have children, and since she loves him she would miss him; but where is the evidence that she couldn't survive without him? He would presumably have survived without her, in the brutish way he survived before her. But surely it is their *interdependence* that is the real point?

I want, now, to read the Diaries as a subtle, sweet-natured send-up of the Strong Man–Weak Woman arrangement; but I'm not sure it's possible to do so, or not entirely. It may be both a send-up and a capitulation.

And Adam has the last word. "Wheresoever she was, *there* was Eden." But the poignancy of those words is utterly unexpected, a cry from the heart. It made me shiver as a child; it does now.

⟳

I was raised as irreligious as a jackrabbit, and probably this is one reason Mark Twain made so much sense to me as a child. Descriptions of churchgoing interested me as the exotic rites of a foreign tribe, and nobody described churchgoing better than Mark Twain did. But God, as I encountered him in my reading, seemed only to cause unnecessary complications, making people fall into strange postures and do depressing things; he treated Beth March abominably, and did his best to ruin Jane Eyre's life before she traded him in for Rochester. I didn't read any of the books in which God is the main character until a few years later. I was perfectly content with books in which he didn't figure at all.

Could anybody but Mark Twain have told the story of Adam and Eve without mentioning Jehovah?

As a heathen child I was entirely comfortable with his version. I took it for granted that it was the sensible one.

As an ancient heathen I still find it sensible, but can better appreciate its originality and courage. The nerve of the man, the marvelous, stunning independence of that mind! In pious, prayerful, censorious, self-righteous Christian America of 1896, or 1996 for that matter, to show God as an unnecessary hypothesis, by letting Eve and Adam cast themselves out of Eden without any help at all from him, and really none from the serpent either—to put sin and salvation, love and death in our own hands, as our own, strictly human business, our responsibility—now that's a free soul, and a brave one.

What luck for a child to meet such a soul when she is young. What luck for a country to have a Mark Twain in its heart.

THINKING ABOUT CORDWAINER SMITH

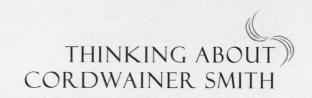

Written for the program booklet of the annual science-fiction confer-ence ReaderCon, of July 1994, this essay was aimed at a sophisticated group of readers familiar with its subject. For those who haven't read the fiction of Cordwainer Smith or James Tiptree Jr., I can only hope it may awaken a curiosity that will lead them to have a look at the works of these intensely original writers. Some points will be clearer if one knows that both writers worked for the U.S. government (the usual explanation of why they used pen names when they wrote fiction), and that Smith, as Paul Linebarger, was a professor of Asiatic Studies at Johns Hopkins, an intelligence agent in China during the Second World War, wrote Psychological Warfare, *long the standard text on the subject, served as a member of the Foreign Policy Association and adviser to John F. Kennedy, and was Sun Yat-sen's godson.*

NAMES

A pen name is a curious device. Actors, singers, dancers use stage names for various reasons, but it seems that not many painters or sculptors or composers make up their name. If you're a German com-poser named Engelbert Humperdinck who wrote the opera *Hansel and Gretel,* you don't do anything about your name, you just live with it, till a hundred years later some dweeb singer comes along and filches it because he thinks it's cute. If you're a French painter named Rosa Bonheur, you don't call yourself Georges Tristesse; you just

paint horses and sign "Rosa" large and clear. But writers, especially
fiction writers, are always making up names. Do they confuse themselves with their characters?

The question isn't totally frivolous. I think most novelists are
aware at times of containing multitudes, of having an uncomfortably
acute sympathy for Multiple Personality Disorder, of not entirely sub-
scribing to the commonsense notion of what constitutes a self.

And there is a distinction, normally, between "the writer" and
"the person." The cult of personality erases this difference; with writers like Lord Byron and Hemingway, as with actors or politicians,
the person disappears in the glare of the persona. Publicity, book
tours, and so on all keep the glare focused. People line up to "meet
the writer," not realising that this is impossible. Nobody can be a
writer during a book signing, not even Harlan Ellison. All they can
write is "To Jane Doe with best regards from George Author"—not
a very interesting story. All their admirers can meet is the person—
who has a lot in common with, but is not, the writer. Maybe nicer,
maybe duller, maybe older, maybe meaner; but the main difference is,
the person lives in this world, but writers live in their imagination,
and/or in the public imagination, which creates a public figure that
lives only in the public imagination.

So the pen name, hiding the person behind the writer, may be essentially a protective and enabling device, as it was for the Brontë sisters and for Mary Ann Evans. The androgynous Currer, Ellis, and
Acton Bell hid Charlotte, Emily, and Anne Brontë from a publicity that
might offend their small community, and also gave their manuscripts a
chance to be read with an unprejudiced eye by editors, who would assume them to be men. George Eliot protected Mary Ann Evans, who
was unrepentantly living in sin, from the dragon of social disapproval.

I think one can assume that these personae also allowed the writers a freedom from inner censors, internalised shames and inhibitions,
notions of what a woman "should" write. The masculine pen name,
oddly enough, frees the woman author from obedience to a masculine

conception of literature and experience. I think James Tiptree Jr. undoubtedly gave Alice Sheldon such freedom.

But with Sheldon we come to another aspect of the pen name: the already public figure who wants or needs a different persona for a different kind of work.

I don't know if there was any actual professional need for Sheldon to be Tiptree; would she have lost a job or come under governmental suspicion if she'd published her stories under her own name? My guess is that her need for the pen name was primarily and intensely personal. She needed to write as somebody other than who she "was." She had led a highly successful career as a woman, but as a writer she needed, at least at first, to present herself, perhaps even to herself, as a man. She found her alter ego on the label of a jar of marmalade. She slipped into the impersonation very comfortably, writing not only stories but letters as James Tiptree Jr., who became a beloved, treasured penfriend to many people. When she began to want to publish as a woman she used only half of her own name, calling herself Raccoona Sheldon (a name that troubles me, because the invented half is so grotesque that it seems a self put-down). Finally, when they blew her cover, she essentially stopped writing. It looks as if the name/mask, whether masculine or feminine, was above all an enabler to her, an escape route from a public self that could not or would not write, into a private self that was all writer.

So how about Professor and Colonel Paul Myron Anthony Linebarger—what was Cordwainer Smith to him? From here on I rely completely and gratefully on the researches of John J. Pierce, the prime authority on Linebarger/Smith's life and writing. In his fine introduction to *The Rediscovery of Man,* Pierce tells us that Linebarger published his book on psychological warfare under his own name, but his first two novels (*Ria* and *Carola*) as Felix C. Forrest. Then, "when people found out who 'Forrest' was, he couldn't write any more." (That sounds like Sheldon.) Pierce goes on: "He tried a spy thriller, *Atomsk,* as Carmichael Smith, but was found out again. He even submitted a manuscript for another novel under his wife's name, but nobody was fooled." Using your wife's name as an alias implies, to me, not only a very good-natured wife, but a very imperative need for a mask. It also implies a quite extraordinary indifference to what is so often of immense importance to a man: that he be perceived, always and totally, as a man.

My guess is that the pen name he finally settled on may have been necessary to save his dignity as an academic and an expert on grave matters, but was equally important to him because it allowed him psychic freedom. Dr. Linebarger had to be respectable and responsible and had to guard his tongue. Cordwainer Smith wrote skiffy and babbled whatever he pleased. The Doctor used his knowledge discreetly to counsel Chiang Kai-shek and advise politicians and diplomats. Mr. Smith let that knowledge out in the open to please the common folk who read popular fiction, and to serve art. Paul was a man. Cordwainer was men, women, animals, a cosmos.

Splitting the personality in this way might signify in most people that they were a bit daft; but all the writers I've been talking about were notably effective people in both incarnations, flesh and paper. Still, their paper selves, having long outlived the "real person," might well ask, Which of us can claim to be real?

WORDS
After all, fiction writers make a reality of words.

The arts of writing all begin in playing with words, wallowing in them, revelling in them, being obsessed by them, finding reality in them. Words are the mud this mudpie's made of. Some writers are cool and masterful and never get their hands dirty, but Cordwainer Smith got muddy from the toes to the top of the head.

Language evidently intoxicated him and sometimes controlled him; rhymes, particularly, and the rhythms of sentences. *Golden the ship was—Oh! Oh! Oh!* That's the last line, and the title, of one of his stories. I have a baseless, unverifiable, perhaps totally mistaken conviction that the line came before the story: that the story grew out of, unfolded from, was compelled to exist by, an unexplained, unattached fragment of language, seven words that took hold of his mind and rocked it and wouldn't let him be until he had made a box of meaning that would hold them: *Golden the ship was—Oh! Oh! Oh!*

This kind of thing is part of his peculiar magic. He knows a powerful phrase or word when he finds one, and uses and repeats it powerfully. I suspect the "Instrumentality" was very little but a word at first, a grand word, which as he used, repeated, explored, explained it, turned out to contain in itself much of the wonderful, semicoherent "future history" of the stories and the novel. The Instrumentality of Mankind—it is a suggestive, complex, multiplex kind of phrase, a Mother Lode phrase that keeps leading to the high-grade ore.

Sometimes I think the words get away from him. The story "Drunkboat" is Arthur Rimbaud getting high on absinthe getting Cordwainer Smith high on *Le Bateau ivre* and sailing out across the galaxy. It's a tour de force. But it's full of awfully bad verse.

> Point your gun at a murky lurky.
> *(Now you're talking ham or turkey!)*
> Shoot a shot at a dying aoudad.
> *(Don't ask the lady why or how, dad!)*

Lord Crudelta, in the story, quotes this as an example of words remaining long after their referents are gone, laboriously explaining that an aoudad was an ancient sheep and that he doesn't know what ham and turkey were, but that children have sung the song for "thousands of years." Well, I don't believe it. No sane child would sing that for five minutes. I think Cordwainer Smith had that stupid aoudad/how dad rhyme in his head and couldn't get it out, and it overcame his better reason and forced itself into the story.

When you let words take you over, as Rimbaud and Smith did, you relinquish control to a sometimes dangerous extent. You can't keep the stupidities and inconsequentialities out, the way a tight-control writer can; you're on a wild ride and you have to take what comes. What comes may be treasure and may be junk. I find much of "Drunkboat" overwritten, straining for effect, starting with its rather pompous claims to fame: "Perhaps it is the saddest, maddest, wildest story in the whole long history of space." . . . "We know his name now. And our children and their children will know it for always." And the story is full of obsessive jingles, "Baiter Gator" and "ochre joker" and so on, which weaken what should be a stunning effect when Rambo/ Rimbaud bursts into a wild flood of rhyming speech. There are too many one-sentence paragraphs, italics, and other heavy devices to show significance. And yet, and yet . . . what a wonderful image, the man swimming, swimming slowly through spacetime, reaching through the walls, seeking his Elizabeth. . . . And the recurrent char-acters, Sir-and-Doctor Vomact, the Lord Crudelta (whose Italian name means what Lord Jestocost's means in Russian), the Instrumentality it-self. "Drunkboat" is a wild jungle of language, grotesque, deformed, obstructive, energetic, vividly alive.

THE MOUSE

I seem to be impelled to discuss stories that I don't particularly like, in-stead of the ones I love, such as "Alpha Ralpha Boulevard," "The Dead Lady of Clown Town," "Mark Elf," "A Planet Named Shayol."

A Smith story that I have always resisted, kept my distance from, is "Think Blue, Count Two." When I reread it some while ago for con-sideration for the *Norton Book of Science Fiction* I saw again what I'd disliked—a pretty girl, blue-eyed, called "doll" and "kitten," a plot that teases by threatening sadism but dodges the threat by rather im-plausible means, and a sentimental ending where the doll-kitten goes off with the deformed sadist, now miraculously cured and tamed. A very *very* romantic story, plunging (as romanticism will) from sappy sweetness to sick cruelty, with not much actual humanity in between. When it came to choosing for the *Norton Book,* I wanted "Alpha

Ralpha Boulevard," which uses these characteristic Smithian themes in a story that is not excessively, but magnificently, romantic—a beautiful, powerful story. When my coeditors argued for other choices, I whined. I wanted "Alpha Ralpha" in that book the way I wanted Fritz Leiber's "The Winter Flies" in it—passionately—because to me they are uniquely valuable, unsurpassed explorations of regions of fiction that are still unfamiliar, still New Found Lands.

Well, so, then I reread "Think Blue" again for this paper. I did so looking for evidence, as it were, of what I don't like in Smith. Served me right.

What I found was that I had misread and underestimated the story shamefully. Indeed the heroine-doll-kitten seems the typical male-fantasy girl, virginal, beautiful, defenseless, with "no skill, no learning, no trained capacities," no threat to nobody, no sir. She's being used to hold the crew together during a long voyage; she has "Daughter Potential," that is, every man will want to protect her, she will keep everybody alive "for her sake." However, in case things get really bad, she has another protection aboard, in the form of one of Smith's unforgettable inventions, a cube of laminated mouse brain.

> We stiffened it with celluprime and then we veneered it down, about seven thousand layers. Each one has plastic of at least two molecular thicknesses. This mouse can't spoil. As a matter of fact, this mouse is going to go on thinking forever. He won't think much, unless we put the voltage on him, but he'll think. And he can't spoil. . . . I told you, this mouse is going to be thinking when the last human being on the last known planet is dead. And it's going to be thinking about that girl. Forever.

The mouse does protect her, through the projection of various fantasies, which I no longer find as implausible as I did, because I now see that in fact she is protectable. She is not the inevitable victim I took her for. Veesey has strength and courage; she meets the danger posed by her psychotic male companions with stoicism: "Life's life, she thought, and I must live it. Here." Her reaction to her own Daughter Potential is stoical endurance—"Is it *child* again? she thought to herself." She's a woman, not a child, and she knows it if they don't. (She is, in fact, remarkably like some of Dickens's much-ridiculed heroines, Lizzie Hexam, Amy Dorrit, Florence Dombey, who, though the male characters see them as childish, and many readers follow suit, are in fact strong, courageous, adult women, survivors against all odds.) She is childlike only in the depth of her innocence. At the most frightening moment she asks the rapist, "Is this what crime is, what you are doing to me?" But the allegory is of an Innocence stronger than Experience—of a genuinely inviolable soul.

And the sick bits, I now realise, are not self-indulgent, as so much literary rape and torture is. Trying to say something seriously about who men are, what their chief problem may be, Smith found these were the images to say it with—the necessary vocabulary.

The apparitions summoned by Sh'san to save Veesey from the men and the men from themselves are much more complicated and psychologically tricky than I had thought. Since they bring about the happy ending, they can partake in high comedy; and they do, especially the last one, the ship's captain:

> "If I stop to think about it, I find myself pretty upsetting. I know that I'm just an echo in your minds, combined with the experience and wisdom which has gone into the cube. So I guess that I do what real people do. I just don't think about it very much. I mind my business." He stiffened and straightened and was himself again. "My own business," he repeated.
>
> "And Sh'san," said Trece, "how do you feel about him?"
>
> A look of awe—almost a look of terror—came upon the captain's face. . . . "Sh'san. He is the thinker of all thinking,

the 'to be' of being, the doer of doings. He is powerful beyond
your strongest imagination. He makes me come living out of
your living minds. In fact," said the captain with a final snarl,
"he is a dead mouse brain laminated with plastic and I have
no idea at all of who *I* am. Good night to you all!"

The captain set his cap on his head and walked straight
through the hull.

This reality-shifting also contains one of Smith's central and to me
most fascinating themes: that of the animal as savior. The engineer
who created the cube imprinted his own personality in it, the minds of
the girl and the two men create the apparitions, the girl's imprinted call
for help switches on the voltage that activates the cube—but the sav-
ing energy lies, finally, in the brain of a dead mouse.

The mouse is worth remembering.

THE UNDERPEOPLE

It's easy to remember Smith's great Underpeople savior figures—D'joan
the dog woman, the pure sacrificial figure; E-tele-keli, man and eagle,
who flies deep under Old Earth; and of course, threading her way like a
wandering red flame through the stories and the novel, C'mell the girly-
girl, all woman and all cat.

In stories where animal and human are mixed in the way Smith
mixed them, the human body dominating but possessing animal char-
acteristics, the effect is usually horrible or pitiful: the Minotaur or the
awful creatures of Dr. Moreau's island.

Here is B'dikkat, the cattle-person of Shayol, Smith's version of the
Minotaur:

An enormous face, four times the size of any human face
Mercer had ever seen, was looking down at him. Huge brown
eyes, cowlike in their gentle inoffensiveness, moved back and

forth as the big face examined Mercer's wrapping. The face was that of a handsome man of middle years, clean-shaven, hair chestnut-brown, with sensual, full lips and gigantic but healthy yellow teeth exposed in a half-smile. The face saw Mercer's eyes open, and spoke with a deep friendly roar.

The mixture is very strange and not horrible at all; the bull and the man are each there, blended but uncontaminated, with their own nature and their own beauty.

When human and animal can mix so completely, they are, by implication, the same. An identity has been asserted.

In Norstrilia, the eponymous setting of Smith's one novel, an immortality drug, stroon, or the santaclara drug, is made from the exudations of enormous, sick sheep. The countryside is dotted with these sheep, big as airplane hangars, immobile, diseased. By their endless dying they furnish untold wealth and eternal life to their human owners.

Animal sacrifice is a very widespread human custom. The little dead mouse, the dying sheep of Norstrilia, may be seen as animal sacrifices to ensure human welfare. But the Underpeople's suffering and their sacrifice in the person of D'joan extend and enlarge the theme. It is unmistakably a human sacrifice—also a fairly widespread human custom. D'joan's life points to Joan of Arc, of course, and behind that, to the humiliation and death of Jesus.

The "Old Strong Religion," one of Smith's fine phrases, is mentioned in several stories, but he never does much with it. In a way it would seem more appropriate if the Old Strong Religion were, not Christianity as it evidently is, but Buddhism. The Compassionate Buddha can be incarnate as any creature, as a mother tiger, as a little jackal, as a bird, as a mouse. Smith does not share the Judeo-Christian exclusive focus on one species, the exclusion from sacredness of everything but the human. His stories say that the death of an animal counts the same, weighs the same, as the death of a human. That animal and human are equally sacred. That salvation can lie in the death of a dog, as in the death of a god.

This is pretty subversive stuff. Smith's attitude towards authority is complex. He loves to tell us about people who are immensely powerful and supernally rich—the Lords and Ladies of the Instrumentality, the Misters and Owners of Norstrilia, such as the boy who bought Old Earth. Linebarger's familiarity with the corridors of power must have fed this fascination, and also fueled Smith's visions of people in power who learn to be worthy of their power, who become just, compassionate, and wise. Their wisdom leads them to subvert their own orderly, static, perfect society, to reinvent freedom, ordaining the Rediscovery of Man, when "everywhere, men and women worked with a wild will to build a more imperfect world."

But wisdom, compassion, and justice fail them when it comes to the Underpeople. Here they still have something to learn. Here the Judeo-Christian division still obtains. The Underpeople are nonpeople, they have no rights, no souls, they are things that exist to serve Man. Like any machine or slave, if useless or rebellious they are to be destroyed. At this point, in this division, lies the ethical crux of Smith's strongest stories.

"Alpha Ralpha Boulevard" serves well to illustrate the themes. In a corridor under the earth (the twelve-mile-high Earthport and the deep underground are recurrent, contrasted loci) the narrator Paul and his Virginia are threatened by a monstrous, Dr. Moreauish, drunken version of the bull-man. They are saved from it by a woman, who tells them, "Come no closer. I am a cat." When Paul thanks her and asks her name, she says, "Does it matter? I'm not a person."

Paul has reacted to her as to a beautiful woman, but Virginia feels "dirtied" by even this contact with an Underperson. At the end, high on the ruined boulevard in the sky, C'mell tries again to save them both. Virginia, horrified that a cat-girl might actually touch her, tries to avoid her and falls to her death. Only Paul, who saw her as human, can be saved. And the reason she wanted to save them was that Paul—unthinkingly, instinctively—had stopped another man from crushing the eggs of some birds.

You saved them. You saved their young, when the red-topped man was killing them all. All of us have been worried about what you true people would do to us when you were free. We found out. Some of you are bad and kill other kinds of life. Others of you are good and protect life.

Thought I, is that all there is to *good* and *bad*?

There is, of course, much more to the story, a marvelously complex one; but at the heart of it is this motif, a familiar one from our secular mythology, our folktales. The girl who saves the ant from the spider's web is saved in turn by the ants, who do her impossible task for her; the prince who sneers at the wolf in the trap is lost in the forest, but the prince who frees the wolf inherits the kingdom. The theme is pagan, entering Christianity only with St. Francis. It is a profound element of Buddhism, Jainism, and other Asian religions; and the sense of the interdependence of human and animal is fundamental to the native religions of North America.

Smith was touching a deep chord here, one that is not often struck in realistic fiction. Science fiction is specifically suited to this theme, since its central subject is the interaction of the human with the non-human, the known/self with the unknown/other. The durable and mysterious power of Cordwainer Smith's stories is not a matter only of their exuberant language and brilliant invention and hallucinatory imagery; there is a deep ground to them, a moral ground, lying in his persuasive conviction of the responsibility of one being for another. "Thought I, is that all there is to *good* and *bad*?"

᛭

Note: Cordwainer Smith's works, published in paperback, are at any given moment mostly out of print. Among them are the story collections *You Will Never Be the Same, Space Lords, Stardreamer,* and various combinations of pieces of what never quite became a finished novel, published under the titles *The Planet Buyer, Quest of the Three Worlds,* and *Norstrilia.*

STRESS-RHYTHM IN POETRY AND PROSE

This investigation and discussion grew out of a workshop on rhythm in language I gave in 1995. It leads to the next essay, on rhythm in Tolkien's work.

GETTING THE BEAT

RHYTHM *Phys., Physiol., etc.*, movement with regular succession of strong and weak elements; regularly recurring sequence of events. —*In literature,* metrical movement determined by various relations of long and short or accented and unaccented syllables; measured flow of words and phrases in verse or prose. *In music,* periodical accent and the duration of notes. *In fine arts,* harmonious correlation of parts; regular succession of opposites. (*The Concise Oxford Dictionary*)

Movement is the first word. Rhythm is a mode of time.

Like time, rhythm can be imagined as linear, events seen as beads strung along a line of intervals, or cyclical: the line becomes a circle, a necklace of beads. Or if the event is singular, the interval can be seen as a circle always coming round to it again: for instance, year as interval, birthday as event. . . .

Identical intervals make a regular rhythm. The more irregular the intervals are, the more alike the events have to be for any rhythm to be recognised.

Rhythm is a physical, material, bodily thing: the drumstick hitting the drumhead, the dancer's pounding feet. Rhythm is a spiritual thing: the drummer's ecstasy, the dancer's joy.

Beginning to consider the rhythms of writing, my mind wandered about among the world's beats: the clock, the heart, the interval between the last meal and the next meal, the alternation of day and night. Trying to understand how and why writing is rhythmical, I thought about mechanical, biological, social, and cosmic rhythms; about the interplay of bodily rhythms with social regularities; about the relation of rhythm and order, rhythm and chaos.

One way to start thinking about such things is to try to listen to your own body's beat.

Many kinds of meditation begin, and some go on, by concentrating your awareness on breathing, nothing but breathing. You sit and you pay attention, full attention, constant attention, to your breath as it goes in your nostrils and comes out. When your attention wanders, you gently bring it back to your nose and the sensation of breathing. In . . . out . . . in . . . out . . . To sit and be fully aware of the air going in and out of your nose and nothing else, this sounds really stupid. If you haven't tried it, try it. It is really stupid. Nothing your intellect can do can help you do it. This must be why so many people for so long have used it as a way towards wisdom.

Rhythm is pulsation. So is life. If they want to know if you're still alive, they feel for your pulse, no? Find your pulse where you can feel it easily and attend to it, its evenness and irregularities. Heartbeat changes a lot, it's seldom metronomically even for long.

And also, attend to the interval *between* beats, thinking of the pulse as a boundary between intervals. Event and interval, like figure and ground, can be reversed.

Walking is a lovely beat. Just walking. Runners like a fast pounding beat, a high stress-rate. That's fine. But it's also pleasant to walk, just walk, in awareness of the steady, subtle, ever-changing rhythms of walking.

T'ai chi walking is interestingly rhythmical. I learned to do it thus: You're barefoot. You stand still for a while. On an inbreath, lift one foot and move it forward. Set it down as you breathe out. The other foot will naturally begin to rise, but its full rise and movement forward must wait for the inbreath. It comes softly down on the outbreath. Meanwhile, the first foot is ready for the inbreath. . . . You aren't going to get very far, walking this way. I used to fall over quite a lot when I first tried it. To keep your balance it helps to set the whole foot down at once, lightly, not striking down heel first, and to be aware of the touch of foot on ground and the touch of ground on foot. This is *very* low stress-rate walking. It's a form of meditation, because you can't think about anything else while doing it.

Meditation is a word often used to mean "thinking" but as I understand it, it means *not* thinking, which is much harder than one would think. In any case, all the meditative practices I know offer an immediate awareness of bodily and other rhythms.

RHYTHM IN LANGUAGE: STRESS

I apologise for the didactic tone of this section. The subject of language rhythms has a technical vocabulary, and as with all such jargons, some words need explaining. The technical word for the beat in language (spoken or written) is *stress*. There are unstressed languages, but English is a language that uses stress.

ENGlish is a LANGuage that Uses STRESS.

Some syllables get said harder than others. That's "stress."

Every English word spoken by itself has at least one stressed syllable, even if it only has one: (WHEN?) Many words, however, when used in sentences, receive no stress: the, of, in, a, when . . . (when USED in SENtences). In normal speech, a stress occurs every few syllables.

(Note: Most of us discovered as children that if you repeat any word aloud, such as the word *syllable—syllable syllable syllable syllable syllable*—or even your own name, it will begin to sound funny and then become meaningless, having been reduced by repetition to pure sound and rhythm, which is all it "really" is. This is important.)

Poetry and prose differ in the *frequency* and the *regularity* of stresses.

Frequency: In poetry, there is often only one unstressed syllable between stressed ones, and seldom more than two (thus: TUM ta TUM, or TUM ta ta TUM, but seldom TUM ta ta ta TUM). Prose often has three or even four unstressed syllables between stressed ones.

In other words, in poetry the intervals are shorter; or, in other other words, in prose the intervals are longer.

If you say more than four unstressed syllables in a row you are likely to find yourself mumbling. That's what mumbling is.

SYLLables in a ROW—that's four. SYLLables in an unexPECted ROW—that's six, and it is so mumbly that in reading it aloud we're likely to put in a substress, perhaps on the "un" of "unexpected," to give it a bit of a beat so that it's easier to say.

Both as readers and as speakers, we want the stresses to occur fairly often, we resist long intervals. We don't really like mumbling.

Regularity: A regularly repeated pattern of stress/unstress, a regular beat, in language, is called *meter*. Meter belongs to poetry. To poetry alone.

Within the realm of poetry, free verse does not have meter. But the stress-count of free verse is high, and it sneaks in a lot of semiregular, sort-of-metrical patterns.

Prose does not have meter. Prose scrupulously avoids any noticeable regularity or pattern of stresses. If prose acquires any noticeable meter for more than a sentence or so (just as if it rhymes noticeably), it stops being prose and becomes poetry.

This is the only difference between prose and poetry that I have ever been certain of.

STRESS-RHYTHM IN POETRY: METRICS

English meter in the earliest days was "accentual," which means people just counted how many stresses per line. The metrical unit in such poetry is the line or the half-line. Each unit has the same number of stresses; but there is no set number of syllables in the line and no set arrangement of stressed and unstressed syllables. Seamus Heaney's translation of *Beowulf* reproduces the four-stress line that breaks into two half-lines:

> Down to the waves then, dressed in the web
> of their chain-mail and warshirts, the young men marched.

By Chaucer's day, English poets had taken to counting syllables along with stresses, and to thinking of the line as divisible into feet. Some poets still argue that you can't put English stockings onto Greek or Latin feet, but most find the concept of the metric foot a useful one. All who do agree that the foot that goes the farthest in English has two syllables, the first unstressed, the second stressed: ta TUM— the iamb.

> "Te he!" quoth she, and clapt the window to.

That line from Chaucer is iambic pentameter, "five-beat iambic." English poetry has over the centuries favored this particular meter. (It has been suggested that this may be because five heartbeats relate to a comfortable breathing rate, so that iambic pentameter fits nicely with the living-breathing-speaking voice.)

Metrical poetry has a regular pattern, yet many, many lines of poems in iambic pentameter do not actually go,

> Te HE! quoth SHE, and CLAPT the WINdow TO—
> ta TUM ta TUM ta TUM ta TUM ta TUM

(or as it's usually written,

$$— \acute{} \ / — \acute{} \ / — \acute{} \ / — \acute{} \ / — \acute{} \ /$$

—a dash for the unstressed syllable, a stroke for the stressed syllable, and a slash to separate the feet).

The pattern is endlessly varied by "substituting" feet—a TUM ta
here, a ta ta followed by a TUM TUM, an unstressed syllable dropped
or added. (All these variant feet have names of their own—trochee,
pyrrhic/spondee, anapest.) The innate stresses of the words, manipulated by the syntax, play against the demand of the regular beat, setting up a syncopation, a tension between expectation and act, which is
surely one of the essential ploys of art.

Here are three lines of Shakespeare, who was, no question about
it, good at this sort of thing:

> Thus conscience does make cowards of us all,
> And thus the native hue of resolution
> Is sicklied o'er with the pale cast of thought.

If you force a pure iambic/ten-syllable line pattern onto these lines
you'll get:

> Thus CONscience DOES make COWards OF us ALL
> And THUS the NAtive HUE of RESoLOOSHN
> Is SICKlied O'ER with THE pale CAST of THOUGHT.

Clearly this won't do. "Of" and "the" are not stressable words. Besides, we aren't rocking in a rocker, we're reading poetry. The natural
stress of the words within the sentence, and the syntactical phrases or
meaning-groups they fall into, are in active tension with the ideal pattern. They fit it, yet they fight it.

I'd speak the lines more or less this way:

Thus CONscience / does make COWards / of us ALL,/
And THUS / the NAtive HUE / of REsoLUtion/
Is SICKlied O'ER / with the PALE CAST / of THOUGHT./

This puts only three stress-beats in the first line, with three unstressed syllables in a row. The second line is regular except for its extra final syllable. The third uses the two-foot variation of two unstressed followed by two stressed syllables.

The poetic heart never follows the metronome. The rhythm of these lines is complex, subtle, and powerful, and that power comes from its syncopation with the ideal or underlying regular pattern.

The first of these lines also demonstrates why the idea of the foot will always be problematic in English. My scanning of it above would give:

$$— \acute{} \ / — — / — \acute{} \ / — — / — \acute{} \ /$$

that is, five feet, iambics alternating with pyrrhics; but reading it as I would speak it aloud, I scan it into three elements or phrases that are not usefully describable as feet at all:

$$— \acute{} \ — \ | \ — — \acute{} \ — \ | \ — — \acute{} \ |$$

So I introduce here the idea of "bars." When I scan either poetry or prose by reading it aloud and listening for the beats, I find it falls into short syntactical groups, which I call bars. I mark them with a vertical slash: |. The intervals between bars may be very slight, or even imperceptible if one is reading or speaking very fluently, but I think they exist; I think they clarify both the thought and the emotion, and are as essential to the rhythm of the poetic line or sentence as stress is. But I'm not certain anybody else would agree with me, or would mark off the bars as I do, so I simply mention it, and hope someone, sometime, who knows more about the subject will tell me what they know.

The *line* is a vexed subject in modern poetry. Many poets argue for reading poetry aloud without any pause at all at the end of lines. But it seems to me the line is part of the pattern, the rhythm, of the poem. In reading free verse, if the voice gives no indication, however slight, of the line end, the hearer cannot know where it is. This reduces the lines to mere typography. The regularity of metrical verse may signal the ear where a line ends, but still it needs some support from the voice. Speaking Shakespeare is a constant compromise between the natural run-on of the voice in dialogue and the beat of the pentameter lines that underlies it. If in search of natural tone the actor completely ignores the lines, the poetry is being read as prose.

Here's a wonderful example of what a poet can do with line: Gwendolyn Brooks's "We Real Cool:"

> We real cool. We
> Left school. We
> Lurk late. We
> Strike straight. We
>
> Sing sin. We
> Thin gin. We
>
> Jazz June. We
> die soon.

And another from John Donne:

> At the round earth's imagin'd corners, blow
> Your trumpets, Angels, and arise, arise
> From Death, you numberless infinities
> Of souls, and to your scatter'd bodies go.

The syntactical phrases break out of the pentameter lines, creating a strong tension. The technical name for a phrase that runs over into the next line is *enjambment*. It is a form of syncopation.

What happens to the rhythm and to the meaning if we take the enjambments out of "We Real Cool"?

> We real cool.
> We left school
> We lurk late . . .

No, I can't go on. We can also desecrate Donne's quatrain by following the syntax and abandoning the pentameter: the same words exactly, but without the rhythmic tension given by enjambment:

> At the round earth's imagin'd corners,
> blow your trumpets, Angels,
> and arise, arise from Death,
> you numberless infinities of souls,
> and to your scatter'd bodies go.

Not only is the structure weakened by the loss of the emphatic rhyme-pattern, but the tense, powerful beat of the lines has gone flabby.

I did not desecrate Brooks and Donne only to show the power of the line in poetry, but also as an indication of why poets may seek strict, formalised patterns to work in. The observation of a pattern, even an arbitrary pattern, can give strength to words that would otherwise wander bleating like lost lambs.

This is why it can be harder to write prose than to write poetry.

STRESS-RHYTHMS IN POETRY: FREE VERSE

Free verse has no regular meter; but there are stress-patterns in most free verse, just as there are often plenty of rhymes and other rhythmic devices, though not in predictable places. Finding the flexible, changing patterns in free verse is a matter of listening intently, using your own ear to catch the poet's beat.

For example, in Whitman's "Out of the Cradle Endlessly Rocking," you'll find the hypnotic, gentle beat of that title line recurring, here and there, changed and varied, throughout the long poem: TUMtata TUMta / TUMtata TUMta. . . .

Free verse that avoids stress patterns and doesn't use the line end as a pause may compensate by other rhythmic devices, other kinds of pattern and recurrence. One is the regular repetition of lines or parts of lines. Left to its own devices, English poetry seems to do this only in refrains; but it has imported exotic forms, such as the sestina and the pantoum, which not only set up a pattern by strict repetition, but control the range of emotion and meaning by restricting the choice of words.

The ideal of free verse is that the poem itself will find/create its own internal pattern, as unpredictable and inevitable as any fir tree, any waterfall.

STRESS-RHYTHMS IN PROSE

Tentatively, I propose the following statement: There are two elements to stress-rhythm in prose: first, actual syllabic stresses; second, syntactical phrases or word groups, following syntax, punctuation, sense, stress, and breath. These groups are what I call "bars."

By reading a passage of prose aloud you will hear both the syllabic stresses and the slight pauses or rise-and-fall of intonation that break the sentence into bars. Almost certainly none of us will read or hear or "scan" it in the same way. That doesn't matter. Prose has a whole lot of latitude.

The thing to remember is that good prose does have a stress-rhythm, subtle and complex and changing though it may be. Dull prose, clunky narrative, hard-to-read textbook stuff, lacks the rhythm that catches and drives and moves the reader's body and mind and heart.

There are no rules for finding and feeling the rhythm of prose. It is a gift, but it is also a learnable skill—learned by practice. Probably the best practice is reading out loud. You know how an uncomprehending reader reads out loud, a scared fourth-grader, stumbling and missing the beats? A poor reader can't dance to the prose.

But the best reader can't make lame prose dance.

The only rule of prose "scansion" I know is: listen to what you are reading (or writing) as closely as you can, listen for its beat, and follow your own ear. There is no right way. The way that sounds right to you is the way. (Tao Rules, OK?) Don't worry if you mark the stresses differently at different readings. Don't worry if others disagree.

Don't WORry if OTHers disaGREE

DON'T WORry if OTHers DISagree

Don't WORry if OTHers DISaGREE

With repetition and emphasis, a regular beat tends to establish itself. My last reading of that casual prose sentence, with just a wee bit of elision, is iambic tetrameter. We are rhythmical animals. But prose refuses to give us predictability. If in prose one sentence is an iambic tetrameter, all you can predict is that the next one won't be. True prose rhythm is always just ahead of us, elusive, running ahead, leading us on.

SCANNING PROSE: EXPERIMENTS IN STRESS PATTERNS

Prose rhythm is made up of many elements, repetitions of sound, parallels in syntax and construction, patterns of imagery, recurrences of mood, but just now I am sticking to the stress, the brute beat of it.

I think that if Virginia Woolf (in the quotation that opens this book) is right, that style is all rhythm—and I think that she is right, and that yes, she is profound—then even just the brute beat of a sentence might tell you something about what the sentence is and does. Do certain kinds of prose have certain characteristic stress-rhythms? Do authors have a characteristic beat of their own?

What follows are some very crude and simple investigations into the stress-rhythms of some bits of prose narrative. Mostly I just wanted to find out what would turn up if I counted the stresses. I had some expectations. I thought I might find clear, immediate differences in the stress-rhythm of different types of prose. And I wondered if I would find measurable differences in the stress-rhythms of different authors.

What I am counting here are *oral* stresses. These are the *rhythms of the voice*—not of silent reading, which is a mysterious activity far too fleet and delicate for my coarse net. It is my strong belief, however, that all prose worth reading is worth reading aloud, and that the rhythms we catch clearly in reading aloud, we also catch unconsciously when reading in silence.

As there are no rules of scansion in prose, anybody's opinion is as good as anybody else's. My method consists of reading the sentences aloud; the second or third time through, I start marking the stresses (an accent mark over stressed syllables).

In many cases you will probably disagree with where I put the stresses. I probably do too. Also, there are (alas) degrees of stress. Some are unmistakable, TUM! some are arguable, TUM; some are weak, a substress, a mere tumlet to get one through a long series of tatas. I may or may not mark these feeble ones. There are many inconsistencies. I have been over these samples many times, but have never arrived at a final judgment in many places; my mind will never be easy about some of my decisions. Anyhow, if you haven't already skipped this section, you can disagree with me by striking out my stresses and putting in your own.

The selection of samples is whimsical. I picked writers whose style interested me and whose books were handy at the moment, and let my finger fall on a passage without any real selection, though I did avoid passages with back-and-forth dialogue. "The Three Bears" is included as an oral touchstone. Twain, Tolkien, and Woolf are here because I admire them as stylists. The textbook was chosen because it is a well-written one, not a horrible example of academic mumble. Darwin is here because I wanted some good mid-Victorian narrative, Austen because I wanted some good pre-Victorian narrative. Stein is here because I thought she'd come out wildly different from all the others, which she didn't.

The stresses are indicated by bold type.

The pauses or subdivisions I call bars are indicated by a vertical slash. A slash means a minimal pause or change of voice quality, a double slash indicates a longer pause. Longer pauses mostly coincide with punctuation, and indeed punctuation is almost always a guide to phrase grouping. In marking these bars, again my decisions were made reading aloud, not silently.

In the Stein passage, punctuation is an urgent necessity; without it the words would fall into a mumble-jumble in which the reader would be hopelessly lost. I had no hesitation in marking the Woolf passage, which to my ear fell inevitably into its brief, melodious elements. I dithered endlessly over the Austen, finding it as hard to chop into bits as a river flowing. Every time I look at it again I mark it differently. This scansion by bars is an even more subjective matter than stress-scansion, and you may find it quite useless. To me it serves to show visually some elements of the rhythmic structure of the prose—the triple patterning of the folktale, and sometimes a hint of metricality, the "bar" becoming a "foot." Also it shows visibly whether the passage uses mostly short, discrete phrases, or longer, more fluid ones, or a mixture and variety.

The passages are of *one hundred syllables* to the dagger (anything past the dagger is not counted). I wanted the samples to be of the same length so I could count and compare various elements.

"The Three Bears" (folktale, oral tradition)

> **Once** upon a **time** | there were **three bears:** | a **great, big Papa Bear;** | a **mid**dle-sized **Mama Bear;** | and a **little** tiny wee **Baby Bear.** ‖ The **Three Bears lived** in the **forest,** | and in **their house** there **was:** | a **great, big bed** for **Papa Bear;** | a **middle-sized bed** for **Mama Bear;** | and a **little** tiny wee **bed** for the **Baby Bear.**

‖ And **at** the **table** ‖ there was a **great, big chair** for **Papa Bear,**
‖ and a **middle-sized chair** for Mama † Bear ‖. . . .

Sentences: 3
Bars: 13
Words: 79
Words of one syllable: 61

   of two syllables: 15

   of three syllables: 3 (counting "middle-sized" as one word; if it is
counted as two words there are no words of more than two syllables)

   There are two series of 3 unstressed syllables, one broken by a bar
line (a comma).

   There are four series of 3 stressed syllables. (These TUM TUM
TUMs are mostly connected with ponderous Papa Bear, while Mama
and Baby Bear get a lighter beat.)

Stresses: 49

Mark Twain: "The Notorious Jumping Frog of Calaveras County"

Well, ‖ **thish**-yer **Smiley** ‖ had **rat**-tarriers, ‖ and **chicken** cocks,
‖ and **tomcats,** ‖ and **all** them **kind** of **things,** ‖ till you **couldn't
rest;** ‖ and you **couldn't fetch no**thing for **him** to **bet** on ‖ but
he'd **match** you. ‖ He **ketched** a **frog one day,** ‖ and **took** him
home, ‖ and **said** he **calc'**lated to **edu**cate him; ‖ and **so** he **never**
done **nothing** for **three months** ‖ but **set** in his **backyard** ‖ and
learn that **frog** to **jump.** ‖ And **you bet** you ‖ he *did* **learn** him,
‖ **too.** ‖ He'd **give** him a lit†tle punch . . .

Sentences: 4
Bars: 19
Words: 85.5
Words of one syllable: 72

   of two syllables: 11 (10.5)

of three syllables: 3 (I count "rat-tarriers" as one word; "thish-yer" and "couldn't" are each two one-syllable words conventionally combined in spelling, or unconventionally in the case of "thish-yer," so that the ratio of monosyllables could go even higher. "Calc'lated" is a four-syllable word cut down to three.)

There are three series of 3 unstressed syllables, but each series is divided by a bar line (comma or period), so mumbling is neatly avoided.

There is one series of 3 stressed syllables.

Stresses: 44

J. R. R. Tolkien: *The Lord of the Rings*

They **now mount**ed their **ponies** | and **rode off** silently **into** the **evening.** || **Darkness came down quickly,** | as they **plod**ded **slowly down**hill and **up again,** | until at **last** they saw **lights** | **twink**ling some **distance ahead.** ||

 Before them **rose Bree hill** | **bar**ring the **way,** || a **dark mass** | against **misty stars;** | and **under** its **western flank** | **nest**led a **large village.** || **Towards it** they **now hurried,** | desiring **only** to **find** a **fire,** | and a **door** be†tween them and the night.

Sentences: 4 plus a paragraph break

Bars: 15

Words: 72

Words of one syllable: 45

 of two syllables: 24

 of three syllables: 2 ("towards" in Tolkien's English is one syllable, but "evening," which I count as two, might be three)

The single series of 3 unstressed syllables is divided by a bar line (comma).

I mark one series of 3 stresses, "**came down quick**ly," which might be disputed, as might my series of 4, "**rose Bree hill bar**ring"—to my ear these phrases do not break down into lighter and heavier stresses,

but insist on being read with a strong, even beat. Also questionable is
my reading "a **dark mass** against **misty stars**," where "against" is de-
prived of its normal stress by—to my ear!—the overriding rhythm of
the phrase.
Stresses: 47

Virginia Woolf: *Between the Acts*

Then something **moved** in the **water**; | her **favorite fantail**. ||
The **golden orfe** followed. || **Then** she had a **glimpse** of **silver**—
|| the **great carp** himself, | who **came** to the **surface** | so **very sel**-
dom. || They **slid on**, | in and **out** | between the **stalks**, | **silver**;
| **pink**; | **gold**; | **splashed**; | **streaked**; | **pied**. ||

    "**Ourselves**," | she **murmured**. || And re**trieving** some **glint**
of **faith** | from the **grey waters**, | **hopefully**, | with**out** much **help**
from **reason**, | she **followed** the **fish**; || the **speckled**, **streaked**,
and **blotched**; || † seeing in that vision beauty, power, and glory
in ourselves.

Sentences: 6 plus a paragraph break
Bars: 24
Words: 75
Words of one syllable: 53
    of two syllables: 19
    of three syllables: 3

There are two series of 3 unstressed syllables, one broken by a bar
line (period).

The unusual series of 7 stressed syllables with only 1 unstressed
syllable in it is marked clearly to be stressed by the comma and semicolons ("**stalks, silver; pink; gold; splashed; streaked; pied**"). It probably raises the stress-count in this selection higher than Woolf's norm.
Stresses: 47

Craig, Graham, et al.: *The Heritage of World Civilizations*

The **new** technology in **textile** manu**facture** | **vastly increased** **cotton** production | and revolutionized a **major** consumer **in**-dustry. || But the in**vention that,** | **more** than **any other**, | per-**mitted** industrialization | to **grow** on itself | and to expand into **one** area of production after ano**ther** | was the **steam engine.** || **This** ma**chine** provided | for the **first time** in hu†man history a steady and essentially unlimited source of inanimate power.

Sentences: 3

Bars: 10

Words: 52.5

Words of one syllable: 25

of two syllables: 14.5

of three syllables: 9

of four syllables: 2

of five syllables: 1

of seven syllables: 1

There are seven series of 3 unstressed syllables, one divided by a bar line, and two series of 4 unstressed syllables.

There are no series of over 2 stresses.

Stresses: 33

Jane Austen: *Pride and Prejudice*

It was **generally** evident whenever they **met,** | that he *did* ad-mire her; | and to *her* it was equally evident | that **Jane** was **yielding** to the **preference** | which **she** had be**gun** to enter**tain** for **him** | from the **first,** || and **was** in a **way** to be **very much** in **love;** || **but** she considered with **pleasure** | that it was **not likely** to be discovered | by the **world** in general, || since **Jane** united with **great strength** † of feeling, a composure of temper and a uniform cheerfulness of manner, which would guard her from the suspicions of the impertinent.

Sentences: 1
Bars: 10
Words: 72
Words of one syllable: 55
   of two syllables: 9
   of three syllables: 9 (I count "generally" as three syllables, "general" as two, "preference" as two; this may be quite wrong for the way Austen would have said the words.)
   There are six series of 3 unstressed syllables, one broken by a bar line, and one series of 4 unstressed syllables.
   There are no series of more than 2 stresses.
   (Note the assonance of the first four stressed syllables. Prose can get this close to rhyme without its being noticeable as anything more than a pleasantly musical quality.)
Stresses: 34

Charles Darwin: *The Voyage of the Beagle*

I **hired** a **Gaucho** to accompany me | on my **ride** to **Buenos Aires**, | **though** with **some difficulty**, | as the **father** of **one man** | I was a**fraid** to **let** him **go**, | and a**nother**, | who **seemed willing**, | I was de**scribed** to me as so **fearful**, | that **I** was a**fraid** to **take** him, | for **I** was **told** | that even if he **saw** an **ostrich** at a **distance**, | he would mis**take** it for an **Indian**, | and would **fly** like the **wind away**. || The † distance to Buenos Aires . . .

Sentences: 1
Bars: 13

Words: 77
Words of one syllable: 58
    of two syllables: 15
    of three syllables: 1
    of four syllables: 2
    There are four series of 3 unstressed syllables, three series of 4 unstressed syllables (one broken by a bar line [comma]), and one series of 5 unstressed syllables, broken by a bar line (comma).
    There are no series of more than 2 stresses.
    (The delicate, humorous metricality of the final phrase "fly like the wind away," is certainly deliberate, involving also a poetic inversion and alliteration.)
Stresses: 35

Gertrude Stein: "My Wife Has a Cow"

Have it as **hav**ing **hav**ing it as **hap**pening, | **hap**pening to **have** it as **hap**pening, | **hav**ing to **have** it as **hap**pening. ‖ **Hap**pening and **have** it as **hap**pening | and **hav**ing to **have** it **hap**pen as **hap**pening, | and my **wife** has a **cow** as **now**, | my **wife hav**ing a **cow** as **now**, | my **wife hav**ing a **cow** as **now** | and **hav**ing a **cow** as **now** | and **hav**ing a **cow** and **hav**ing a **cow now**, | my **wife** has a **cow** † and now.

Sentences: 2
Bars: 10
Words: 76
Words of one syllable: 59
    of two syllables: 10
    of three syllables: 7 (all the same word, "happening")
    There are five series of 3 unstressed syllables and one series of 4, broken by a bar line (comma).
    There are no series of more than 2 stresses, and only two series of 2.

That the stresses almost all occur singly gives the sentences a peculiar, rocking gait. A fairly consistent three-foot metric beat based on "**hap**pening" continues with "**wife** has a" and is then replaced by a different beat beginning with the double stress "**wife hav**ing." Given these semiregular beats, the repetition of words, the repeated rhyme "cow /now," and the alliteration on "h," this passage is probably best regarded as possibly a poem, anyhow not exactly prose. But the stress count is much the same as in my other, narrative samples.
Stresses: 38

ᔕ

Judson Jerome, in *Poetry: Premeditated Art,* a useful and interesting book, says that poetry averages 40 to 60 stresses per 100 syllables, while prose averages about 20 to 40. My samples of prose run higher than that. He says that the maximum number of nonstressed syllables between stresses in poetry, on average, is 0 to 2, while in prose it's 2 to 4, while the maximum possible number of unstressed syllables in a row is 6 to 7. I've seldom found even four unstressed syllables in a row occurring in good prose.

Here's my count of how our prose samples vary in the number of stressed syllables, and some other counts and comparisons, which I find fascinating and you may wish to sink deep in the Sea of Unread Statistics.

ᔕ

Per 100-syllable sample:
Number of stresses, most to fewest:
    "Three Bears," Woolf: 48
    Tolkien: 47
    Twain: 44
    Stein: 38
    Darwin: 35
    Austen: 33
    Craig: 32

Number of words, most to fewest:

     Twain: 85.5

     "Three Bears:" 79

     Darwin: 77

     Stein: 76

     Woolf: 75

     Austen, Tolkien: 72

     Craig: 52.5

Number of sentences, most to fewest:

     Woolf: 6

     Twain, Tolkien: 4

     "Three Bears," Craig: 3

     Stein: 2

     Darwin: 1

     Austen: 1

Number of bars, most to fewest:

     Woolf: 24

     Twain: 19

     Tolkien: 15

     "Three Bears," Darwin: 13

     Craig, Austen, Stein: 10

Number of one-syllable words, most to fewest:

     Twain: 72

     "Three Bears":62

     Stein: 59

     Darwin: 58

     Austen: 55

     Woolf: 53

     Tolkien: 45

     Craig: 25

Two-syllable words, most to fewest:

> Tolkien: 24
> Woolf: 19
> Darwin, "Three Bears," Craig: 15
> Twain, Stein: 10
> Austen: 7

Three-syllable words, most to fewest:

> Austen: 10
> Craig: 9
> Stein: 7
> Woolf, Twain, "Three Bears": 3
> Tolkien: 2
> Darwin: 1

Words over three syllables:

> "Three Bears," Austen, Stein, Woolf, Twain, Tolkien: 0
> Darwin: 1 of four syllables
> Craig: 4, 2 of four syllables, 1 of five, 1 of seven.

Various interesting factoids emerge:

- that Virginia Woolf and "The Three Bears" have the same stress-count;
- that Mark Twain uses more one-syllable words than a folktale;
- that in even a readable textbook more than half the words are polysyllables;
- that Woolf writes the shortest sentences of the lot and Austen the longest;
- and so on.

The samples are far too small and the method of counting stresses too subjective for any conclusions at all to be drawn. That Jane

Austen's stress-count is almost the same as that of the textbook is, how-ever, a good indication that merely counting stresses is not going to give us any solid indications of the quality—in all senses—of the prose.

None the less I found it an interesting and worthwhile exercise, the simple doing of which intensified and refined my awareness of the rhythms of prose.*

BEYOND STRESS
Long Prose Rhythms

Stress-units are the smallest elements of prose rhythm, and the most purely physical. The frequency of stressed syllables and the handling of the beat so that it's neither jerky nor monotonous are essential ele-ments of the character of the prose sentence.

Thus the sentence itself, as I tried to show in my analyses of pas-sages above, is a rhythmic but never regularly rhythmic element of prose.

Other elements of prose rhythm are vastly longer and larger, and far more elusive.

Rhythm is repetition. In a prose narrative, which must "move" with the events it tells, what can be repeated without losing the narra-tive impulse? What events can recur (of course with variations) to form the long rhythmic patterns of narrative?

Recurrent events in a narrative have to do with sound (the words, phrases, sentences) and they have to do with meaning (the content of the words—images, described actions, moods, themes).

There is repetition, much more repetition, even in very sophisticated narrative, than one might expect.

---

* I want to thank Dell Hymes for giving me the whole idea of reading prose this way—though of course he bears no responsibility for my extensions and misuses. His work with the written version of oral narrative is stunning in its revelation of complex, conscious, formal pattern in Native American narratives long considered "artless," "primitive," etc.

Repetition of Words or Phrases

Virginia Woolf's novel *Between the Acts* offers a simple, straightforward example of the repetition of a phrase throughout a long narrative. An amateur pageant is being performed outdoors, with some recorded music, and the old phonograph hidden in the bushes keeps going "Chuff . . . chuff . . . chuff. . . ." The chuffing of the phonograph, varied slightly in the wording, recurs as a refrain throughout a whole section of the book. It seems insignificant, but it's so effective that when the phonograph stops, you miss it—in a sense, a whole new rhythm is set up by the lack of that repetition.

Another kind of repetition is a characteristic phrase, a character tag; in *David Copperfield,* for instance, Mr. Micawber's ever-hopeful "in case anything turns up." Having a character say the same thing often enough that you come to wait for it can be a mechanically humorous contrivance; but Dickens is not a mechanical writer, and when the Micawbers are on the brink of ruin, the repetition darkens humor into irony, sympathy, and pain. Fiction can take a trivial event or even a single word and repeat it in different contexts, changing and deepening its meaning every time, and intensifying the structure of the narrative.

This is worth thinking about. In school we got red circles on our paper for saying "repetition" four times in one paragraph. We're taught to avoid unintentional repetition of words or phrases. So we may have come to feel distrust or disdain for repetition as a device. But the power of deliberate repetition in a narrative is both great and legitimate.

Repetition of Images, Actions, Moods, and Themes

The next essay in this book is a study of the rhythmic structures in a chapter of Tolkien's *Lord of the Rings*. It continues the investigation of what these rhythmic structures may be and do. To sum it up very briefly: I found that many of the events and scenes, though each is vivid and particular, repeat or will be repeated by other events and images within the chapter and throughout the book, relating all the parts of the story by alluding back to or foreshadowing events, scenes, images, movements, relations, acts, responses, moods. Every part of the chapter is part of the pattern of the whole chapter, and the greater whole, the book, is immensely self-referential, largely through semirepetition, variations on the same themes.

I think this is how a well-written narrative works—through endlessly complex rhythmic correspondences. Its coherence is established by inner references and backward-looking or forward-looking semirepetitions. If they are pure repetitions, adding no new vision or emotion, the story loses narrative drive (pure repetition is better suited to ritual than to narrative). If the rhythms become predictable, the coherence of the story is mechanical. But if the repetitions vary, echoing and foreshadowing others with continuous and developing invention, the narration has the forward movement we look for in a story, while maintaining the complexity and integrity proper to a living creature or a work of art: a *rhythmic* integrity, a deep beat to which the whole thing moves.

RHYTHMIC PATTERN IN
THE LORD OF THE RINGS

This piece, growing out of my attempts to study and consider the rhythms of prose and written for my own amusement, happily found a home in Karen Haber's anthology of writing on Tolkien, Meditations on Middle Earth, published in 2001. I have added a brief note about the film version of the first book of the Trilogy, released late in the same year.

Since I had three children, I've read Tolkien's Trilogy aloud three times. It's a wonderful book to read aloud or (consensus by the children) listen to. Even when the sentences are long, their flow is perfectly clear, and follows the breath; punctuation comes just where you need to pause; the cadences are graceful and inevitable. Like Dickens and Virginia Woolf, Tolkien must have heard what he wrote. The narrative prose of such novelists is like poetry in that it wants the living voice to speak it, to find its full beauty and power, its subtle music, its rhythmic vitality.

Woolf's vigorous, highly characteristic sentence rhythms are surely and exclusively prose: I don't think she ever uses a regular beat. Dickens and Tolkien both occasionally drop into metrics. Dickens's prose in moments of high emotional intensity tends to become iambic, and can even be scanned: "It is a far, far better thing that I do/than I have ever done." The hoity-toity may sneer, but this iambic beat is tremendously effective—particularly when the metric regularity goes unnoticed as such. If Dickens recognised it, it didn't bother him. Like most really great artists, he'd use any trick that worked.

Woolf and Dickens wrote no poetry. Tolkien wrote a great deal, mostly narratives and "lays," often in forms taken from the subjects of his scholarly interest. His verse often shows extraordinary intricacy of meter, alliteration, and rhyme, yet is easy and fluent, sometimes excessively so. His prose narratives are frequently interspersed with poems, and once at least in the Trilogy he quietly slips from prose into verse without signalling it typographically. Tom Bombadil, in *The Fellowship of the Ring,* speaks metrically. His name is a drumbeat, and his meter is made up of free, galloping dactyls and trochees, with tremendous forward impetus: Tum tata Tum tata, Tum ta Tum ta. . . . "You let them out again, Old Man Willow! What be you a-thinking of? You should not be waking. Eat earth! Dig deep! Drink water! Go to sleep! Bombadil is talking!" Usually Tom's speech is printed without line breaks, so unwary or careless silent readers may miss the beat until they *see* it as verse—as song, actually, for when his speech is printed as verse Tom is singing.

As Tom is a cheerfully archetypal fellow, profoundly in touch with, indeed representing the great, natural rhythms of day and night, season, growth and death, it's appropriate that he should talk in rhythm, that his speech should sing itself. And, rather charmingly, it's an infectious beat; it echoes in Goldberry's speech, and Frodo picks it up. "Goldberry!" he cries as they are leaving. "My fair lady, clad all in silver green! We have never said farewell to her, nor seen her since that evening!"

If there are other metric passages in the Trilogy, I've missed them. The speech of the elves and noble folk such as Aragorn has a dignified, often stately gait, but not a regular stress-beat. I suspected King Théoden of iambics, but he only drops into them occasionally, as all measured English speech does. The narrative moves in balanced cadences in passages of epic action, with a majestic sweep reminiscent of epic poetry, but it remains pure prose. Tolkien's ear was too good and too highly trained in prosody to let him drop into meter unknowingly.

Stress-units—metric feet—are the smallest elements of rhythm in literature, and in prose probably the only quantifiable ones. A while ago I got interested in the ratio of stresses to syllables in prose, and did some counting.

In poetry, by and large, one syllable out of every two or three has a beat on it: Tum ta Tum ta ta Tum Tum ta, and so on. . . . In narrative prose, that ratio goes down to one beat in two to four: ta Tum tatty Tum ta Tum tatatty, and so on. . . . In discursive and technical writing the ratio of unstressed syllables goes higher; textbook prose tends to hobble along clogged by a superfluity of egregiously unnecessary and understressed polysyllables.

Tolkien's prose runs to the normal narrative ratio of one stress every two to four syllables. In passages of intense action and feeling the ratio may get pretty close to 50 percent, like poetry, but still, except for Tom, it is irregular, it can't be scanned.

Stress-beat in prose is fairly easy to identify and count, though I doubt any two readers of a prose passage would mark the stresses in exactly the same places. Other elements of rhythm in narrative are less physical and far more difficult to quantify, having to do not with an audible repetition, but with the pattern of the narrative itself. These elements are longer, larger, and very much more elusive.

Rhythm is repetition. Poetry can repeat anything—a stress-pattern, a phoneme, a rhyme, a word, a line, a stanza. Its formality gives it endless liberty to establish rhythmic structure.

What is repeatable in narrative prose? In oral narrative, which generally maintains many formal elements, rhythmic structure may be established by the repetition of certain key words, and by grouping events into similar, accumulative semirepetitions: think of "The Three Bears" or "The Three Little Pigs." European story uses triads; Native American story is more likely to do things in fours. Each repetition both builds the foundation of the climactic event, and advances the story.

Story moves, and normally it moves forward. Silent reading doesn't need repetitive cues to keep the teller and the hearers oriented, and people can read much faster than they speak. So people accustomed to silent reading generally expect narrative to move along pretty steadily, without formalities and repetitions. Increasingly, during the past century, readers have been encouraged to look at a story as a road we're driving, well paved and graded and without detours, on which we go as fast as we possibly can, with no changes of pace and certainly no stops, till we get to—well—to the end, and stop.

"There and Back Again": in Bilbo's title for *The Hobbit,* Tolkien has already told us the larger shape of his narrative, the direction of his road.

The rhythm that shapes and directs his narrative is noticeable, was noticeable to me, because it is very strong and very simple, as simple as a rhythm can be: two beats. Stress, release. Inbreath, outbreath. A heartbeat. A walking gait—but on so vast a scale, so capable of endlessly complex and subtle variation, that it carries the whole enormous narrative straight through from beginning to end, from There to Back Again, without faltering. The fact is, we *walk* from the Shire to the Mountain of Doom with Frodo and Sam. One, two, left, right, on foot, all the way. And back.

What are the elements that establish this long-distance walking pace? What elements recur, are repeated with variations, to form the rhythms of prose? Those that I am aware of are: Words and phrases. Images. Actions. Moods. Themes.

Words and phrases, repeated, are easy to identify. But Tolkien is not, after all, telling his story aloud; writing prose for silent, and sophisticated, readers, he doesn't use key words and stock phrases as storytellers do. Such repetitions would be tedious and faux-naive. I have not located any "refrains" in the Trilogy.

As for imagery, actions, moods, and themes, I find myself unable to separate them usefully. In a profoundly conceived, craftily written novel such as *The Lord of the Rings,* all these elements work together indissolubly, simultaneously. When I tried to analyse them out I just unraveled the tapestry and was left with a lot of threads, but no picture. So I settled for bunching them all together. I noted every repetition of any image, action, mood, or theme without trying to identify it as anything other than a repetition.

I was working from my impression that a dark event in the story was likely to be followed by a brighter one (or vice versa); that when the characters had exerted terrible effort, they then got to have a rest; that each action brought a reaction, never predictable in nature, because Tolkien's imagination is inexhaustible, but more or less predictable in kind, like day following night, and winter after fall.

This "trochaic" alternation of stress and relief is of course a basic device of narrative, from folktales to *War and Peace;* but Tolkien's reliance on it is striking. It is one of the things that make his narrative technique unusual for the mid–twentieth century. Unrelieved psychological or emotional stress or tension, and a narrative pace racing without a break from start to climax, characterise much of the fiction of the time. To readers with such expectations, Tolkien's plodding stress/relief pattern seemed and seems simplistic, primitive. To others it may seem a remarkably simple, subtle technique of keeping the reader going on a long and ceaselessly rewarding journey.

I wanted to see if I could locate the devices by which Tolkien establishes this master rhythm in the Trilogy; but the idea of working with the whole immense saga was terrifying. Perhaps some day I or a braver reader can identify the larger patterns of repetition and alternation throughout the narrative. I narrowed my scope to one chapter, the eighth of volume 1, "Fog on the Barrow Downs": some fourteen pages, chosen almost arbitrarily, though I did want a selection with some traveling in it, journey being such a large component of the story. I went through the chapter noting every major image, event, and feeling-tone and particularly noting recurrences or strong similarity of words, phrases, scenes, actions, feelings, and images. Very soon, sooner than I expected, repetitions began to emerge, including a positive/negative binary pattern of alternation or reversal.

These are the chief recurrent elements I listed (page references are to the George Allen & Unwin edition of 1954):

- A vision or vista of a great expanse (three times: in the first paragraph; in the fifth paragraph; and on page 157, when the vision is temporal—back into history)
- The image of a single figure silhouetted against the sky (four times: Goldberry, page 147; the standing stone, page 148; the barrow-wight, page 151; Tom, pages 153 and 154. Tom and Goldberry are bright figures in sunlight, the stone and the wraith are dark looming figures in mist)
- Mention of the compass directions—frequent, and often with a benign or malign connotation
- The question "Where are you?" three times (page 150, when Frodo loses his companions, calls, and is not answered; page 151, when the barrow-wight answers him; and Merry, on page 154, "Where did you get to, Frodo?" answered by Frodo's "I thought that I was lost" and Tom's "You've found yourself again, out of the deep water")
- Phrases describing the hill country through which they ride and walk, the scent of turf, the quality of the light, the ups and downs, and the hilltops on which they pause: some benign, some malign
- Associated images of haze, fog, dimness, silence, confusion, unconsciousness, paralysis (foreshadowed on page 148 on the hill of the standing stone, intensified on page 149 as they go on, and climaxing on page 150 on the barrow), which reverse to images of sunlight, clarity, resolution, thought, action (pages 151–153)

What I call reversal is a pulsation back and forth between polarities of feeling, mood, image, emotion, action—examples of the stress/release pulse that I think is fundamental to the structure of the book. I listed some of these binaries or polarities, putting the negative before the positive, though that is not by any means always the order of occurrence. Each such reversal or pulsation occurs more than once in the chapter, some three or four times.

darkness/daylight
resting/traveling on
vagueness/vividness of perception
confusion of thought/clarity
sense of menace/of ease
imprisonment or a trap/freedom
enclosure/openness
fear/courage
paralysis/action
panic/thoughtfulness
forgetting/remembering
solitude/companionship
horror/euphoria
cold/warmth

These reversals are not simple binary flips. The positive causes or grows from the negative state, and the negative from the positive. Each yang contains its yin, each yin contains its yang. (I don't use the Chinese terms lightly; I believe they fit with Tolkien's conception of how the world works.)

Directionality is extremely important all though the book. I believe there is no moment when we don't know, literally, where north is, and what direction the protagonists are going. Two of the wind rose points have a pretty clear and consistent emotional value: east has bad connotations, west is benign. North and south vary more, depending on where we are in time and space; in general I think north is a melancholy direction and south a dangerous one. In a passage early in the chapter, one of the three great "vistas" offers us the whole compass view, point by point: west, the Old Forest and the invisible, beloved Shire; south, the Brandywine River flowing "away out of the knowledge of the hobbits"; north, a "featureless and shadowy distance"; and east, "a guess of blue and a remote white glimmer . . . the high and distant mountains"—where their dangerous road will lead them.

The additional points of the Native American and the airplane compass—up and down—are equally firmly established. Their connotations are complex. Up is usually a bit more fortunate than down, hilltops better than valleys; but the Barrow Downs—hills—are themselves an unlucky place to be. The hilltop where they sleep under the standing stone is a bad place, but there is a *hollow* on it, as if to contain the badness. *Under* the barrow is the worst place of all, but Frodo gets there by climbing *up* a hill. As they wind their way downward, and northward, at the end of the chapter, they are relieved to be leaving the uplands; but they are going back to the danger of the Road.

Similarly, the repeated image of a figure silhouetted against the sky—above seen from below—may be benevolent or menacing.

As the narrative intensifies and concentrates, the number of characters dwindles abruptly to one. Frodo, afoot, goes on ahead of the others, seeing what he thinks is the way out of the Barrow Downs. His experience is increasingly illusory—two standing stones like "the pillars of a headless door," which he has not seen before (and will not see when he looks for them later)—a quickly gathering dark mist, voices calling his name (from the eastward), a hill which he must climb "up and up," having (ominously) lost all sense of direction. At the top, "It was wholly dark. 'Where are you?' he cried out miserably." This cry is unanswered.

When he sees the great barrow loom above him, he repeats the question, "angry and afraid"—"'Where are you?'" And this time he is answered, by a deep, cold voice out of the ground.

The key action of the chapter, inside the barrow, involves Frodo alone in extreme distress, horror, cold, confusion, and paralysis of body and will—pure nightmare. The process of reversal—of escape—is not simple or direct. Frodo goes through several steps or stages in undoing the evil spell.

Lying paralysed in a tomb on cold stone in darkness, he *remembers* the Shire, Bilbo, his life. Memory is the first key. He thinks he has come to a terrible end, but refuses to accept it. He lies "thinking and getting a hold on himself," and as he does so, light begins to shine.

But what it shows him is horrible: his friends lying as if dead, and "across their three necks lay one long naked sword."

A song begins—a kind of limping, sick reversal of Tom Bombadil's jolly caroling—and he sees, unforgettably, "a long arm groping, walking on its fingers towards Sam . . . and towards the hilt of the sword that lay upon him."

He stops thinking, loses his hold on himself, forgets. In panic terror, he considers putting on the Ring, which has lain so far, all through the chapter, unmentioned in his pocket. The Ring, of course, is the central image of the whole book. Its influence is utterly baneful. Even to think of putting it on is to imagine himself abandoning his friends and justifying his cowardice—"Gandalf would admit that there had been nothing else he could do."

His courage and his love for his friends are stung awake by this *imagination:* he escapes temptation by immediate, violent (re)action: he seizes the sword and strikes at the crawling arm. A shriek, darkness, he falls forward over Merry's cold body.

With that touch, his memory, stolen from him by the fog-spell, returns fully: he remembers the house under the Hill—Tom's house. He remembers Tom, who is the earth's memory. With that he recollects himself.

Now he can remember the spell that Tom gave him in case of need, and he speaks it, calling at first "in a small desperate voice," and then, with Tom's name, loud and clear.

And Tom answers: the immediate, right answer. The spell is broken. "Light streamed in, the plain light of day."

Imprisonment, fear, cold, and solitude reverse to freedom, joy, warmth, and companionship . . . with one final, fine touch of horror: "As Frodo left the barrow for the last time he thought he saw a severed hand wriggling still, like a wounded spider, in a heap of fallen earth." (Yang always has a spot of yin in it. And Tolkien seems to have had no warm spot for spiders.)

This episode is the climax of the chapter, the maximum of stress, Frodo's first real test. Everything before it led towards it with increasing tension. It is followed by a couple of pages of relief and release. That the hobbits feel hungry is an excellent sign. After well-being has been restored, Tom gives the hobbits weapons, knives forged, he tells them rather somberly, by the Men of Westernesse, foes of the Dark Lord in dark years long ago. Frodo and his companions, though they don't know it yet, are of course themselves the foes of that lord in this age of the world. Tom speaks—riddlingly, and not by name—of Aragorn, who has not yet entered the story. Aragorn is a bridge figure between the past and the present time, and as Tom speaks, the hobbits have a momentary, huge, strange vision of the depths of time, and heroic figures, "one with a star on his brow"—a foreshadowing of their saga, and of the whole immense history of Middle Earth. "Then the vision faded, and they were back in the sunlit world."

Now the story proceeds with decreased immediate plot tension or suspense, but undecreased narrative pace and complexity. We are going back towards the rest of the book, as it were. Towards the end of the chapter the larger plot, the greater suspense, the stress they are all under, begin again to loom in the characters' minds. The hobbits have fallen into a frying pan and managed to get out of it, as they have done before and will do again, but the fire in Mount Doom still burns.

They travel on. They walk, they ride. Step by step. Tom is with them and the journey is uneventful, comfortable enough. As the sun is setting they reach the Road again at last, "running from South-west to

North-east, and on their right it fell quickly down into a wide hollow." The portents are not too good. And Frodo mentions—not by name—the Black Riders, to avoid whom they left the Road in the first place. The chill of fear creeps back. Tom cannot reassure them: "Out east my knowledge fails." His dactyls, even, are subdued.

He rides off into the dusk, singing, and the hobbits go on, just the four of them, conversing a little. Frodo reminds them not to call him by his name. The shadow of menace is inescapable. The chapter that began with a hopeful daybreak vision of brightness ends in a tired evening gloom. These are the final sentences:

> Darkness came down quickly, as they plodded slowly downhill and up again, until at last they saw lights twinkling some distance ahead.
>
> Before them rose Bree-hill barring the way, a dark mass against misty stars; and under its western flank nestled a large village. Towards it they now hurried, desiring only to find a fire, and a door between them and the night.

These few lines of straightforward narrative description are full of rapid reversals: darkness/lights twinkling—downhill/up again—the rise of Bree-hill/the village under it (*west* of it)—a dark mass/misty stars—a fire/the night. They are like drumbeats. Reading the lines aloud I can't help thinking of a Beethoven finale, as in the Ninth Symphony: the absolute certainty and definition of crashing chord and silence, repeated, repeated again. Yet the tone is quiet, the language simple, and the emotions evoked are quiet, simple, common: a longing to end the day's journey, to be inside by the fire, out of the night.

After all, the whole Trilogy ends on much the same note. From darkness into the firelight. "Well," Sam says, "I'm back."

There and back again. . . . In this single chapter, certain of the great themes of the book, such as the Ring, the Riders, the Kings of the West, the Dark Lord, are struck once only, or only obliquely. Yet this small part of the great journey is integrally part of the whole in event and imagery: the barrow-wight, once a servant of the Dark Lord, appears even as Sauron himself will appear at the climax of the tale, looming, "a tall dark figure against the stars." And Frodo defeats him, through memory, imagination, and unexpected act.

The chapter itself is one "beat" in the immense rhythm of the book. Each of its events and scenes, however vivid, particular, and local, echoes or recollects or foreshadows other events and images, relating all the parts of the book by repeating or suggesting parts of the pattern of the whole.

I think it is a mistake to think of story as simply moving forward. The rhythmic structure of narrative is both journeylike and architectural. Great novels offer us not only a series of events, but a *place,* a landscape of the imagination which we can inhabit and return to. This may be particularly clear in the "secondary universe" of fantasy, where not only the action but the setting is avowedly invented by the author. Relying on the irreducible simplicity of the trochaic beat, stress/unstress, Tolkien constructs an inexhaustibly complex, stable rhythmic pattern in imagined space and time. The tremendous landscape of Middle Earth, the psychological and moral universe of *The Lord of the Rings,* is built up by repetition, semirepetition, suggestion, foreshadowing, recollection, echo, and reversal. Through it the story goes forward at its steady, human gait. There, and back again.

᧤

Note (2002): I enjoyed the film of *The Fellowship of the Ring* immensely, and feel an awed admiration for the scriptwriters who got so much of the story and the *feeling* of the story into the brevity of a movie. I was sorry not to see the barrow-wight's hand crawling towards Frodo, but they were very wise to leave out Tom—wise in all their omissions. Nothing was disappointing but the orcs, standard-issue slimy monsters with bad teeth, bah. I expected that the greatest difference between the book and the film might be a difference of pace;

and it is. The film begins at a proper footpace, an old man jogging along in a pony cart . . . but soon it's off at a dead run, galloping, rushing, leaping through landscapes, adventures, marvels, and perils, with barely a pause at Rivendell to discuss what to do next. Instead of the steady rhythm of breathing, you can't even catch your breath.

I don't know that the filmmakers had much choice about it. Movie audiences have been trained to expect whiz-bang pacing, an eye-dazzling ear-splitting torrent of images and action leaving no time for thought and little for emotional response. And the audience for a fantasy film is assumed to be young, therefore particularly impatient.

Watching once again the wonderful old film *Chushingura,* which takes four hours to tell the (comparatively) simple story of the Forty-seven Ronin, I marveled at the quiet gait, the silences, the seemingly aimless lingering on certain scenes, the restraint that slowly increases tension till it gathers tremendous force and weight. I wish a Tolkien film could move at a pace like that. If it was as beautiful and well written and well acted as this one is, I'd be perfectly happy if it went on for hours and hours. . . . But that's a daydream.

And I doubt that any drama, no matter how un-whiz-bang, could in fact capture the singular gait that so deeply characterises the book. The vast, idiosyncratic prose rhythms of *The Lord of the Rings,* like those of *War and Peace,* have no counterpart in Western theatrical writing.

So all I wish is that they'd slowed down the movie, every now and then, even just held still for a moment and let there be a rest, a beat of silence. . . .

THE WILDERNESS WITHIN

THE SLEEPING BEAUTY AND "THE POACHER"
AND A PS ABOUT SYLVIA TOWNSEND WARNER

This piece was written as a contribution to the anthology Mirror, Mirror on the Wall: Women Writers Explore Their Favorite Fairy Tales, *edited by Kate Bernheimer in 1998. Francine Prose's piece about the Sleeping Beauty, which I mention here, is also in that anthology. My story "The Poacher" can be found in my collection* Unlocking the Air.

Influence—the anxiety of influence—it's enough to give you influenza. I've come to dread the well-intended question, "What writer or writers influenced you as a writer?"

What writer or writers didn't? How can I name Woolf or Dickens or Tolstoy or Shelley without implying that a hundred, a thousand other "influences" didn't matter?

I evade: telling the questioners they really don't want to hear about my compulsive reading disorder, or changing the playing field—"Schubert and Beethoven and Springsteen have had a great influence on my writing"—or, "Well, that would take all night, but I'll tell you what I'm reading right now," an answer I learned from being asked the question. A useful question, which leads to conversation.

Then there was the book *The Anxiety of Influence.* Yes, I know who's afraid of Virginia Woolf. Still I'm faintly incredulous when I hear that phrase used seriously. The book about being anxious because you learned things from other writers came out at the same time that a lot of us were energetically rejoicing in the rediscovery and reprinting of older and earlier woman writers, the rich inheritance that had been withheld from all writers by the macho literary canon.

While these guys were over there being paranoid about influence, we were over here celebrating it.

Well, all right; if some authors feel threatened by the very existence of other, older writers, what about *fairy tales?* Stories so old they don't even *have* writers? That should bring on a regular panic attack.

That the accepted (male) notion of literary influence is appallingly simplistic is shown (first—not last, but first) by the fact that it overlooks, ignores, disdains the effect of "preliterature"—oral stories, folktales, fairy tales, picture books—on the tender mind of the prewriter.

Such deep imprints are, of course, harder to trace than the effect of reading a novel or a poem in one's teens or twenties. The person affected may not be conscious of such early influences, overlaid and obscured by everything learned since. A tale we heard at four years old may have a deep and abiding effect on our mind and spirit, but we aren't likely to be clearly aware of it as adults—unless asked to think about it seriously. And the person affected may be deeply unwilling to achieve consciousness of such influences. If "seriousness" is limited to discourse of canonical Literature, we may well be embarrassed to mention something that some female relative read aloud to us after we'd got into bed in our jammies with our stuffed animals. Yet it may have formed our imagination more decisively than anything we ever read.

I have absolutely no idea of when I first heard or read the tale of the Sleeping Beauty. I don't even remember (as I do for some stories) the illustrations, or the language, of a certain edition. I certainly read it for myself as a child in several collections, and again in various forms when I was reading aloud to my own children. One of those versions was a charming Czech-made book, an early example of the Pop-Up genre. It was good magic, the way the thorny paper rose hedge leapt up around the little paper castle. And at the end everybody in the castle woke, just as they ought to, and got right up off the page.

But when did I first learn that that was what they ought to do?

The Sleeping Beauty is one of the stories that I've "always known," just as it's one of the stories that "we all know." Are not such stories part of our literary inheritance? Do they not influence us?

Does that make us anxious?

Francine Prose's article on the Sleeping Beauty elegantly demonstrates, by the way, that we *don't* know the stories we think we've always known. I had the twelfth fairy and the whole spindle business clear in my mind, but all that after-the-marriage hanky-panky was news to me. As I knew it, as most Americans know it, the story ends with the prince's kiss and everybody getting ready for the wedding.

And I wasn't aware that it held any particular meaning or fascination for me, that it had "had any influence" on me, until, along in my sixties, I came on Sylvia Townsend Warner's evocation of the tale in a tiny poem (it is in her *Collected Poems*):

The Sleeping Beauty woke:
The spit began to turn,
The woodmen cleared the brake,
The gardener mowed the lawn.
Woe's me! And must one kiss
Revoke the silent house, the birdsong wilderness?

As poetry will do, those words took me far beyond themselves, straight through the hedge of thorns, into the secret place.

For all its sweet brevity, the question asked in the last two lines is a total "revisioning" of the story, a subversion of it. Almost, it revokes it.

The pall of sleep that lies upon the house and grounds is supposedly the effect of a malicious spell, a curse; the prince's kiss that breaks the spell is supposed to provide a happy ending. Townsend Warner asks, was it a curse, after all? The thorn hedge broken, the cooks growling at their porridge pots, the peasants laboring again at their sowing or harvesting, the cat leaping upon the mouse, Father yawning and scratching his head, Mother jumping up sure that the servants have been misbehaving while she was asleep, Beauty staring in some confusion at the smiling young man who is going to carry her off and make her a wife—everything back to normal, everyday, commonplace, ordinary life. The silence, the peace, the magic, gone.

Really, it is a grand, deep question the poet asks. It takes me into the story as no Freudian or Jungian or Bettelheimian reduction of it does. It lets me see what *I* think the story is about.

I think the story is about that still center: "the silent house, the birdsong wilderness."

That is the image we retain. The unmoving smoke above the chimney top. The spindle fallen from the motionless hand. The cat asleep near the sleeping mouse. No noise, no bustle, no busyness. Utter peace. Nothing moving but the slow subtle growth of the thorn bushes, ever thicker and higher all about the boundary, and the birds who fly over the high hedge, singing, and pass on.

It is the secret garden; it is Eden; it is the dream of utter, sunlit safety; it is the changeless kingdom.

Childhood, yes. Celibacy, virginity, yes. A glimpse of adolescence: a place hidden in the heart and mind of a girl of twelve or fifteen. There she is alone, all by herself, content, and nobody knows her. She is thinking: *Don't wake me. Don't know me. Let me be. . . .*

At the same time she is probably shouting out of the windows of other corners of her being, *Here I am, do come, oh do hurry up and come!* And she lets down her hair, and the prince comes thundering up, and they get married, and the world goes on. Which it wouldn't do if she stayed in the hidden corner and renounced love marriage childbearing motherhood and all that.

But at least she had a little while by herself, in the house that was hers, the garden of silence. Too many Beauties never even know there is such a place.

⤺

Townsend Warner's lines haunted my mind for some while before I realised that her question had led me not only into the folktale of the Sleeping Beauty but into a story I had to write about it. In this case, the influence was almost direct. I am not anxious about it in any way. I am cheerfully grateful.

My story is called "The Poacher." Its title describes exactly what I, the author, was doing: poaching on the folktale's domain. Trespassing, thieving. Hunting. Tracking down something that happened in the place where nothing happens.

In my story a peasant boy lives at the edge of a forest where he poaches and gathers a very poor living for himself, a nasty father, and a gentle stepmother. (I find reversing stereotypes a simple but inexhaustible pleasure. The stepmother is not much older than he is, and there is a sexual yearning between them that can find no solace.) He discovers the great hedge where it cuts across a far part of the forest. This impenetrable, thorny, living wall fascinates him. He keeps going back to it, exploring along it. When he realises that it forms a circle, a complete defense of something within it, some *other place,* he resolves to get through it.

As we know from the tale, the magic hedge is yards thick, yards high, and regrows two razor-thorned shoots for every one that's cut, so anybody trying to get through it gives up pretty soon. The twelfth fairy's spell decreed that it would stand for a hundred years. Only when the hundred years are up will a certain prince appear with a certain sword, which will cut through the monstrous tangle like a hot knife through butter.

Our peasant boy doesn't know that, of course. He doesn't really know anything. He is dirt poor and ignorant. He has no way out of his life. There is no way out of his life. He starts trying to cut through the hedge.

And he keeps it up for years, with the poor tools he has, slowly, slowly defeating the ever-regrowing vitality of the thorn trees, pushing a narrow, choked opening through the trunks and branches and endless shoots and tangles, doggedly returning and returning; until at last he gets through.

He does not break the spell; that is what the prince will do. He has broken *into* the spell. He has entered it.

It is not he who will revoke it. Instead, he will do what the prince cannot do. He will enjoy it.

He wanders about the fields and gardens inside the great hedge wall, and sees the bee sleeping on the flower, and the sheep and cattle sleeping, and the guardians asleep by the gate. He enters the castle (for in the tale as I knew it, Beauty's father is the king of the realm). He wanders among the sleeping people. My poacher says then, "I knew already that they were all asleep. It was very strange, and I thought I should be afraid; but I could not feel any fear." He says, "I knew I trespassed, but I could not see the harm."

He's hungry, as he has been all his life. "The venison pastry that the chief cook had just taken out of the oven smelled so delicious that hungry flesh could not endure it. I arranged the chief cook in a more comfortable position on the slate floor of the kitchen, with his hat crumpled up for a pillow; and then I attacked the great pie, breaking off a corner with my hands and cramming it in my mouth. It was still warm, savory, succulent. Next time I came through the kitchen, the pastry was whole, unbroken. The enchantment held. Was it that, as a dream, I could change nothing of this deep reality of sleep?"

So he stays there. He has always been alone, that is nothing new; and now he is not hungry. Not even sexually, for he shares a sleeping peasant girl with her sleeping lover, and she smiles with pleasure in her sleep, and there is no harm in it, for the spell holds: nothing can be changed, or broken, or hurt. What more can he desire?

Speech, perhaps, which he never had much of in his old life either. Here there is no one to answer if he speaks; but he has vast leisure, time without end, and so he teaches himself to read. He reads the princess's book of fairy tales. He knows then where he is. Perhaps he knows what more there is to desire.

He knows who the princess is. "I knew that she, she alone in all the castle, might wake at any moment. I knew that she, alone of all of them, all of us, was dreaming. I knew that if I spoke in that tower room, she would hear me: maybe not waken, but hear me in her sleep, and her dreams would change." He knows that to break the spell, all he need do is move the spindle in her hand so that its tip does not prick into her thumb. "If I did that, if I moved the spindle, a drop of red blood would well up slowly on the delicate little cushion of flesh above the joint. And her eyes would open. Her eyes would open slowly; she would look at me. And the enchantment would be broken, the dream at an end."

᠆

My story, like Townsend Warner's poem, merely asks a question. It does not alter anything. All will go on as told. The prince will come; his kiss will wake his virgin bride. I and my poacher had no desire to change the story. We were both just glad to get into it. To be there, awake.

Thinking about it now, I believe that the tale is as impregnable and unassailable as its hedge of thorns. We can play variations round about it, imagine peasant trespassers, or rapist princes, happy or unhappy endings, as we please. We can define it; we can defile it. We can retell it to improve its morality, or try to use it to deliver a "message." When we're done, it will still be there: the place within the thorn-hedge. The silence, the sunlight, the sleepers. The place where nothing changes. Mothers and fathers will read the tale to their children, and it will have an influence upon those children.

The story is, itself, a spell. Why would we want to break it?

᠆

POSTSCRIPT (2003):
I want to take this opportunity to pay a little further tribute to Sylvia Townsend Warner, whom I had the great good fortune to meet. When

we were in England in 1976, our friend Joy Finzi knew how much I admired Sylvia's work, and thought she might enjoy meeting me. So, after talking me up a bit, I imagine, and giving Sylvia some of my poems, she drove me to the cottage on the river in Dorset where Sylvia had lived for many years, first with her lover Valentine Ackland, then alone. The place is marvelously described in her letters and turns up in several of her stories. It was a sort of a naiad of a house that seemed to be only partly above water, with bits of beautiful, muddy, unkempt garden, and the murmur of the river all around it. We had a cup of tea in a sort of sunroom at the front of the house. Antiquities from Valentine's antiques shop still stood or lay about here and there, or possibly they were part of the furniture. Sylvia smoked more or less continuously, as she had done for sixty years or so, and it was impressive to see the golden-brown walls of the interior rooms, which had been white; smoke varnish lay so thick on the glass of the pictures that you couldn't make out the pictures. Of course, some of it may have been wood smoke from the fireplaces, too, in that dank place. Sylvia was old, and tired, and reserved, and kind, and keen as a splinter of diamond. She said she liked one of my poems, "Ars Lunga," which is about being a storyteller, and since then I have liked that poem better myself. I asked her about one of her stories, which I had read long ago in the *New Yorker* and had forgotten the name of, about a nice English family on a picnic. At the end of the story, a stranger sees them: one of them is wearing a bloodstained Indian shawl, two of them are in eighteenth-century costume, the father is sitting on the ground listening to an enormous music box, while the mother approaches with a bird cage. All this has come to seem perfectly reasonable to us, as it does to the family, because we know why it is so, but the stranger does not, and the reversal of viewpoint is revelatory and ravishingly funny. Sylvia smiled happily at my description and said, "Oh yes I do remember that," but she couldn't remember what it was called either, or where I could find it. No wonder. She had published nine volumes of stories (and this is not in any of them; it is "A View of Exmoor," in the posthumous collection *One Thing Leading to Another*). She also published seven novels, of which *Lolly Willowes* is perhaps still the most amazing, though I love *The True Heart* and *The Corner That Held Them* as well. Her last major work was a stunning biography of T. H. White. Her poetry has been collected at last, her brilliant letters and her heartbreaking journal have been published. I think she is still esteemed at something like her worth in her own country, though she seems largely forgotten here, where most of her stories were first published. I hold it one of the dearest honors of my life that I knew her for an hour.

OFF THE PAGE: LOUD COWS

A Talk and a Poem about
Reading Aloud

"Off the Page" was a talk for a conference on Women and Language held by graduate students of the Department of Linguistics at the University of California in Berkeley, in April 1998. In getting it ready for this book, I didn't change the informality of the language, since the piece not only is about reading aloud to a live audience but was written for performance. The audience was by no means all women, but they were more receptive to uncomforting remarks about gender equality than most academic groups. I have performed the poem "Loud Cows" at that meeting, in New York, and elsewhere, and it appears as a frontispiece in The Ethnography of Reading, *edited by Jonathan Boyarin.*

What happened to stories and poems after the invention of printing is a strange and terrible thing. Literature lost its voice. Except on the stage, it was silenced. Gutenberg muzzled us.

By the time I got born the silence of literature was considered an essential virtue and a sign of civilisation. Nannies and grannies told stories aloud to babies, and "primitive" peoples spoke their poems, poor illiterate jerks, but the real stuff, literature, was literally letters, letterpress, little black noiseless marks on paper. And libraries were temples of the goddess of silence attended by vigilant priestesses going *Shhhh*.

If you listen to the first Caedmon tape of poets reading, which was a landmark, you'll hear T. S. Eliot going *adduh, adduh* in this dull grey mutter, and Elizabeth Bishop going *gnengnengne* in a low flat whine. They were good poets who'd been taught poetry was to be seen not heard, and thought the music in their verse should be a secret between the poet and the reader—like the music that people who know how to read music hear when they read a score. Nobody was playing the music of poetry out loud.

Until Dylan Thomas. You know the Caedmon tape of him reading at Columbia in 1952? I was there at that reading, and you can hear me—in the passionate silence of the audience listening to that passionate voice. Not a conspiracy of silence, but a participatory silence, a community collaboration in letting him let the word loose aloud. I left that reading two feet above the ground, and it changed my understanding of the art forever.

So then there were the Beat poets, all posing and using and screwed up by testosterone, but at least audible, and Ginsberg's "Howl," which from the title on is a true performance piece that will not lie down quietly on the paper and be good. And ever since then, our poets have been noisy. Now God knows there are too many open-mike readings in the world; but better drivel at an open mike than silence from a closed mouth. And we have the voices of all recent poets on tape, so we can hear their word on their breath, with their heartbeat in it. Whereas of the greatest English writer of the twentieth century we have one tiny BBC recording: about ninety seconds of Virginia Woolf's voice reading a little essay. But in it you hear an invaluable hint of the rhythm that she said was where all the words began for her, the mysterious rhythm of her own voice.

It wasn't till the seventies, I think, that publishers realised they could sell more books by sending the author to two hundred cities in eight days to sign them—and then realised that people like not only to see the author sit and grin and write its name, but also to hear the author stand up and read its story. So now you here in Berkeley have Black Oak and Cody's, and we in Portland have Powell's and the Looking Glass, and Seattle has Elliott Bay Books running two readings a day every day of the week, and people come. They come to be read to. Some of them want books signed and some of them want to ask weird questions, but most of them want to be read to. To hear the word.

One reason I think this is a restoration of an essential function of literature is that it is reciprocal: a social act. The audience is part of the performance. A lecture isn't reciprocal, it's a talking-to. There were professors at Harvard when I was there who would give you a C if you *breathed* during a lecture. But the hush during a performance is alive and responsive, as at the theater. Nothing kills a play like a dead audience. This response is recognised and called for in all oral literatures. Zunis listening to a narrative recital say a word, *eeso,* meaning yes, OK, about once a minute and whenever appropriate. In oral cultures generally, kids are taught to make these soft response-noises; if they don't, it's assumed they weren't listening and they're sent out in disgrace. Any Baptist preacher who doesn't hear Yes Lord! and Amen! pretty often knows he's lost the congregation. In poetry readings, big groups or small, the convention is mostly a little soft groan or *hahh* at a striking line or at the end. In prose readings the response convention is even subtler, except for laughter, but there are audible responses which the reader counts on just as the actor does.

I learned that once for all at a reading I did in Santa Barbara. They had no lights on the audience, so I was facing this black chasm, and no sound came out of it. Total silence. Reading to pillows. Despair. Afterwards the students came around all warm and affectionate and said they'd loved it, but it was too late, I was a wreck. They'd been so laid back or so respectful or something they hadn't given me any response, and so they hadn't been working with me; and you can't do it alone.

It was men who first got poetry off the page, but the act was of great importance to women. Women have a particular stake in keeping the oral functions of literature alive, since misogyny wants women to be silent, and misogynist critics and academics do not want to hear the woman's voice in literature, in any sense of the word. There is solid evidence for the fact that when women speak more than 30 percent of the time, men perceive them as dominating the conversation; well, similarly, if, say, two women in a row get one of the big annual literary awards, masculine voices start talking about feminist cabals, political correctness, and the decline of fairness in judging. The 30 percent rule is really powerful. If more than one woman out of four or five won the Pulitzer, the PEN/Faulkner, the Booker— if more than one woman in ten were to win the Nobel literature prize—the ensuing masculine furore would devalue and might destroy the prize. Apparently, literary guys can only compete with each other. Put on a genuinely equal competitive footing with women, they get hysterical. They just have to have their voices heard 70 percent of the time.

Well, when feminism got reborn, it urged literary women to raise their voices, to yell unladylikely, to shoot for parity. So ever since, we have been grabbing the mike and letting loose. And it was this spirit of *hey, let's make a lot of noise* that carried me into experimenting with performance poetry. Not performance art, where you take your clothes off and dip yourself in chocolate or anything exciting like that, I'm way too old for that to work at all well and also I am a coward. But just letting my own voice loose, getting it off the page. Making female noises, shrieking and squeaking and being *shrill,* all those things that annoy people with longer vocal cords. Another case where the length of organs seems to be so important to men.

I read this piece, "Loud Cows," on tape at first but then didn't know what to do with the tape, so I do it live; and it's never twice the same, and though it has been printed, it really needs you, the audience, to be there, going *eeso, eeso!* So I'll end up now by performing it, in the hope of sending you away from this great conference with the memory of seeing an old woman mooing loudly in public.

LOUD COWS

It's allowed. It is allowed, we are allowed**SILENCE!**

It is allowed. It IS allowed. It IS allowed**SILENCE!!**

it *used* to be allowed.

SI—EE—LENTSSSSS.

I-EE AM THE AWE—THOR.

REEEED MEEE IN SI-EE-LENT AWE.

> but it's aloud.
> it *is* aloud.

A word is a noise a word is a noise
A word is a NOISE a NOISE a *NOISE* ——

> AWWWWw.

The word is aloud. The word is a loud thing.
The loud word is allowed, aloud to be, the loud word allows to be,
it allows as how.

> **but**
> GUNS have si-len-cers.
> Gumments have sssi-len-sssers.
> So do Private SseC-tors.

Words are to be-hayve.
To lie sigh-lent-ly on pages being good.
To keep their covers over them.
Words are to be clean.
To be neat.
To be seen   not   heard.

Words are the children of the fathers who say**SILENCE!**
who say **BANG!** you're dead!

But:
the word is longer than daddy and louder than bang.
And all that silent words forbid **DO NOT TRESPASS KEEP OUT**
    SILENCE!
And all that silent words forbid,
loud words allow to be.

All, all walls fall.

I say aloud: All walls all fall.
    It is aloud, it is allowed to be loud,
    and I say it is aloud LOUDly
    loudness allowing us to BE us — SO —

MOOOOOOOOOOOO**OOVE OH**-ver —

here come the **LOUD COWS** right **NOW!**

Moooooooooving throoooooough the silences

Mooooooooing in the Libraries

LOUD COWS in the sacred groves *(sssssh! don't wake daddy!)*

MOOO-**OOOO-OOOOVE** along there,

MOOOOOOVe along,
        JUMP! over the
                moooOOOOOOOON!

LOUD cows LOUD **COWS**
Loud **SOWS LOUD SOWS** now
      mouthing sounds**HEY!**

IT IS ALOUD!

DISCUSSIONS
AND OPINIONS

FACT AND/OR/PLUS FICTION

In 1998 the editors of the interesting litcrit magazine Paradoxa *asked me to contribute to an issue on "the future of narrative," and this was the result. I have edited and fiddled with it here and there.*

In earlier times, when we divided narrative into the secular and the sacred, factuality and invention were both considered to be properties of the former, and Truth the quality of the latter. With the decline of a consensus opinion concerning Truth, the difference between fact and fiction began to take on more importance, and we took to dividing narrative into fiction and nonfiction.

This division, maintained by publishers, librarians, booksellers, teachers, and most writers, I find to be fundamental to my own concept of narrative and its uses. The file in my computer that I'm using now is labelled "Nonfiction in Progress," as distinct from the "Fiction in Progress" file. But, perhaps as part of the postmodern boundary breakdown, some files are coalescing; a lot of fiction seems to be getting into certain types of nonfiction. I like genre transgression, but this may involve more than genre. To start thinking about it, I called as usual on the OED.

FICTION:
[1, 2—obsolete usages]

3.a. The action of 'feigning' or inventing imaginary inci-
dents, existences, states of things, etc., whether for the purpose
of deception or otherwise. [. . .] Bacon, 1605: ". . . so great an
affinitie hath fiction and beleefe." [. . .]

b. That which, or something that, is imaginatively invented; feigned existence, event, or state of things; invention as
opposed to fact. [First citation 1398.]

4. The species of literature which is concerned with the
narration of imaginary events and the portraiture of imaginary
characters; fictitious composition. Now, usually, prose novels
and stories collectively; the composition of works of this class.
[First citation 1599.]

(Definitions 5 and after concern nonliterary and derogatory uses of
the word—deliberate falsehood, moonshine, yarn spinning, and so on.)

As for the word *nonfiction*, it isn't in the OED. Probably if I went
to a contemporary American dictionary I'd find it, but not having
one, and having found the thesaurus in my Macintosh a nice source
of current usage, I asked it for its synonyms and antonyms to "fiction." It gave me "story" as the principal synonym, then "unreality,"
and then "drama, fantasy, myth, novel, romance, legend, tale." All
these synonyms except "unreality" have to do with the literary use of
the word.

The principal antonym is "actuality," then "authenticity, biography, certainty, circumstance, event, face [?], fact, genuineness, happening, history, incident, occurrence, reality." Only two of the antonyms
refer to literature: history and biography.

The antonyms didn't include "nonfiction," which I thought a quite
common word by now. I tried the thesaurus with "nonfiction." All it
could give me was what it calls a Close Word—"fiction."

Is my Macintosh telling me the words "fiction" and "nonfiction"
are so close in meaning they can be used interchangeably?

Possibly this is what is happening.

⟨

A good deal has been said and written here and there about this blurring of definition or melding of modes, though I don't know of a methodical or scholarly study. Most of what I've read on the subject has been by nonfiction writers defending their use of techniques and freedoms that have been seen as pertaining properly or only to fiction. Their arguments include the following: Since total accuracy is impossible, invention in a purportedly factual report is inevitable; since nobody perceives the same event the same way, factuality is always in question; artistic license may reach a higher form of authenticity than mere accuracy; and (therefore? anyhow?) writers have the right to write a story the way they want to.

The journalist Janet Malcolm, sued by her interviewee Jeffrey Masson for deliberate and defamatory misquotation, defended her form of journalism in a *New Yorker* article with such arguments. Perhaps she was inspired by Truman Capote, who called his *In Cold Blood* (also published in the *New Yorker*) a "nonfiction novel," apparently to elevate it above mere reportage and incidentally defend himself from accusations of playing a bit fast and loose with facts. Some nonfiction writers vigorously defend their use of invented elements in their work. Others take it for granted and are surprised by objections.

In conversation, I have heard that "nature writing" often contains a good deal of invention, and that some well-known nature writers admit without shame to faking observations and relating experiences that didn't occur. But the principal entryway of fiction into nonfiction seems to be via autobiographical writing—the memoir or "personal essay." Two relevant quotes from reviewers (for which I thank Sara Jameson, who sent them to me): W. S. Di Piero, in the *New York Times Book Review* of March 8, 1998:

> Remembering is an act of the imagination. Any account we
> make of our experience is an exercise in reinventing the self.

Even when we think we're accurately reporting past events, persons, objects, places, and their sequence, we're theatricalizing the self and its world.

I find the term "reinventing the self" interesting. Who did the original invention? Is the implication that of an eternal self-invention, the relationship of which to experience or reality is unimportant? The word "theatricalizing" is also interesting; *theatrical* isn't a neutral word, but loaded with connotations of exaggeration and emotional falsehood.

In the same issue, Paul Levy wrote: "All autobiographers have a problem conjuring with the truth. My own strategy is to regard writing about oneself as inadvertent fiction."

"Conjuring" has the same ring to it as "theatricalizing"—autobiography as sleight of hand, doves out of thin air. The phrase "inadvertent fiction" not only disclaims the writer's responsibility, but offers irresponsibility as a strategy. This approach certainly could slide an autobiographer over the difficulties faced by writers unwilling to regard their art as inadvertent.

A related argument concerns objectivity, famed cornerstone of the scientific method, which many scientists now consider, as a realistic criterion of even the most painstakingly factual report of an experiment or observation, illusory. Feminists add that, as an ideal, it is in many ways undesirable.

Anthropologists have generally come to admit that accounts of ethnographical observations from which the observer is omitted contain a profound element of falsification. Ethnography these days is full of postmodern uncertainties, ellipses, and self-reflexivities, sometimes to the point of appearing to be less about the natives' behavior than the ethnographer's soul. Claude Lévi-Strauss's *Tristes Tropiques,* the founding classic of this subtle and risky genre, exhibits its value when performed by a truly searching, skillful subjectivity.

In writing this essay I consciously include my subjective reactions and partialities as part of the process and lay no claim to either objectivity or authority. This is, to put it mildly, not how I was taught to write at Harvard in the forties. To me it seems perfectly appropriate to what I am doing, which is mostly speculation and opinion (as were most of the authoritatively phrased and apparently egoless papers produced at Harvard in the forties).

If, however, I were an eyewitness journalist charged with describing an event, if I were writing a biography, or an autobiography, could I not claim a genuine authority, based not only on knowledge (research), perceptivity, and inclusiveness but also on a strenuous attempt to be objective?

When scientists come out and state that they *cannot* achieve objectivity, and historians follow suit, a certain demoralisation may follow. Objectivity was an ideal to journalists, too. If the scientists abandon it, why should a poor stiff working part-time for the local foreign-corporation-owned rag even try for it?

Yet most journalists still profess the ideal of objective reporting, even when it comes to highly subjective matters. No proper journalist has ever admitted that anybody who does or suffers anything that brings them into public attention, intentionally or not, has any right to privacy. But in practice, journalists respect privacy when they describe objective actions and speech, leaving subjective motives, thoughts, and feelings to be deduced from the description; and outside the tabloids, most journalists do that. Serious journalism defines itself by the avoidance of speculation presented as fact.

Though they may have abandoned the claim to objectivity, serious history and biography define themselves in the same way. As soon as the writer tells us what Napoleon murmured to Josephine in bed and how Josephine's heart went pitpat, we know we're nearer Oz than Paris.

Many readers, of course, want Oz, not Paris. They're reading for the story, and don't care if the story is inaccurate or if the characters make a travesty of the historical figures they're based on.

Why, then, are they reading history rather than a novel? Is it because they distrust the novel as being "made up," while the narrative that calls itself history or biography, however dishonest, is "real"?

Such a bias, reflecting the Puritan judgmentalism so common in American minds, turns up in many and unlikely places. I hear a ring of such absolutism in both the *New York Times Book Review* quotations above, with their emphasis on "theatricality" and "conjuring." You can't tell the whole truth; nothing less will do; so you fake it.

But it's equally possible that many or most American readers are genuinely indifferent to the distinction of fiction from nonfiction. These categories mean little or nothing in preliterate cultures, and even now, when the written word is the word that counts, ever more so as we increasingly communicate via electronic media, perhaps they are not generally seen as carrying any great intellectual or ethical significance.

This perception may be in part connected to the increasing electronicisation of writing. In so far as writing becomes electronic, surely its categories and genres will change. So far, the new technology has influenced fiction only by opening to the novelist the garden of forking paths accessible through hypertext. Genuinely interactive fiction, where the reader would control the text equally with the writer, remains hype or a promise (or, to some, a threat). As for nonfiction, it seems that scant care for accuracy and fact checking, along with wide tolerance of hearsay and opinion, characterise a lot of what passes for information on the Internet. The transitory nature of Net communication encourages a freedom like that of private conversation. Rumor-mongering, gossip, pontification, unverified quotation, and backchat all flow freely through cyberspace, shortcutting the skills and/or self-restraints of both fiction and factual writing. The pseudo-oral, pseudonymous, transitory character of electronic writing encourages an easy abdication of the responsibility that accrues to print. But that responsibility may be truly out of place in the Net. A new form of writing has to develop its own aesthetic and ethic. That's to come. In this essay I'm talking about print, the essence of which is that it gives writing reproducible permanence. All permanence in human terms involves responsibility.

〜

A group I belong to that gives annual awards to writers got a letter recently asking us to divide our nonfiction prize into two—one for historical nonfiction and one for creative nonfiction. The first term was new to me, the second was familiar.

Writing workshops and programs all over the country now offer courses in "creative nonfiction." The arts of scientific, historical, and biographical narrative are rarely if ever taught in such programs (or anywhere else). Autobiography, however, has been increasingly popular in the writing programs. It may be taught as journal writing or as therapy through self-expression. When it has more literary goals, it is called creative nonfiction, personal essay, and memoir.

The writer of a memoir, like the responsible biographer, ethnographer, or journalist, used to describe what other people did and said, leaving what they may have felt and thought as implications to be drawn by the reader or as authorial speculation identified as such. The autobiographer limited her account to her own memory of how her uncle Fred looked as he ate the grommet, what she heard him say when he'd swallowed it, and what she thought about it. The only sensations and emotions she described were her own.

According to those who defend the use of fictional devices and elements in nonfiction, the memoirist is justified in telling us how, as he swallowed it, Fred vividly recalled the slightly oily taste of the first grommet he ever ate, fifty years ago in Indiana, and how bittersweet the memory was to him.

Many writers and readers of creative nonfiction hold that such ascription of inward thought or feeling, if it's based on a knowledge of Fred's character, is legitimate. It does no harm to Fred (who died in 1980 of a surfeit of grommets), and no harm to the reader, who after all will almost certainly know Fred only in and through the story, just as if he were a character in a novel.

But who is to certify the writer's knowledge of her uncle's character as accurate, unbiased, reliable? Possibly her aunt, but we're not likely to have the chance to consult her aunt. The memoirist's responsibility seems to me to be exactly that of the ethnographer: not to pretend to objectivity, but also not to pretend to be able to speak for anybody but oneself. To assign oneself the power to tell us what another person thought or felt is, to my mind, co-optation of a voice: an act of extreme disrespect. The reader who accepts the tactic colludes in the disrespect.

~

Characters "come alive" in a story, fictive or factual, they "seem real," not, of course, through the mere report of their actions and words, but by selection, suppression, rearrangement, and interpretation of that material. I take it this is what Mr. Di Piero, quoted above, meant by "Remembering is an act of the imagination." (It may be what Genly Ai, in my novel *The Left Hand of Darkness,* meant by saying that he was taught on his home world that "Truth is a matter of the imagination"; but Genly, of course, wasn't real.)

The most cogent argument in support of the use of invention in nonfiction is, then: as fiction involves the arrangement, manipulation, and interpretation of inventions, so creative nonfiction involves the arrangement, manipulation, and interpretation of actual events. A short story is an invention, a memoir is a reinvention, and the difference between them is negligible.

I accept the terms, but the conclusion makes me uneasy.

It's not just that many readers evidently don't know whether a story they just read is factual, invented, or a mixture, and don't care. They do care, in the sense that I discussed above: American readers tend to value factuality over invention, reality over imagination. They're uncomfortable with the fictivity of fiction.

Perhaps this is why they beg novelists to tell them, "Where do you get your ideas from?" The only honest answer is of course "I make them up," but that's not the answer they want. They want specific sources. In my experience, most readers vastly exaggerate the dependence of fiction on research and immediate experience. They assume that characters in a story are "taken" from somebody the author knows, "based on" a specific person used as "copy," and believe that a story or novel is necessarily preceded by "research."

(This latter illusion may rise from the necessity most writers are under of writing applications for grants. You can't tell the guys with the money that you don't actually need to spend six months in the Library of Congress doing research for your novel. You've been drawing maps of Glonggo ever since you were ten, you worked out the curious mores and social structure of the Glonggovians when you were twenty, the plot and characters of *Thunder-Lords of Glonggo* are ready and waiting in your mind, and all you need is the six months to write the story and some peanut butter to live on. But peanut butter and made-up stories aren't what grants are given for. Grants are for serious things, like research.)

The notion that fictional characters are all portraits of actual people probably arises from natural vanity and paranoia, and is encouraged by the power fantasies of some fiction writers (you're nothing to me but copy). Tracing back elements of great novel characters—Jane Eyre, Natasha, Mrs. Dalloway—to this or that element of real people the writer knew is an entertaining and sometimes revealing critico-biographical game. But involved in all such searches for the nonfiction in the fiction is, I suspect, a distrust of the fictive, a resistance to admitting that novelists *make it up*—that fiction is not reproduction, but invention.

If invention is so much distrusted, why is it admitted where it doesn't belong?

Maybe this insistence that fiction is "really" not made up but derived immediately from fact is what has established the confusion of modes that, as if reciprocally, permits the entry of fictional data into purported nonfiction.

⤻

Nothing comes from nothing. The novelist's "ideas" do come from somewhere. The poet Gary Snyder's finely unpoetic image of composting is useful here. Stuff goes into the writer, a whole lot of stuff, not notes in a notebook but everything seen and heard and felt all day every day, a lot of garbage, leftovers, dead leaves, eyes of potatoes, artichoke stems, forests, streets, rooms in slums, mountain ranges, voices, screams, dreams, whispers, smells, blows, eyes, gaits, gestures, the touch of a hand, a whistle in the night, the slant of light on the wall of a child's room, a fin in a waste of waters. All this stuff goes down into the novelist's personal compost bin, where it combines, recombines, changes; gets dark, mulchy, fertile, turns into ground. A seed falls into it, the ground nourishes the seed with the richness that went into it, and something grows. But what grows isn't an artichoke stem and a potato eye and a gesture. It's a new thing, a new whole. It's *made up*.

That's how I understand the process of using fact, experience, memory, in fictional narrative.

It seems to me the process of using fact, experience, memory in nonfiction is entirely different. In a memoir, the artichoke stem remains itself. The remembered light that slants across the wall can be placed and dated: a room in a house in Berkeley in 1936. These memories are immediate to the writer's mind. They weren't composted, but saved.

Memory is an active and imperfect process. Memories are shaped and selected, often profoundly, in that process. Like souls in heaven, they are saved, but changed. When the writer comes to make them into a coherent story, in the interests of clarity, comprehensibility, impetus, and other aims of narrative art, they'll be selected from, emphasised, omitted, interpreted, and thoroughly worked over.

Nothing in these processes makes them fictional. They're still, to the best of the author's ability, genuine memories.

But if the remembered facts are deliberately changed or rearranged, they become false. If the artichoke stem is made a zinnia because the writer finds the zinnia more aesthetically effective, if the light falls aslant on the wall in 1944 because that date fits more conveniently into the narrative, they're no longer facts or memories of facts. They are fictional elements in a piece that calls itself nonfiction. And when in reading a memoir I suspect or identify such elements, they cause me intense discomfort.

I'll let Tolstoy tell me what Napoleon thought and felt, because, although his novel is full of well-researched historical facts, that's not why I'm reading it. I'm reading it for the values proper to the novel, as a work of invention. If certain aspects of the author's uncle Fred get into a short story where he's called Cousin Jim and eats washers, I'll accept their rubbery taste without a qualm, because it's a story, and I take Cousin Jim to be a fictional character. It's when I'm not quite sure what I'm reading that qualms arise.

It can happen even when there is a surfeit of fact in what calls itself fiction.

Reading for a jury for a fiction award, I fretted to a fellow juror about one of the books: was it really a novel? It read like a pure relation of the author's boyhood, an honest, accurate, touching memoir barely disguised with a few name changes. How could we tell? "The author calls it a novel," said my friend, "and so I read it as fiction and judge it as such." Dealer's call. If the writer calls it nonfiction, read it as fact; if the writer calls it a novel, read it as fiction.

I tried. I couldn't do it. Fiction involves invention; fiction *is* invention. I can't read a book in which nothing is invented as a novel. I couldn't give a fiction award to a book that contains only facts. Any more than I could give a prize for journalism to *The Lord of the Rings*.

ς

A real novel, an entirely fictive and imaginative tale, can contain vast amounts of fact without being any less fictional for it. Historical fiction and science fiction (which, by the way, often really does require research) may be full of solid, useful information concerning an era or a body of knowledge. The ploy of the whole realistic genre is to put invented characters into a framework of reproduced actuality—imaginary toads in a real garden, to twist Marianne Moore. All fiction serves later generations as descriptive evidence of its time, place, society; for keen observation and recording of ordinary people's lives, very little ethnography has ever equalled the novel.

But it doesn't work the other way. The historian, biographer, anthropologist, autobiographer, nature writer, have to use real gardens *and* real toads. Therein lies their proper creativity: not in inventing, but in making recalcitrant reality into a story without faking it.

Anything written contains an implicit contract, which can be honored or broken in the writing, or in the reading, or in the presentation by the publisher.

The first and most tenuous and intangible contract is between the writer and his or her conscience, and goes something like this: In this piece I will try to tell my story truly, using the means I find appropriate to the form, whether fiction or nonfiction.

Then there's a more verifiable agreement between the writer and the reader, the terms of which vary immensely, depending, in the first place, on the sophistication of both. An experienced reader may follow a sophisticated writer through a whole gallery of tricks and illusions with perfect confidence that there will be no aesthetic betrayal. For more naive readers, however, the terms of the contract depend largely on how the writer—and publisher—present the work: as factual, imaginative, or a mixture of the two.

Reader as well as writer can twist the terms of this contract, reading a novel as if it were an account of actual events, or a piece of reportage as if it were pure invention.

Despite the great affinitie of fiction and beleefe, only the very innocent believe what novelists tell them. But an attitude of distrust towards nonfiction may well be the result of experience. One has been disappointed so often.

For though a whole swarm of facts in a novel doesn't in the least invalidate the invention as a whole, every fictive or even inaccurate element in a narrative that presents itself as factual puts the whole thing at risk. To pass a single invention off as a fact is to damage the credibility of the rest of the narrative. To keep doing so is to disauthenticate it entirely.

Lincoln's aphorism about fooling people applies, as usual. The writer who reports inaccurately or presents invention as fact is, consciously or not, exploiting the reader's ignorance. Only the informed reader is aware that the contract has been violated. If amused enough, this reader may privately rewrite the contract, reading the so-called nonfiction as mere entertainment, hokum—fiction in the OED's fifth definition.

Perhaps the terms of the contract are currently being rewritten by the writers. Perhaps the whole idea of a contract is hopelessly prepostmodern, and readers are coming to accept false data in nonfiction as calmly as they accept factual information in fiction.

Certainly we've become so numbed by the quantity of unverifiable information poured out upon us that we admit factoids as more or less equivalent to facts. And with the same numbness, we're generally acceptant of hype of all kinds—advertising, stories about celebrity figures, political "leaks," patriotic and moralistic declarations, and so on—reading it without much caring if the material is credible or that we're being treated as objects of manipulation.

If this nondistinction of the fictive and the factual is a general trend, maybe we should celebrate it as a victory of creativity over unimaginative, indiscriminate factualism. I worry about it, however, because it seems to me that by not distinguishing invention from lying it puts imagination itself at risk.

Whatever "creative" means, I don't think the term can fairly be applied to falsification of data and memories, whether intentional or "inevitable."

Excellence in nonfiction lies in the writer's skills in observing, organising, narrating, and interpreting facts—skills entirely dependent on imagination, used not to invent, but to connect and illuminate observation.

Writers of nonfictional narrative who "create" facts, introduce inventions, for the sake of aesthetic convenience, wishful thinking, spiritual solace, psychic healing, vengeance, profit, or anything else, aren't using the imagination, but betraying it.

AWARD AND GENDER

This was given as a talk and a handout at the Seattle Book Fair in 1999.

In 1998 I was on a jury of three choosing a literary prize. From 104 novels, we selected a winner and four books for the shortlist, arriving at consensus with unusual ease and unanimity. We were three women, and the books we chose were all written by women. The eldest and wisest of us said, Ouch! If a jury of women picks only women finalists, people will call us a feminist cabal and dismiss our choices as prejudiced, and the winning book will suffer for it.

I said, But if we were men and picked all books by men, nobody would say a damn thing about it.

True, said our Wise Woman, but we want our winner to have credibility, and the only way three women can have credibility as a jury is to have some men on the short list.

Against my heart and will, I agreed. And so two women who should have been there got bumped from our shortlist, and the two men whose books we had placed sixth and seventh got on it.

ᔆ

Literary awards used to be essentially literary events. Though a prize such as the Pulitzer certainly influenced the sale of the book, that wasn't all it was valued for. Since the takeover of most publishing houses by their accounting departments, the financial aspect of the literary award has become more and more important.

These days, literary prizes carry a huge weight in fame, money, and shelf longevity.

But only some of them. Certain awards are newsworthy and success-assuring: most of them are not. The selection of which prize is sure to hit the headlines and which is ignored seems to be almost totally arbitrary. The media follow habit without question. Hysteria about the Booker Prize is assured; general indifference to the PEN Western States Award is certain.

Most writers who have served on award juries agree that the field of finalists is often so qualitatively even that selection of a single winner is essentially arbitrary. Many also agree that the field of finalists often contains books so various in nature and intent that the selection of a single winner is, again, essentially arbitrary. But a single winner is what is demanded of them, so they provide it. Then publishers capitalise on it, bookstores fawn on it, libraries stock their shelves with it, while the shortlist books are forgotten.

I feel that the competitive, single-winner pattern is suited to sports events but not to literature, that the increasingly exaggerated dominance of the "big" awards in the field of fiction is pernicious, and that the system inevitably perpetuates cronyism, geographical favoritism, gender favoritism, and big-name syndrome.

Of these, gender favoritism particularly irks me. It is so often and so indignantly denied that I began to wonder if I was irked over nothing. I decided to try to find if my impression that the great majority of literary awards went to men had any foundation in fact. To establish my facts, I limited my study to fiction.

If more men than women publish fiction, that would of course justify an imbalance towards male prizewinners. So to start with I did some gender sampling of authors of novels and story collections published in various periods from 1996 to 1998. My time was limited and my method was crude. The numbers (only about a thousand writers in all) may not be large enough to be statistically significant. My author-gender count covers only four recent years, while my figures on the awards go back decades. (A study on author gender in fiction in the whole twentieth century would be a very interesting subject for a thesis.) My sources were *Publishers Weekly* for general fiction, *What Do I Read Next?* for genre fiction, and the *Hornbook* for children's books. I counted authors by sex, omitting collaborations and any names that were not gender identifiable. (My genre sources identified aliases. Rumor has it that many romances are written by men under female pen names, but I found only one transgenderer—a woman mystery writer who used a male name.)

AUTHOR GENDER
Summations
(see Details of the Counts and Awards, below)

> General fiction: 192 men, 167 women: slightly more men than
> women.
> Genre fiction: 208 men, 250 women: more women than men
> Children's books and young adult: 83 men, 161 women: twice
> as many women as men
> All genres: 483 men, 578 women: about 5 women to 4 men.

Eighty of the authors in my Genre category were romance writers, all women; if you consider them as probably balanced by predominantly male-written genres such as sports, war, and porn, which I did not have figures for, you might arrive at parity. It looks as if, overall, as many women as men, perhaps slightly more women than men, write and publish novels and stories.

Author gender in fiction is pretty near 1:1.

Now for the gender counts and ratios for literary prizes. Ideally I would have listed the shortlists or runners-up where available, but given the shortness of time in which I had to prepare this paper, and the shortness of life, I list only winners. (Information on most awards, including shortlists, winners, and sometimes jurors, is accessible at libraries and on the Net.)

The years covered are the years the prize has been given, up to 1998—these spans of course vary greatly. The oldest is the Nobel Prize in Literature.

I did not try to find out the gender composition of the juries of any of these awards, though many are on record. I wish I had the time to go into this and find out whether juries are gender balanced or not, whether the balance has changed over time, and whether gender composition influences their choices. One might well assume that men tend to pick men and women women, but if juries are even moderately balanced between men and women, my figures do not support this assumption. It looks as if men and women tend to pick men.

Most awards are chosen by a judge or panel of judges, but some genre prizes are voted by readers or (in the case of the Nebula Award) fellow writers in the genre.

(In this context I want to point out that the MacArthur "genius awards" are nominated by "experts" chosen by the MacArthur Foundation, and the winners are selected by a board chosen by the Foundation—a *permanently secret* board, whose members are therefore, in the true meaning of the word, irresponsible. In all the arts awards given by the MacArthur Foundation, I find the 3:1 gender ratio—three men to one woman—so consistent that I must assume it is the result of deliberate policy.)

Gender Ratio of Literary Prizes, Male to Female

(in order of most extreme imparity to nearest parity)

Nobel Prize in Literature, 10:1

PEN/Faulkner Award for Fiction, 8:1

Edgar Grand Master Award (mystery), 7:1

National Book Award (now American Book Award), 6:1

World Fantasy Lifetime Achievement Award, 6:1

Pulitzer Prize for Literature, since 1943, 5:1

Edgar Award for Best Novel, since 1970 (mystery), 5:1

Hugo Award (science fiction) (reader vote), 3:1

World Fantasy Best Novel Award, 3:1

Newbery Award (juvenile), 3:1

Nebula Award (science fiction) (voted by fellow writers), 2.4:1

Pulitzer Prize for Literature, till 1943, 2:1

Edgar Award for Best Novel, till 1970 (mystery), 2:1

Booker Prize, 2:1

Some Observations

Though the number of men and women writing literary fiction is nearly equal, the "big" literary awards, Nobel, National Book Award, Booker, PEN, Pulitzer, give 5.5 prizes to men for every 1 to a woman. Genre awards average 4 to 1, so a woman stands a better chance of getting a prize if she writes genre fiction.

Among all the prizes I counted, the ratio is 4.5:1—for every woman who gets a fiction prize, four and a half men do; or, to avoid the uncomfortable idea of half-men, you can say that nine men get a prize for every two women who do.

Except in the Nobel, which gave three women prizes in the nineties, there was no gain in gender parity in these prizes during the twentieth century, and in some cases a drastic decline. I broke the figures for the

Pulitzer into before and after 1943, and the Edgar Best Novel into before and after 1970, to demonstrate the most notable examples of this decline. There would have to have been a massive change in author gender, a great increase in the number of men writing fiction in these fields, to explain or justify the increasing percentage of male award winners. I do not have the figures, but my impression is that there has not been any such great increase; my guess is that the fifty-fifty ratio of men and women writing fiction has been fairly constant through the twentieth century.

In children's literature, where by my rough count there are twice as many women authors, men win three times as many prizes as women.

Nearly two-thirds of mystery writers are women, but men get three times as many prizes as women, and since 1970, five times as many.

The inescapable conclusion is that prize juries, whether they consist of readers, writers, or pundits, through conscious or unconscious prejudice, reward men four and a half times more than women.

The escapable conclusion is that men write fiction four and a half times better than women. This conclusion appears to be acceptable to many people, so long as it goes unspoken.

Those of us who do not find it acceptable have to speak.

Literary juries and the sponsors of awards need to have their prejudices queried and their consciousness raised. The perpetuation of gender prejudice through literary prizes should be challenged by fair-minded writers by discussions such as this, by further and better research, and by letters of comment and protest to the awarding bodies, to literary publications, and to the press.

DETAILS OF THE COUNTS AND AWARDS

This appendix is for people who enjoy details and want to see how my system of determining author gender and gender parity worked, or suggest how it might be improved, enlarged, and updated—a job I would gladly hand on to anybody who wants to undertake it. . . . And I have made some notes and observations on various outcomes and oddities.

Author Gender (Novels and Story Collections)
(MF indicates male to female)

"Literary" Fiction

> Hardcover: men 128, women 98. MF ratio 1.3:1
> Trade paperback: men 64, women 69. MF ratio near parity

"Genre" Fiction

> Mystery: men 52, women 72. MF ratio 0.7:1
> Romance: men 0, women 80. MF ratio 0:1
> Western: men 60, women 22. MF ration 3:1
> Fantasy: men 39, women 40. MF ratio near parity.
> Science fiction: men 57, women 35. MF ratio 1.6:1

"Juvenile" Fiction

> Children, age 6–12: men 80, women 117. MF ratio 0.7:1
> Young adult: men 23, women 44. MF ratio 1:2

Summary

> "Literary" fiction: men 192, women 167
> "Genre" fiction: men 208, women 249
> "Juvenile" fiction: men 103, women 161

These categories, derived from my reference sources, should be taken with extreme distrust, which is why I put them in quotes. Genre, as generally understood, is itself a suspect concept. Many of the books could well have been listed in two or even three categories.

Total Count of Gender of Authors of Novels and Story Collections

Total authors: 1,080
Men 503, women 577
Approximate MF ratio 5:6

Author Gender in Awards Given to Novels and Story Collections

The Nobel Prize in Literature (voted by a special board)

Between 1901 and 1998, the prize was given 91 times (it was not given 7 times, notably during World War Two). It has been split twice between two men and once between a man and a woman, so that the totals have decimals.

Men 85.5, women 8.5. MF ratio almost exactly 10:1

The years women were given the Nobel for Literature were 1909, 1926, 1928, 1938, 1945, 1966, 1991, 1993, 1996: pretty much one woman per decade, till the nineties when three women were given prizes.

The Pulitzer Prize for Literature (voted by a jury of writers)

Given since 1918, with six no-award years.

Men 50, women 23. MF ratio just over 2:1

The ratio has declined severely from parity since 1943. Of the 23 awards to women, 12 were given in the 25 years 1918–1943, but only 11 in the 54 years 1944–1998. Since 1943, though half or more of the shortlist authors are often women, 5 out of 6 winners have been men (MF ratio 5:1).

The Booker Prize (voted by a jury of writers and critics)

Given since 1969.

Men 21, women 11. MF ratio 2:1

This ratio has been pretty steady over 30 years, remaining the nearest parity of the prizes I examined.

The National Book Award/American Book Award

Given since 1950, with various types of jury, various sponsors, and several changes of category in fiction, so it is hard to count. As well as I can determine, the "Best Novel" award (excluding genre and juvenile) has been as follows:

Men 43, women 7. MF ratio 6:1

The PEN/Faulkner Award for Fiction (voted by a jury)

Given since 1981.

Men 17, women 2. MF ratio 8.5: 1

As there are always women on the shortlist for the PEN/Faulkner, I was startled, in fact shocked, to discover how few have been given the award. This prize is almost as male oriented as the Nobel.

The Nebula Award (science fiction and fantasy; voted by public nomination and secret ballot of members of the Science Fiction and Fantasy Writers' Association)

Given since 1965.

Men 24, women 10. MF ratio 2.4:1

The Hugo Award (science fiction; voted by ballot of members of the World Science Fiction Convention)

Given since 1953.

Men 36, women 11. MF ratio 3:1

I find it interesting that these two balloted awards, the Nebula selected by writers and the Hugo by fans, are nearer parity than several juried awards, and far nearer parity than the similarly balloted Edgar.

The World Fantasy Award (given by a jury, plus an anonymous decision)

Best Novel (split awards cause decimals):
    Men 18.5, women 5.5. MF ratio 3:1

Lifetime Achievement (16 awards plus a 5-way split):
    Men 17, women 3. MF ratio 6:1

The Edgar Award

Best Novel (mystery; voted by the members of the Mystery Writers of America)
    Given since 1946.
    Men 39, women 13. MF ratio 3:1
    This ratio is for the whole 52 years. From 1946 to 1970, 16 men and 8 women were given the prize, making the ratio 2:1. But in the 28 years since 1970, despite the fact that considerably more women than men write mysteries, only 5 women have won "Best Novel," making the MF ratio almost 5:1.

Grand Master

First given in 1955, to Agatha Christie. For the next 15 years, only men were made Grand Masters. By 1998, of the 46 Grand Masters, 35 were men, 8 women—but 3 of those 8 women shared a single award. No men have been asked to share their Grand Mastery. Counting the 3-in-1 as a single award, the MF ratio is 7:1.

The Newbery Award (for excellence in children's literature; voted by a "panel of experts")

Given since 1922.

1922–1930, all the awards went to men; 1931–1940, all to women. From 1941 to 1998, men 34, women 12. Although only 1 out of 3 authors of books for children and young adults is a man, since 1941 the prize has been given to a man 3 times out of 4.

I found the history of the Newbery, in several respects, the most troubling of all. It is a powerful award, guaranteeing long-term prestige and success, since booksellers as a rule feature Newbery (and Caldecott—an art award) books preeminently, and sometimes almost solely, in their juvenile department. Since the prejudice shown in this single aspect appears so blatant, should other aspects of the judging process of the Newbery perhaps be examined and discussed?

ON GENETIC DETERMINISM

I wrote this piece as a reader's personal response to a text. Finding myself troubled by many of E. O. Wilson's sweeping statements, I tried to figure out what was troubling me. I did it in writing because I think best in writing. An amateur responding to a professional is likely to make a fool of herself, and no doubt I've done just that; but I decided to publish the piece. I am not pitting my opinions against scientific observation; I am pitting my opinions against a scientist's opinions. Opinions and assumptions, when presented by a distinguished scientist, are likely to be mistaken for scientific observations—for fact. And that was what troubled me.

In his very interesting autobiography, *Naturalist,* E. O. Wilson summarises the statement of the biological foundations of human behavior made in his book *Sociobiology:*

Genetic determinism, the central objection raised against [*Sociobiology*], is the bugbear of the social sciences. So what I said that can indeed be called genetic determinism needs saying here again. My argument ran essentially as follows: Human beings inherit a propensity to acquire behavior and social structures, a propensity that is shared by enough people to be called human nature. The defining traits include division of labor between the sexes, bonding between parents and children, heightened altruism toward closest kin, incest avoidance, other forms of ethical behavior, suspicion of strangers, tribalism, dominance orders within groups, male dominance overall, and territorial aggression over limiting [limited?] resources. Although people have free will and the choice to turn in many directions, the channels of their psychological development are nevertheless—however much we might wish otherwise—cut more deeply by the genes in certain directions than in others. So while cultures vary greatly, they inevitably converge toward these traits. . . . The important point is that heredity interacts with environment to create a gravitational pull toward a fixed mean. It gathers people in all societies into the narrow statistical circle that we define as human nature. (E. O. Wilson, *Naturalist*, pp. 332, 333)

That human beings inherit a propensity to acquire behavior and that the construction of society is one of these behaviors, I agree. Whether anything worth the risk is to be gained by calling this propensity "human nature," I wonder. Anthropologists have excellent justification for avoiding the term *human nature,* for which no agreed definition exists, and which all too easily, even when intended as descriptive, is applied prescriptively.

Wilson states that the traits he lists constitute a "narrow statistical circle that we define as human nature." Like Tonto, I want to ask, "Who 'we,' white man?" The selection of traits is neither complete nor universal, the definitions seem sloppy rather than narrow, and the statistics are left to the imagination. More statistics and completer definitions are to be found in *Sociobiology,* of course; but Wilson's own statement of what the book says is as accurate and complete as it is succinct, so that I think it fair to address my arguments to it.

Taking it, then, phrase by phrase:

Division of labor between the sexes:
This phrase means only that in all or most known societies men and women do different kinds of work; but since it is very seldom understood in that strict meaning, it is either ingenuous or disingenuous to use it in this context without acknowledging its usual implications. Unless those implications are specifically denied, the phrase "division of labor between the sexes" is understood by most readers in this society to imply specific *kinds* of gender-divided work, and so to imply that *these* are genetically determined: our genes ensure that men hunt, women gather; men fight, women nurse; men go forth, women keep the house; men do art, women do domestic work; men function in the "public sphere," women in the "private," and so on.

No anthropologist or person with an anthropological conscience, knowing how differently work is gendered in different societies, could accept these implications. I don't know what implications, if any, Wilson intended. But as this kind of unstated extension of reductionist statements does real intellectual and social damage, reinforcing prejudices and bolstering bigotries, it behooves a responsible scientist to define his terms more carefully.

As some gendered division of labor exists in every society, I would fully agree with Wilson if he had used a more careful phrasing, such as "some form of gender construction, including gender-specific activities."

Bonding between parents and children; heightened altruism toward closest kin; suspicion of strangers:
All these behaviors are related, and can be defined as forms of "selfish gene" behavior; I think they have been shown to be as nearly universal among human beings as among other social animals. But in human beings such behavior is uniquely, and universally, expressed in so immense a range of behaviors and social structures, of such immense variety and complexity, that one must ask if this range and complexity,

not present in any animal behavior, is not as genetically determined as the tendencies themselves.

If my question is legitimate, then Wilson's statement is unacceptably reductive. To focus on a type of human behavior shared with other animals, but to omit from the field of vision the unique and universal character of such behavior among humans, is to beg the question of how far genetic determination of behavior may extend. Yet that is a question that no sociobiologist can beg.

Tribalism:

I understand tribalism to mean an extension of the behavior just mentioned: social groups are extended beyond immediate blood kin by identifying nonkin as "socially kin" and strangers as nonstrangers, establishing shared membership in constructs such as clan, moiety, language group, race, nation, religion, and so on.

I can't imagine what the mechanism would be that made this kind of behavior genetically advantageous, but I think it is as universal among human groups as the behaviors based on actual kinship. If universality of a human behavior pattern means that it is genetically determined, then this type of behavior must have a genetic justification. I think it would be a rather hard one to establish, but I'd like to see a sociobiologist try.

Incest avoidance:

Here I'm uncertain about the evolutionary mechanism that enables the selfish gene to recognise a selfish gene that is too closely akin, and so determines a behavior norm. If there are social mechanisms preventing incest among the other primates, I don't know them. (Driving young males out of the alpha male's group is male-dominant behavior serving only incidentally and ineffectively as incest prevention; the alpha male does mate with his sisters and daughters, though the young males have to go find somebody else's.)

I'd like to know whether Wilson knows what the general incidence of incest among mammals is, and whether he believes that incest is "avoided" among humans any more than it is among apes, cats, wild horses, and so on. Do all human societies ban incest? I don't know; it was an open question, last I heard. That most human societies have cultural strictures against certain types of incest is true; that many human societies fail as often as not to implement them is also true. I think in this case Wilson has confused a common cultural dictum or desideratum with actual behavior; or else he is saying that our genes program us to *say* we must not do something, but do not prevent us from *doing* it. Now those are some fancy genes.

Dominance orders within groups:
Here I suspect Wilson's anthropology is influenced by behaviorists' experiments with chickens and primatologists' observations of apes more than by anthropologists' observation of human behavior in groups. Dominance order is very common in human societies, but so are other forms of group relationship, such as maintaining order through consensus; there are whole societies in which dominance is not the primary order, and groups in most societies in which dominance does not function at all, difficult as this may be to believe at Harvard. Wilson's statement is suspect in emphasising one aspect of behavior while omitting others. Once again, it is reductive. It would be more useful if phrased more neutrally and more accurately: perhaps, "tendency to establish structured or fluid social relationships outside immediate kinship."

Male dominance overall:
This is indeed the human social norm. I take it that the genetic benefit is that which is supposed to accrue in all species in which the male displays to the female to attract her choice and/or drives away weaker males from his mate or harem, thus ensuring that his genes will dominate in the offspring (the *male* selfish gene). Species in which this kind of behavior does not occur (including so close a genetic relative as the

bonobo) are apparently not considered useful comparisons or paradigms for human behavior.

That male aggressivity and display behavior extend from sexuality to all forms of human social and cultural activity is indubitable. Whether this extension has been an advantage or a liability to our genetic survival is certainly arguable, probably unprovable. It certainly cannot simply be assumed to be of genetic advantage in the long run to the human, or even the male human, gene. The "interaction of heredity with environment" in this case has just begun to be tested, since only in the last hundred years has there been a possibility of *unlimited* dominance by any subset of humanity, along with *unlimited*, uncontrollable aggressivity.

Territorial aggression over limiting [sic] *resources:*
This is evidently a subset of "male dominance overall." As I understand it, women's role in territorial aggression has been subsidiary, not institutionalised, and seldom even recognised socially or culturally. So far as I know, all organised and socially or culturally sanctioned aggression over resources or at territorial boundaries is entirely controlled and almost wholly conducted by men.

It is flagrantly false to ascribe such aggression to scarcity of resources. Most wars in the historical period have been fought over quite imaginary, arbitrary boundaries. It is my impression of warlike cultures such as the Sioux or the Yanomamo that male aggression has no economic rationale at all. The phrase should be cut to "territorial aggression," and attached to the "male dominance" item.

Other forms of ethical behavior:
This one's the big weasel. What forms of ethical behavior? Ethical according to whose ethics?

Without invoking the dreaded bogey of cultural relativism, I think we have a right to ask anybody who asserts that there are universal human moralities to list and define them. If he asserts that they are genetically determined, he should be able to specify the genetic mechanism and the evolutionary advantage they involve.

Wilson appends these "other forms" to "incest avoidance," which is thus syntactically defined as ethical behavior. Incest avoidance certainly involves some genetic advantage. If there are other behaviors that involve genetic advantage and are universally recognised as ethical, I want to know what they are.

Not beating up old ladies might be one. Grandmothers have been proved to play a crucial part in the survival of grandchildren in circumstances of famine and stress. Their genetic interest of course is clear. I doubt, however, that Wilson had grandmothers in mind.

Mother-child bonding might be one of his "other forms of ethical behavior." It is tendentious, if not hypocritical, to call it "bonding between parents and children" as Wilson does, since it is by no means a universal cultural expectation that the male human parent will, or should, bond with his child. The biological father is replaced in many cultures by the mother's brother, or serves only as authority figure, or (as in our culture) is excused from responsibility for children he sired with women other than his current wife. A further danger in this context is that the mother-child bond is so often defined as "natural" as to be interpreted as subethical. A mother who does not bond with her child is defined less as immoral than as inhuman. This is an example of why I think the whole matter of ethics, in this context, is a can of actively indefinable worms far better left unopened.

Perhaps that's why Wilson left these "other ethical behaviors" so vague. Also, if he had specified as ethical such behavior as, say, cooperation and mutual aid between individuals not blood kin, he would have risked his credibility with his fellow biologists still trained to interpret behavior strictly in the mechanistic mode.

Finally, I wonder if genetic determinism as such really is "the bugbear of the social sciences." Academics are the very model of territorialism, and some social scientists certainly responded with fear and fury to what they saw as Wilson's aggression when he published *Sociobiol-*

ogy. But on the whole, Wilson's statement seems a little paranoid, or a little boastful.

The controversy and animus aroused by *Sociobiology* might have been avoided if the author had presented his determinism in more precise, more careful, less tendentious, less anthropologically naive terms. If in fact his theory is not a bugbear to the social sciences, it's because it has not proved itself useful or even relevant to them.

I'd find his arguments far more interesting if he had genuinely taken pains to extend his reductive theory to explain specifically human behavior, including the elaboration of the gender-based, kin-based repertory of behaviors we share with animals into the apparently infinite varieties of human social structures and the endless complexities of culture. But he has not done so.

There are social scientists and humanists, as well as determinists, who would argue that it's the vast range and complexity of human behavioral options, in origin genetically determined, that gives us what may ultimately be the illusion of free will. But Wilson, having raised this question in *Naturalist,* ducks right under it with a flat statement of belief that "people have free will." The statement as such is meaningless. I am not interested in his beliefs. He is not a religious thinker or a theologian but a scientist. He should speak as such.

ABOUT FEET

Watching a ballroom dancing competition on television, I was fascinated by the shoes the women wore. They were dancing in strapped stiff shoes with extremely high heels. They danced hard, heel and toe, kicking and prancing, clapping their feet down hard and fast with great precision. The men wore flat-heeled shoes, conformed to the normal posture of the foot. One of them had flashing jewels on the outer side of each shoe. His partner's shoes were entirely covered with the flashing jewels, which must have made the leather quite rigid, and the heels were so high that her own heels were at least three inches above the balls of her feet, on which all her weight was driven powerfully again and again. Imagining my feet in those shoes, I cringed and winced, like the Little Mermaid walking on her knives.

The question has been asked before but I haven't yet got an answer that satisfies me: why do women cripple their feet while men don't?

It's not a very long step to China, where women broke the bones of their daughters' feet and strapped the toes under the ball of the foot to create a little aching useless ball of flesh, stinking of pus and exudations trapped in the bindings and folds of skin: the Lotus Foot, which was, we are told, sexually attractive to men, and so increased the marriageability and social value of the woman.

Such attraction is comprehensible to me as a perversity. A gendered perversity. How many women would be attracted by a man's feet deliberately deformed, dwarfed, and smelling of rot?

So there is the question again. Why? Why do we and why don't they?

Well, I wonder, did some Chinese women find other women's Lotus Feet sexually attractive?

Certainly both men and women may find cruelty and suffering erotic. One person hurts the other so that one or both can feel a sexual thrill that they wouldn't feel if neither was frightened or in pain. As in having a child's foot broken and bound into a rotting lump and then getting an erection from fondling the rotting lump. Sadism and masochism: a sexuality dependent on pain and cruelty.

To let sexual feeling be aroused by pain and cruelty may be better—we are often told it is better—than not having any sexual feeling at all. I'm not sure. For whom is it better?

I'd like to think Chinese women looked with pity, with terror, at one another's Lotus Feet, that they flinched and cringed when they smelled the smell of the bindings, that children burst into tears when they saw their mother's Lotus Feet. Girl children, boy children. But what do I know?

I can understand why a mother would "give" her daughter Lotus Feet, would break the bones and knot the bindings; it's not hard at all to understand, to imagine the circumstances that would lead a mother to make her daughter "marriageable," that is, saleable, acceptable to her society, by torturing and deforming her.

Love and compassion, deformed, act with immense cruelty. How often have Christians and Buddhists thus deformed a teaching of compassion?

And fashion is a great power, a great social force, to which men may be even more enslaved than the women who try to please them by obeying it. I have worn some really stupid shoes myself in the attempt to be desirable, the attempt to be conventional, the attempt to follow fashion.

But that another woman would desire her friend's Lotus Feet, find them erotic, can I imagine that? Yes, I can; but I learn nothing from it. The erotic is not the sum of our being. There is pity, there is terror.

I look at the ballroom dancer's rigid glittering shoes with dagger heels that will leave her lame at fifty, and find them troubling and fascinating. Her partner's flat shiny shoes are boring. His dancing may be thrilling, but his feet aren't. And male ballet dancers' feet certainly aren't attractive, bundled into those soft shoes like big hotdog buns. The uncomfortable fascination comes only when the women get up on their pointes with their whole body weight on the tips of their toes, or prance in their dagger heels, and suffer.

Of course this is a sexual fascination, eroticism explains everything. . . . Well, does it?

Bare feet are what I find sexy—the supple, powerful arch, the complex curves and recurves of the dancer's naked foot. Male or female.

I don't find shod feet erotic. Or shoes, either. Not my fetish, thanks. It's the sense of what dancers' shoes are doing to the dancer's feet that fascinates me. The fascination is not erotic, but it is physical. It is bodily, it is social, ethical. It is painful. It troubles me.

And I can't get rid of the trouble, because my society denies that it is troubling. My society says it's all right, nothing is wrong, women's feet are there to be tortured and deformed for the sake of fashion and convention, for the sake of eroticism, for the sake of marriageability, for the sake of money. And we all say yes, certainly, all right, that is all right. Only something in me, some little nerves down in my toes that got bent awry by the stupid shoes I wore when I was young, some muscles in my instep, some tendon in my heel, all those bits of my body say No no no no. It isn't all right. It's all wrong.

And because my own nerves and muscles and tendons respond, I can't look away from the dancer's dagger heels. They pierce me.

Our mind, denying our cruelty, is trapped in it. It is in our body that we know it, and so perhaps may see how there might be an end to it. An end to fascination, an end to obedience, a beginning of freedom. One step towards it. Barefoot?

DOGS, CATS, AND DANCERS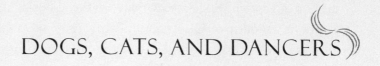

THOUGHTS ABOUT BEAUTY

*An earlier version of this piece was published in 1992 in the "Reflec-
tions" section of Allure magazine, where it was retitled "The Stranger
Within." I have fiddled around with it a good bit since then.*

Dogs don't know what they look like. Dogs don't even know what
size they are. No doubt it's our fault, for breeding them into such
weird shapes and sizes. My brother's dachshund, standing tall at
eight inches, would attack a Great Dane in the full conviction that
she could tear it apart. When a little dog is assaulting its ankles the
big dog often stands there looking confused—"Should I eat it? Will it
eat me? I *am* bigger than it, aren't I?" But then the Great Dane will
come and try to sit in your lap and mash you flat, under the impression that it is a Peke-a-poo.

My children used to run at sight of a nice deerhound named Teddy,
because Teddy was so glad to see them that he wagged his whiplash tail
so hard that he knocked them over. Dogs don't notice when they put
their paws in the quiche. Dogs don't know where they begin and end.

Cats know exactly where they begin and end. When they walk
slowly out the door that you are holding open for them, and pause,
leaving their tail just an inch or two inside the door, they know it. They
know you have to keep holding the door open. That is why their tail
is there. It is a cat's way of maintaining a relationship.

Housecats know that they are small, and that it matters. When a cat meets a threatening dog and can't make either a horizontal or a vertical escape, it'll suddenly triple its size, inflating itself into a sort of weird fur blowfish, and it may work, because the dog gets confused again—"I thought that was a cat. Aren't I bigger than cats? Will it eat me?"

Once I met a huge, black, balloonlike object levitating along the sidewalk making a horrible moaning growl. It pursued me across the street. I was afraid it might eat me. When we got to our front steps it began to shrink, and leaned on my leg, and I recognised my cat, Leonard; he had been alarmed by something across the street.

Cats have a sense of appearance. Even when they're sitting doing the wash in that silly position with one leg behind the other ear, they know what you're sniggering at. They simply choose not to notice. I knew a pair of Persian cats once; the black one always reclined on a white cushion on the couch, and the white one on the black cushion next to it. It wasn't just that they wanted to leave cat hair where it showed up best, though cats are always thoughtful about that. They knew where they looked best. The lady who provided their pillows called them her Decorator Cats.

A lot of us humans are like dogs: we really don't know what size we are, how we're shaped, what we look like. The most extreme example of this ignorance must be the people who design the seats on airplanes. At the other extreme, the people who have the most accurate, vivid sense of their own appearance may be dancers. What dancers look like is, after all, what they do.

I suppose this is also true of fashion models, but in such a limited way—in modeling, what you look like *to a camera* is all that matters. That's very different from really living in your body the way a dancer does. Actors must have a keen self-awareness and learn to know what their body and face are doing and expressing, but actors use words in their art, and words are great illusion makers. A dancer can't weave that word screen around herself. All a dancer has to make her art from is her appearance, position, and motion.

The dancers I've known have no illusions or confusions about what space they occupy. They hurt themselves a lot—dancing is murder on feet and pretty tough on joints—but they never, ever step in the quiche. At a rehearsal I saw a young man of the troupe lean over like a tall willow to examine his ankle. "Oh," he said, "I have an owie on my almost perfect body!" It was endearingly funny, but it was also simply true: his body is almost perfect. He knows it is, and knows where it isn't. He keeps it as nearly perfect as he can, because his body is his instrument, his medium, how he makes a living, and what he makes art with. He inhabits his body as fully as a child does, but much more knowingly. And he's happy about it.

I like that about dancers. They're so much happier than dieters and exercisers. Guys go jogging up my street, thump thump thump, grim faces, glazed eyes seeing nothing, ears plugged by earphones—if there was a quiche on the sidewalk, their weird gaudy running shoes would squish right through it. Women talk endlessly about how many pounds last week, how many pounds to go. If they saw a quiche they'd scream. If your body isn't perfect, punish it. No pain no gain, all that stuff. Perfection is "lean" and "taut" and "hard"—like a boy athlete of twenty, a girl gymnast of twelve. What kind of body is that for a man of fifty or a woman of any age? "Perfect"? What's perfect? A black cat on a white cushion, a white cat on a black one . . . A soft brown woman in a flowery dress . . . There are a whole lot of ways to be perfect, and not one of them is attained through punishment.

Every culture has its ideal of human beauty, and especially of female beauty. It's amazing how harsh some of these ideals are. An anthropologist told me that among the Inuit people he'd been with, if you could lay a ruler across a woman's cheekbones and it didn't touch her nose, she was a knockout. In this case, beauty is very high cheekbones and a very flat nose. The most horrible criterion of beauty I've yet met is the Chinese bound foot: feet dwarfed and crippled to be three inches long increased a girl's attractiveness, therefore her money value. Now that's serious no pain no gain.

But it's all serious. Ask anybody who ever worked eight hours a day in three-inch heels. Or I think of when I was in high school in the 1940s: the white girls got their hair crinkled up by chemicals and heat so it would curl, and the black girls got their hair mashed flat by chemicals and heat so it wouldn't curl. Home perms hadn't been invented yet, and a lot of kids couldn't afford these expensive treatments, so they were wretched because they couldn't follow the rules, the rules of beauty.

Beauty always has rules. It's a game. I resent the beauty game when I see it controlled by people who grab fortunes from it and don't care who they hurt. I hate it when I see it making people so self-dissatisfied that they starve and deform and poison themselves. Most of the time I just play the game myself in a very small way, buying a new lipstick, feeling happy about a pretty new silk shirt. It's not going to make me beautiful, but it's beautiful itself, and I like wearing it.

People have decorated themselves as long as they've been people. Flowers in the hair, tattoo lines on the face, kohl on the eyelids, pretty silk shirts—things that make you feel good. Things that suit you. Like a white pillow suits a lazy black cat. . . . That's the fun part of the game.

One rule of the game, in most times and places, is that it's the young who are beautiful. The beauty ideal is always a youthful one. This is partly simple realism. The young *are* beautiful. The whole lot of 'em. The older I get, the more clearly I see that and enjoy it.

But it gets harder and harder to enjoy facing the mirror. Who is that old lady? Where is her *waist?* I got resigned, sort of, to losing my dark hair and getting all this limp grey stuff instead, but now am I going to lose even that and end up all pink scalp? I mean, enough already. Is that another mole or am I turning into an Appaloosa? How large can a knuckle get before it becomes a kneejoint? I don't want to see, I don't want to know.

And yet I look at men and women my age and older, and their scalps and knuckles and spots and bulges, though various and interesting, don't affect what I think of them. Some of these people I consider to be very beautiful, and others I don't. For old people, beauty doesn't come free with the hormones, the way it does for the young. It has to do with bones. It has to do with who the person is. More and more clearly it has to do with what shines through those gnarly faces and bodies.

⸾

I know what worries me most when I look in the mirror and see the old woman with no waist. It's not that I've lost my beauty—I never had enough to carry on about. It's that that woman doesn't look like me. She isn't who I thought I was.

My mother told me once that, walking down a street in San Francisco, she saw a blonde woman coming towards her in a coat just like hers. With a shock, she realised she was seeing herself in a mirrored window. But she wasn't a blonde, she was a redhead!—her hair had faded slowly, and she'd always thought of herself, seen herself, as a redhead . . . till she saw the change that made her, for a moment, a stranger to herself.

We're like dogs, maybe: we don't really know where we begin and end. In space, yes; but in time, no.

All little girls are supposed (by the media, anyhow) to be impatient to reach puberty and to put on "training bras" before there's anything to train, but let me speak for the children who dread and are humiliated by the changes adolescence brings to their body. I remember how I tried to feel good about the weird heavy feelings, the cramps, the hair where there hadn't been hair, the fat places that used to be thin places. They were supposed to be good because they all meant that I was Becoming a Woman. And my mother tried to help me. But we were both shy, and maybe both a little scared. Becoming a woman is a big deal, and not always a good one.

When I was thirteen and fourteen I felt like a whippet suddenly trapped inside a great lumpy Saint Bernard. I wonder if boys don't often feel something like that as they get their growth. They're forever being told that they're supposed to be big and strong, but I think some of them miss being slight and lithe. A child's body is very easy to live in. An adult body isn't. The change is hard. And it's such a tremendous change that it's no wonder a lot of adolescents don't know who they are. They look in the mirror—that is me? Who's me?

And then it happens again, when you're sixty or seventy.

Cats and dogs are smarter than us. They look in the mirror, once, when they're a kitten or a puppy. They get all excited and run around hunting for the kitten or the puppy behind the glass . . . and then they get it. It's a trick. A fake. And they never look again. My cat will meet my eyes in the mirror, but never his own.

Who I am is certainly part of how I look and vice versa. I want to know where I begin and end, what size I am, and what suits me. People who say the body is unimportant floor me. How can they believe that? I don't want to be a disembodied brain floating in a glass jar in a sci-fi movie, and I don't believe I'll ever be a disembodied spirit floating ethereally about. I am not "in" this body, I *am* this body. Waist or no waist.

But all the same, there's something about me that doesn't change, hasn't changed, through all the remarkable, exciting, alarming, and disappointing transformations my body has gone through. There is a person there who isn't only what she looks like, and to find her and know her I have to look through, look in, look deep. Not only in space, but in time.

I am not lost until I lose my memory.

᠊ᔓ᠊

There's the ideal beauty of youth and health, which never really changes, and is always true. There's the ideal beauty of movie stars and advertising models, the beauty-game ideal, which changes its rules all the time and from place to place, and is never entirely true. And there's an ideal beauty that is harder to define or understand, because it occurs not just in the body but where the body and the spirit meet and define each other. And I don't know if it has any rules.

One way I can try to describe that kind of beauty is to think of how we imagine people in heaven. I don't mean some literal Heaven promised by a religion as an article of belief; I mean just the dream, the yearning wish we have that we could meet our beloved dead again. Imagine that "the circle is unbroken," you meet them again "on that beautiful shore." What do they look like?

People have discussed this for a long time. I know one theory is that everybody in heaven is thirty-three years old. If that includes people who die as babies, I guess they grow up in a hurry on the other side. And if they die at eighty-three, do they have to forget everything they've learned for fifty years? Obviously, one can't get too literal with these imaginings. If you do, you run right up against that old, cold truth: you can't take it with you.

But there is a real question there: How do we remember, how do we *see,* a beloved person who is dead?

My mother died at eighty-three, of cancer, in pain, her spleen enlarged so that her body was misshapen. Is that the person I see when I think of her? Sometimes. I wish it were not. It is a true image, yet it blurs, it clouds, a truer image. It is one memory among fifty years of memories of my mother. It is the last in time. Beneath it, behind it is a deeper, complex, ever-changing image, made from imagination, hearsay, photographs, memories. I see a little red-haired child in the mountains of Colorado, a sad-faced, delicate college girl, a kind, smiling young mother, a brilliantly intellectual woman, a peerless flirt, a serious artist, a splendid cook—I see her rocking, weeding, writing, laughing—I see the turquoise bracelets on her delicate, freckled arm— I see, for a moment, all that at once, I glimpse what no mirror can reflect, the spirit flashing out across the years, beautiful.

That must be what the great artists see and paint. That must be why the tired, aged faces in Rembrandt's portraits give us such delight: they show us beauty not skin-deep but life-deep. In Brian Lanker's album of photographs *I Dream a World,* face after wrinkled face tells us that getting old can be worth the trouble if it gives you time to do some soul making. Not all the dancing we do is danced with the body. The great dancers know that, and when they leap, our soul leaps with them—we fly, we're free. And the poets know that kind of dancing. Let Yeats say it:

> O chestnut tree, great-rooted blossomer,
> Are you the leaf, the blossom or the bole?
> O body swayed to music, O brightening glance,
> How can we know the dancer from the dance?

COLLECTORS, RHYMESTERS, AND DRUMMERS

Some thoughts on beauty and on rhythm, written for my own enter-tainment early in the 1990s, and revised for this book.

COLLECTORS

People collect things. So do some birds and small mammals. The viz-cacha, or bizcacha, is a little rodent that digs holes in Patagonia and the pampa and looks like a very round prairie dog with rabbity ears. Charles Darwin says:

> The bizcacha has one very singular habit: namely, dragging every hard object to the mouth of its burrow: around each group of holes many bones of cattle, stones, thistle-stalks, hard lumps of earth, dry dung, etc., are collected into an irregular heap. . . . I was credibly informed that a gentleman, when rid-ing on a dark night, dropped his watch; he returned in the morning, and by searching the neighborhood of every bizcacha hole in the line of road, as he expected, he soon found it. This habit of picking up whatever may be lying on the ground any-where near its habitation, must cost much trouble. For what purpose it is done, I am quite unable to form even the most re-mote conjecture: it cannot be for defence, because the rubbish is chiefly placed above the mouth of the burrow. . . . No doubt

there must exist some good reason; but the inhabitants of the country are quite ignorant of it. The only fact which I know analogous to it is the habit of that exraordinary Australian bird the Calodera maculata, which makes an elegant vaulted passage of twigs for playing in, and which collects near the spot, land and sea-shells, bones, and the feathers of birds, especially bright colored ones. (*The Voyage of the Beagle*, chapter 7)

Anything that left Charles Darwin unable to form even the most remote conjecture has got to be worth thinking about.

Pack rats and some magpies and crows are, I gather, more selective than bizcachas. They too take hard objects, but keep them in their nest, not outside the front door; and the objects are generally notable in being shiny, or shapely, or in some way what we would call pretty—like the gentleman's watch. But, like the bizcacha's clods and bits of dung, they are also notable in being absolutely useless to the collector.

And we have no idea what it is they see in them.

The male bowerbird's collection of playpretties evidently serves to attract the female bowerbird, but has anyone observed crows or magpies using their buttons, spoons, rings, and can-pulls to enhance their allure? It seems rather that they hide them where nobody else can see them. I don't believe anyone has seen a female pack rat being drawn to the male pack rat by the beauty of his collection (hey, honey, wanna come down and see my bottletops?).

My father, an anthropologist with interests that ranged from biology to aesthetics, kept a semipermanent conversation going—like the famous thirty-year-long poker game in Telluride—on the subject of what beauty is. Hapless visiting scholars would find themselves at our dinner table hotly discussing the nature of beauty. An aspect of the question of particular interest to anthropology is whether such concepts as beauty, or gender, are entirely constructed by each society, or whether we can identify an underlying paradigm, a universal agreement, throughout most or all societies, of what is man, what is woman, what is beautiful. Somewhere in the discussion, as it gathered weight, my father would get sneaky, cross species, and bring in the pack rat.

It is curious that evidence for what looks like an aesthetic sense— a desire for objects because they are perceived as desirable in themselves, a willingness to expend real energy acquiring something that has no practical end at all—seems to turn up only among us, some lowly little rodents, and some rowdy birds. One thing we three kinds of creature have in common is that we are nest builders, householders, therefore collectors. People, rats, and crows all spend a good deal of time gathering and arranging building materials, and bedding, and other furniture for our residences.

But there are many nesters in the animal kingdom, far closer to us genetically than birds or rodents. What about the great apes? Gorillas build a nest every night. Zoo orangs drape themselves charmingly with favorite bits of cloth or sacking. If we shared any collecting tastes with our closest relatives, it might indicate a "deep grammar" of beauty—a "deep aesthetic"?—in all us primates, or at least in the big fancy ones.

But alas I know no evidence of wild apes collecting or prizing objects because they seem to find them pretty. They examine objects of interest with interest, but that's not quite the same as stealing something because it's small and shiny and hiding it away as a treasure. Intelligence and the sense of beauty may overlap, but they aren't the same thing.

Chimpanzees have been taught or allowed to paint, but their motivation seems to be interactive rather than aesthetic: they appreciate color and evidently enjoy the act of whacking the paint on the canvas, but they don't initiate anything remotely like painting on their own in the wild; and they don't prize their own paintings. They don't hide them, hoard them. It appears that they're motivated to paint because people they like want them to paint. Their reward is less the painting than the approval of these people. But a crow or a pack rat will risk its life to steal something that offers no reward of any kind except its own shiny self. And it will hoard that stolen object of beauty, treasuring and rearranging it in its collection, as if it were as precious as an egg or an infant.

The interplay of the aesthetic with the erotic is complex. The peacock's tail is beautiful to us, sexy to the peahen. Beauty and sexual attractiveness overlap, coincide. They may be deeply related. I think they should not be confused.

We find the bowerbird's designs exquisite, the perfume of the rose and the dance of the heron wonderful; but what about such sexual attractors as the chimp's swollen anus, the billy goat's stink, the slime trail a slug leaves for another slug to find so that the two slugs can couple, dangling from a slime thread, on a rainy night? All these devices have the beauty of fitness, but to define beauty as fitness would be even more inadequate than most reductionist definitions.

Darwin was never reductionist. It is like him to say that the bowerbird makes its elegant passage "for playing in"—thus leaving the bowerbird room to play, to enjoy his architecture and his treasures and his dance in his own mysterious fashion. We know that the bower is attractive to female bowerbirds, that they are drawn to it, thus becoming sexually available to the male. What attracts the females to the bower is evidently its aesthetic qualities—its architecture, its orderliness, the brightness of the colors—because the stronger these qualities are, the greater the observable attraction. But we do not know why. Least of all, if the sole end and purpose of the bower is to attract female bowerbirds, do we know why *we* perceive it as beautiful. We may be the wrong sex, and are certainly the wrong species.

So: What is beauty?

Beauty is small, shapely, shiny things, like silver buttons, which you can carry home and keep in your nest/box.

That's certainly not a complete answer, but it's an answer I can accept completely—as far as it goes. It's a beginning.

And I think it interesting, puzzling, important that my appreciation of small, hard, shapely, shiny things is something I share with bizcachas, pack rats, crows, and magpies, of both sexes.

RHYMESTERS

Humpback whales sing. The males sing mostly in breeding season, which implies that their songs play a role in courtship. But both sexes sing; and each humpback population or nation has its distinctive song, shared by all citizens. A humpback song, which may last as much as half an hour, has a complex musical organisation, structured by phrases (groups of notes that are the same or nearly the same in each repetition) and themes (groups of repeated similar phrases).

While the humpbacks are in northern waters they don't sing very much, and the song remains the same. When they regroup in the south, they all sing more, and the national anthem begins changing. Both the song and the changes in it may well serve to confirm community (like street slang, or any group jargon, or dialect). Every member of the community learns the current version, even when it is changing rapidly. After several years the whole tune has been radically altered. "We will sing to you a new song."

Writing in *Natural History,* in March 1991, Kary B. Payne asks two questions of the whales: How do you remember your song, and why do you change it? She suggests that rhyme may help in remembering. Whale songs with a complex set of themes include "rhymes"— phrases that end similarly—and these rhymes link one theme to the next. As for the second question, why they keep changing and transforming their communal song, she says, "Can we speculate about this, and about whales' use of rhymes, without thinking of human beings and wondering about the ancient roots in nature of even our aesthetic behavior?"

Payne's article reminded me irresistibly of the poet/linguist Dell Hymes's work on oral narratives in his book *In Vain I Tried to Tell You* and other books and articles. One such observation (summarised very crudely) is of the value of the repetitive locutions that mark divisions in Native American oral narratives. Such locutions often begin a sentence, and if translated appear as something like "So, then . . ." or "Now, next it happened . . ." or just "And." Often discarded as meaningless, as noise, by translators intent on getting the story and its "meaning," these locutions serve a purpose analogous to rhyme in English poetry: they signal the *line,* which, when there is no regular meter, is a fundamental rhythmic element; and they may also cue the larger, structural rhythmic units that shape the composition.

Following such cues, what was heard, translated, and presented as a "primitive," purely didactic, moralising story, given what shape it has merely by the events it relates, now can be appreciated as subtly formal art, in which the form shapes the material, and in which the seemingly utilitarian narrative may actually be the means towards an essentially aesthetic end.

In oral performance, repetition does not serve only to help the performer remember the text. It is a, perhaps the, fundamental structuring element of the piece: whether it takes the form of the repetitive beat of meter, or the regular sound-echo of rhyme, or the use of refrain and other repeated structures, or the long and subtle rhythm of the lines in unmetered poetry and formal oral narrative. (To these latter are related the even longer and more elusive rhythms of written prose.)

All these uses of repetition do seem to be akin to the whales' rhymes.

As for why the whales sing, it is certainly significant that they sing most, or the males sing most, in mating season. But if you can say a song lasting half an hour performed by a hundred individuals in chorus is a mating call, then you can say a Beethoven symphony is a mating call.

Sometimes Freud sounds as if that's what he thought. If (as he said) the artist is motivated to make art by the desire for "fame, money, and the love of beautiful women," then indeed Beethoven wrote the Ninth because it was mating season. Beethoven was marking his territory.

There is plenty of sexuality in Beethoven's music, which as a woman one may sometimes be rather edgily aware of—thump, thump, thump, BANG!—but testosterone goes only so far. The Ninth Symphony reaches way, way beyond it.

The male song sparrow sings when his little gonads swell as the light grows in the spring. He sings useful information, didactically and purposefully: I am a song sparrow, this is my territory, I rule this roost, my loud sweet voice indicates my youth and health and wonderful capacity to breed, come live with me and be my love, teediddle *wee*too, iddle iddle iddle! And we hear his song as very pretty. But for the crow in the next tree, "caw," said in several different tones, serves exactly the same function. Yet to us, "caw" has negative aesthetic value. "Caw" is ugly. The erotic is not the beautiful, nor vice versa. The beauty of birdsong is incidental to its sexual or informational function.

So why do songbirds go to such elaborate, formalised, repetitive trouble, learning and passing songs down from generation to generation as they do, when they could say "caw" and be done with it?

I propose an anti-utilitarian, nonreductionist, and of course incomplete answer. The bowerbird builds his bower to court his lady, but also, in Darwin's lovely phrase, "for playing in." The song sparrow sings information, but plays with it as he does so. The functional message becomes complicated with a lot of "useless noise" because the pleasure of it—the beauty of it, as we say—is the noise: the trouble taken, the elaboration and repetition, the play. The selfish gene may be using the individual to perpetuate itself, and the sparrow obeys; but, being an individual not a germ cell, he values individual experience, individual pleasure, and to duty adds delight. He plays.

After all, sex, mere sex, may or may not be pleasurable. There's no way to check with slugs or squids, and judging by the hangdog expression on the faces of dogs having sex, and the awful things cats say while having sex, and the experience of the male black widow spider, I should say that if sex is bliss sometimes it doesn't much look like it. But sex is inarguably our duty to our genes or our species. So maybe, to make the duty more enjoyable, you play with it. You fancy it up, you add bells and whistles, tails and bowers, pleasurable complications and formalities. And if these become an end in themselves, as pleasures are likely to do, you end up singing for the joy of singing. Any useful, dutifully sexual purpose of the song has become secondary.

We don't know why the great whales sing. We don't know why pack rats hoard bottlecaps. We do know that young children love to sing and to be sung to, and love to see and possess pretty, shiny things. Their pleasure in such things precedes sexual maturation and seems to be quite unconnected to courtship, sexual stimulation, or mating.

And while song may affirm and confirm community, stealing silver watches certainly does not. We cannot assume that beauty is in the service of either sexuality or solidarity.

I wonder if complication and uselessness are not key words in this meditation. The pack rat seems like a little museum curator, because she has complicated her nest-building instinct with "meaningless noise"—collecting perfectly useless objects for the pleasure of it. The humpback whales can be mentioned along with Beethoven because by adding "meaningless noise" to simple mating calls and statements of community, they elaborated them into symphonies.

My husband's Aunt Pearle employed a useful craft, crochet, with the useful purpose of making a bedspread. By making useless, highly rhythmic variations on plain crochet stitch, she complicated the whole act enormously, because she enjoyed doing so. After months of pleasurable work, she completed a beautiful thing: a "Spiderweb" coverlet, which she gave us. Although it does indeed cover a bed, it isn't, as we women say, for everyday. It is useful, but not simply useful. It is *much more than* useful. It was made to put on the bed when guests are coming, to give them the pleasure of seeing its complex elegance, and the compliment of being given more than is strictly necessary—a surplus, a treat. We take what's useful and play with it—for the beauty of it.

SILENT DRUMMERS

When people are talking about beauty in art they usually take their examples from music, the fine arts, dance, and poetry. They seldom mention prose.

When prose is what's being talked about, the word *beauty* is seldom used, or it's used as mathematicians use it, to mean the satisfying, elegant resolution of a problem: an intellectual beauty, having to do with ideas.

But words, whether in poetry or in prose, are as physical as paint and stone, as much a matter of voice and ear as music, as bodily as dancing.

I think it is a major error in criticism ever to ignore the words. Literally, the words: the sound of the words—the movement and pace of sentences—the rhythmic structures that the words establish and are controlled by.

A pedagogy that relies on the "Cliff Notes" sort of thing travesties the study of literature. To reduce the aesthetic value of a narrative to the ideas it expresses, to its "meaning," is a drastic impoverishment. The map is not the landscape.

In poetry, the auditory and rhythmic reality of language has stayed alive all through the centuries of the Gutenberg Hegemony. Poetry has always been said or read aloud. Even in the inaudible depths of modernism, T. S. Eliot was persuaded to mumble into a microphone. And ever since Dylan Thomas wowed 'em in New York, poetry has reclaimed its proper nature as an audible art.

But prose narrative has been silent for centuries. Printing made it so.

Book-circuit readings by novelists and memoirists are popular now, and recorded readings of books have gone some way towards restoring aurality to prose; but it is still generally assumed, by writer and by critic, that prose is read in silence.

Reading is performance. The reader—the child under the blanket with a flashlight, the woman at the kitchen table, the man at the library desk—*performs* the work. The performance is silent. The readers hear the sounds of the words and the beat of the sentences only in their inner ear. Silent drummers on noiseless drums. An amazing performance in an amazing theater.

What is the rhythm the silent reader hears? What is the rhythm the prose writer follows?

While she was writing her last novel, *Pointz Hall,* which she refers to below as PH, and which when it was published became *Between the Acts,* Virginia Woolf wrote in her diary:

> It is the rhythm of a book that, by running in the head, winds one into a ball: and so jades one. The rhythm of PH (the last chapter) became so obsessive that I heard it, perhaps used it, in every sentence I spoke. By reading the notes for memoirs I broke this up. The rhythm of the notes is far freer and looser. Two days of writing in that rhythm has completely refreshed me. So I go back to PH tomorrow. This I think is rather profound. (Virginia Woolf, *Diary,* 17 November 1940)

Fourteen years before this diary notation made near the end of her life, Woolf wrote the passage I used to open this book and for its title, where she speaks of prose rhythm and the wave that "breaks and tumbles in the mind." In it she also, lightly, called her remarks on the rhythm of narrative "profound." In both these passing notes on the rhythm of narrative, she knew, I think, that she was onto something big. I only wish she'd gone on with it.

In a letter in 1926, Woolf said that what you start with, in writing a novel, "is a world. Then, when one has imagined this world, suddenly people come in." (Letter 1618) First comes the place, the situation, then the characters arrive with the plot. . . . But *telling* the story is a matter of getting the beat—of becoming the rhythm, as the dancer becomes the dance.

And reading is the same process, only far easier, not jading: because instead of having to discover the rhythm beat by beat, you can let your-self follow it, be taken over by it, you can let the dance dance you.

↳

What is this rhythm Woolf talks about? Prose scrupulously avoids any clear regular beat or recurrent cadence. Are there, then, deeply synco-pated patterns of stress? Or does the rhythm occur in and among the sentences—in the syntax, linkage, paragraphing? Is that why punctua-tion is so important to prose (whereas it often matters little in poetry, where the line replaces it)? Or is prose narrative rhythm established as well in even longer phrases and larger structures, in the occurrence of events and recurrence of themes in the story, the linkage and counter-point of plot and chapter?

All these, I think. There are a whole lot of rhythms going in a well-written novel. Together, in their counterpoint and syncopation and union, they make the rhythm of that novel, which is unlike any other, as the rhythms of a human body in their interplay make up a rhythm unique to that body, that person.

↳

Having made this vast, rash statement, I thought I should try to see if it worked. I felt I should be scientific. I should do an experiment.

It is not very rash to say that in a sentence by Jane Austen there is a balanced rhythm characteristic of all good eighteenth-century narra-tive prose, and also a beat, a timing, characteristic of Jane Austen's prose. Following what Woolf said about the rhythm of *Pointz Hall*, might one also find a delicate nuancing of the beat that is characteris-tic of *that particular* Jane Austen novel?

I took down my Complete Austen and, as in the *sortes Vergilianae* or a lazy consultation of the *I Ching*, I let the book open where it wanted. First in *Pride and Prejudice*, and copied out the first para-graph my eyes fell on. Then again in *Persuasion*.

From *Pride and Prejudice*:

More than once did Elizabeth in her ramble within the Park, unexpectedly meet Mr Darcy. — She felt all the perverseness of the mischance that should bring him where no one else was brought: and to prevent its ever happening again, took care to inform him at first, that it was a favourite haunt of hers. — How it could occur a second time therefore was very odd! — Yet it did, and even a third.

From *Persuasion:*

To hear them talking so much of Captain Wentworth, repeating his name so often, puzzling over past years, and at last ascertaining that it *might,* that it probably *would,* turn out to be the very same Captain Wentworth whom they recollected meeting, once or twice, after their coming back from Clifton: — a very fine young man: but they could not say whether it was seven or eight years ago, — was a new sort of trial to Anne's nerves. She found, however, that it was one to which she must enure herself.

Probably I'm fooling myself, but I was quite amazed at the result of this tiny test.

Pride and Prejudice is a brilliant comedy of youthful passions, while *Persuasion* is a quiet story about a misunderstanding that ruins a life and is set right only when it's almost too late. One book is April, you might say, and the other November.

Well, the four sentences from *Pride and Prejudice,* separated rather dramatically by a period and a dash in each case, with a colon breaking the longest one in two, are all quite short, with a highly varied, rising rhythm, a kind of dancing gait, like a well-bred young horse longing to break out into a gallop. All are entirely from young Elizabeth's point of view, in her own mental voice, which on this evidence is lively, ironical, and naive.

Though the paragraph from *Persuasion* is longer, it is in only two sentences; the long first one is full of hesitations and repetitions, marked by eight commas, two colons, and two dashes. Its abstract subject ("to hear them") is separated from its verb ("was") by several lines, all having to do with other people's thoughts and notions. The protagonist of the sentence, Anne, is mentioned only in the next-to-last word. The sentence that follows, wholly in her own mental voice, has a brief, strong, quiet cadence.

I do not offer this little analysis and comparison as proof that any paragraph from *Pride and Prejudice* would have a different rhythm from any sentence in *Persuasion;* but as I said, it surprised me—the rhythms were in fact so different, and each was so very characteristic of the mood of the book and the nature of the central character.

But of course I am already persuaded that Woolf was right, that every novel has its characteristic rhythm. And that if the writer hasn't listened for that rhythm and followed it, the sentences will be lame, the characters will be puppets, the story will be false. And that if the writer can hold to that rhythm, the book will have some beauty.

What the writer has to do is listen for that beat, hear it, keep to it, not let anything interfere with it. Then the reader will hear it too, and be carried by it.

༆

A note on rhythms that I was aware of in writing two of my books:

Writing the fantasy novel *Tehanu,* I thought of the work as riding the dragon. In the first place, the story demanded that I be outdoors while writing it—which was lovely in Oregon in July, but inconvenient in November. Cold knees, wet notebook. And the story came not steadily, but in flights—durations of intense perception, sometimes tranquil and lyrical, sometimes frightening—which most often occurred while I was waking, early in the morning. There I would lie and ride the dragon. Then I had to get up, and go sit outdoors, and try to catch that flight in words. If I could hold to the rhythm of the dragon's flight, the very large, long wingbeat, then the story told itself, and the people breathed. When I lost the beat, I fell off, and had to wait around on the ground until the dragon picked me up again.

Waiting, of course, is a very large part of writing.

Writing "Hernes," a novella about ordinary people on the Oregon coast, involved a lot of waiting. Weeks, months. I was listening for voices, the voices of four different women, whose lives overlapped throughout most of the twentieth century. Some of them spoke from a long time ago, before I was born, and I was determined not to patronise the past, not to take the voices of the dead from them by making them generalised, glib, quaint. Each woman had to speak straight from her center, truthfully, even if neither she nor I knew the truth. And each voice must speak in the cadence characteristic of that person, her own voice, and also in a rhythm that included the rhythms of the other voices, since they must relate to one another and form some kind of whole, some true shape, a story.

I had no dragon to carry me. I felt diffident and often foolish, listening, as I walked on the beach or sat in a silent house, for these soft imagined voices, trying to hear them, to catch the beat, the rhythm, that makes the story true and the words beautiful.

I do think novels are beautiful. To me a novel can be as beautiful as any symphony, as beautiful as the sea. As complete, true, real, large, complicated, confusing, deep, troubling, soul enlarging as the sea with its waves that break and tumble, its tides that rise and ebb.

*An unpublished piece in which I return to and go on from some of the
themes and speculations of the essay "Text, Silence, Performance" in
my previous nonfiction collection* Dancing at the Edge of the World.

MODELS OF COMMUNICATION

In this Age of Information and Age of Electronics, our ruling concept
of communication is a mechanical model, which goes like this:

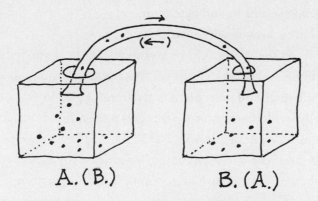

A. (B.)   B. (A.)

Fig. 1.

Box A and box B are connected by a tube. Box A contains a unit
of information. Box A is the transmitter, the sender. The tube is how
the information is transmitted—it is the medium. And box B is the

receiver. They can alternate roles. The sender, box A, codes the information in a way appropriate to the medium, in binary bits, or pixels, or words, or whatever, and transmits it via the medium to the receiver, box B, which receives and decodes it.

A and B can be thought of as machines, such as computers. They can also be thought of as minds. Or one can be a machine and the other a mind.

If A is a mind and B a computer, A may send B information, a message, via the medium of its program language: let's say A sends the information that B is to shut down; B receives the information and shuts down. Or let's say I send my computer a request for the date Easter falls on this year: this request requires the computer to respond, to take the role of box A, which sends that information, via its code and the medium of the monitor, to me, who now take the role of box B, the receiver. And so I go buy eggs, or don't buy eggs, depending on the information I received.

This is supposed to be the way language works. A has a unit of information, codes it in words, and transmits to B, who receives it, decodes it, understands it, and acts on it.

Yes? This is how language works?

As you can see, this model of communication as applied to actual people talking and listening, or even to language written and read, is at best inadequate and most often inaccurate. We don't work that way.

We only work that way when our communication is reduced to the most rudimentary information. "STOP THAT!" in a shout from A is likely to be received and acted on by B—at least for a moment.

If A shouts, "The British are coming!" the information may serve as information—a clear message with certain clear consequences concerning what to do next.

But what if the communication from A is, "I thought that dinner last night was pretty awful."

Or, "Call me Ishmael."

Or, "Coyote was going there."

Are those statements information? The medium is the speaking voice, or the written word, but what is the code? What is A *saying?*

B may or may not be able to decode, or "read," those messages in a literal sense. But the meanings and implications and connotations they contain are so enormously complex and so utterly contingent that there is no one right way for B to decode or to understand them. Their meaning depends almost entirely on who A is, who B is, what their relationship is, what society they live in, their level of education, their relative status, and so on. They are full of meaning and of meanings, but they are not information.

In such cases, in most cases of people actually talking to one another, human communication cannot be reduced to information. The message not only involves, it *is,* a *relationship* between speaker and hearer. The medium in which the message is embedded is immensely complex, infinitely more than a code: it is a language, a function of a society, a culture, in which the language, the speaker, and the hearer are all embedded.

"Coyote was going there." Is the information being transmitted by this sentence—does it "say"—that an actual coyote actually went somewhere? Actually, no. The speaker is not talking about a coyote. The hearer knows that.

What would be the primary information obtained by a hearer who heard those words spoken, in their original language and in the context where they might have been spoken? Probably something like: Ah, Grandfather is going to tell us a story about Coyote. Because "Coyote was going there" is a cultural signal, like "Once upon a time": a ritual formula, the implications of which include the fact that a story's about to be told, right here, right now; that it won't be a factual story but will be myth, or true story; in this case a true story about Coyote. Not a coyote but Coyote. And Grandfather knows that we understand the signal, we understand what he's saying when he says, "Coyote was going there," because if he didn't expect us to at least partly understand it, he wouldn't or couldn't say it.

In human conversation, in live, actual communication between or among human beings, everything "transmitted"—everything said—is shaped as it is spoken by actual or anticipated response.

Live, face-to-face human communication is intersubjective. Intersubjectivity involves a great deal more than the machine-mediated type of stimulus-response currently called "interactive." It is not stimulus-response at all, not a mechanical alternation of precoded sending and receiving. Intersubjectivity is mutual. It is a *continuous interchange* between two consciousnesses. Instead of an alternation of roles between box A and box B, between active subject and passive object, it is a *continuous intersubjectivity that goes both ways all the time.*

"There is no adequate model in the physical universe for this operation of consciousness, which is distinctively human and which signals the capacity of human beings to form true communities." So says Walter Ong, in *Orality and Literacy.*

My private model for intersubjectivity, or communication by speech, or conversation, is amoebas having sex. As you know, amoebas usually reproduce by just quietly going off in a corner and budding, dividing themselves into two amoebas; but sometimes conditions indicate that a little genetic swapping might improve the local crowd, and two of them get together, literally, and reach out to each other and meld their pseudopodia into a little tube or channel connecting them. Thus:

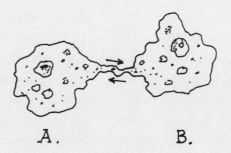

A.   B.

Fig. 2.

Then amoeba A and amoeba B exchange genetic "information," that is, they literally give each other inner bits of their bodies, via a channel or bridge which is made out of outer bits of their bodies. They hang out for quite a while sending bits of themselves back and forth, mutually responding each to the other.

This is very similar to how people unite themselves and give each other parts of themselves—inner parts, mental not bodily parts—when they talk and listen. (You can see why I use amoeba sex not human sex as my analogy: in human hetero sex, the bits only go one way. Human hetero sex is more like a lecture than a conversation. Amoeba sex is truly mutual because amoebas have no gender and no hierarchy. I have no opinion on whether amoeba sex or human sex is more fun. We might have the edge, because we have nerve endings, but who knows?)

Two amoebas having sex, or two people talking, form a community of two. People are also able to form communities of many, through sending and receiving bits of ourselves and others back and forth continually—through, in other words, talking and listening. Talking and listening are ultimately the same thing.

It is literacy that confuses this whole issue of communication by language. I don't want to get into what literacy does to the human mind, though I highly recommend Walter Ong's books on the subject. All I want to emphasise at this point is that literacy is very recent, and still not at all universal. Most people during most of the history of mankind have been, and still are, oral/aural people: people who speak and listen. Most people, most of the time, do not put words in writing, do not read, are not read to. They speak and they listen to speech.

Long, long after we learned how to talk to each other, millennia or hundreds of millennia later, we learned to write down our words. That was only about thirty-five hundred years ago, in certain restricted parts of the world.

Writing existed for three millennia, important to powerful people, seemingly unimportant to most people. Its use and uses spread. Then came printing.

With printing, literacy quite soon developed from a special craft, useful to privileged men to increase their knowledge and power, into a basic tool, a necessity for ordinary existence for ordinary people, particularly if they were seeking not to be poor and powerless.

And so effective is printed writing as a tool that those of us who use it have tended to privilege it as the most valid form of human communication. Writing has changed us, the way all our tools change us, till we have come to take it for granted that speech doesn't matter; words don't count till they're written down. "I give you my word" doesn't count for much until I've signed the contract. And we judge an oral culture, a culture that does not use writing, as essentially inferior, calling it "primitive."

Belief in the absolute superiority of literacy to orality is ingrained in us literates—not without cause. Illiterates in a literate culture are terribly disadvantaged. We have arranged our North American society over the last couple of centuries so that literacy is a basic requirement for full membership.

If we compare literate and nonliterate societies, it appears that literate societies are *powerful* in ways nonliterate societies aren't. Literate culture is *durable* in ways nonliterate culture is not. And literate people may have more *breadth* and *variety* of knowledge that nonliterate people. They are better informed. They are not necessarily wiser. Literacy does not make people good, intelligent, or wise. Literate societies are superior in some ways to nonliterate societies, but literate people are not superior to oral people.

What do anthropologists, who ought to know better, mean when they speak of "the primitive mind," or *La Pensée Sauvage* (how should Lévi-Strauss's title be translated—"How Savages Think"?)—What is a "savage," what does "primitive" mean? Almost inevitably it means "preliterate." "Primitives" are people who haven't learned to write— yet. They can only talk. They are therefore inferior to anthropologists and others who can read and can write.

And indeed literacy confers such power on its owners that they can dominate illiterates, as the literate priestly and noble castes dominated illiterate medieval Europe; as literate men dominated women as long as women were kept illiterate; as literate businessmen dominate illiterate inner-city people; as English-literate corporations dominate illiterate or non-English-literate workers. If might makes right, orality is wrong.

⌇

These days, not only do we have literacy to confuse this whole issue of human communication by language, we also have what Ong calls "secondary orality."

Primary orality refers to people who talk but don't write—all the people we refer to as primitive, illiterate, preliterate, and so on. Secondary orality comes long after literacy, and derives from it. It is less than a hundred years old. Secondary orality is radio, TV, recordings, and such: in general, what we call "the media."

A good deal of media presentation has a script and is therefore primarily written and secondarily oral; but these days, its most meaningful distinction from primary orality is that the speaker has *no present audience*.

If instead of writing this, I were giving a speech, your being in the same room listening to me would be a necessary condition of my talking. That's primary orality: a *relationship* of speaker and listeners.

President Lincoln stands up and begins, "Fourscore and seven years ago," to a crowd of more or less interested people at Gettysburg. His voice (said to have been rather thin and soft) makes a relationship between him and them, establishing community. Primary orality.

Grandfather tells a Coyote tale to a circle of grown-ups and kids on a winter evening. The story affirms and explains their community as a people and among other living beings. Primary orality.

The anchorman on the six o'clock news stares out of the box, not at us, because he can't see us, because we aren't where he is, or even when he is; he is in Washington, D.C., two hours ago, reading what he says off a running tape. He can't see us or hear us, nor can we see or hear him. We see and hear an image, a simulacrum of him. There is no relationship between us and him. There is no interchange, no mutuality, between us and him. There is no intersubjectivity. His communication goes one way and stops there. We receive it, if we choose to. Our behavior, even our presence or absence, makes absolutely no difference to what he says or how he says it. If nobody was listening he would not know it and would go right on talking exactly the same way (until his sponsors found out, eventually, from the Nielsen ratings, and fired him). Secondary orality.

I read this speech into a recorder and it is taped; you buy it and listen to it. You hear the sound of my voice, but we have no actual relationship, any more than we would if you were reading the piece in print. Secondary orality.

⸒

Like the telephone, private writing, the personal letter, the private e-mail, is direct communication—conversation—mediated by technology. Amoeba A extends a pseudopodium and sends little bits of itself out to a distant amoeba B, who incorporates the material sent out and may respond to it. The telephone made immediate conversation at a distance possible; in written letters, there is an interval between messages; e-mail allows both interval and immediate exchange.

My model of printed public writing and of secondary orality is a box A shooting information out into a putative spacetime that may or may not contain many box Bs to receive it—maybe nobody—possibly an Audience of Millions (see figure 3).

Conversation is a mutual exchange or interchange of acts. Transmission via print and the media is one-way; its mutuality is merely virtual or hopeful.

Yet local, immediate community can be built upon both literacy and secondary orality. Schools and colleges are centers of the printed word, whether on paper or electronic, and are genuine if limited communities. Bible-study groups, reading clubs, fan clubs, are small

A.

Fig. 3.

printed-word-centered subcommunities, where, as in colleges, people talk about what they read. Newspapers and magazines create and foster opinion groups and facilitate communities based on information, such as sports fans comparing scores.

As for the audience of secondary orality—aside from that factitious entity the "studio audience," which is actually part of the performance—many people watch certain TV programs not because they particularly like them but because they can talk about them with other people at work next day: they use these programs as social bonding material. But the media audience is for the most part a tenuous, widely

scattered semicommunity or pseudocommunity, which can be esti-
mated and gauged only by market research and opinion polls, and becomes actual only in political situations such as a polling place on
election day, or in the response to a terrible event.

The community created by printing and by secondary orality is not
immediate; it is virtual. It can be enormous—the size of America. Indeed it may be literacy more than any other factor that has enabled or
coerced us to live in huge nation-states instead of tribes and city-states.
Possibly the Internet will allow us to outgrow the nation-state. Although the Global Village McLuhan dreamed of is at present a City of
Night, a monstrous force for cultural reductionism and internationally
institutionalised greed, who knows? Perhaps we shall soar electronically to some arrangement that works better than capitalism.

But so vast a community must remain more concept than tangible
fact. Written word, printed word, reproduced speech, filmed speech,
the telephone, e-mail: each medium links people, but it does not link
them physically, and whatever community it creates is essentially a
mental one.

Let me not to the marriage of true minds admit impediment. It is
marvelous that we can talk to living people ten thousand miles away
and hear them speak. It is marvelous that by reading their words, or
seeing a film of them, we may feel communion even with the dead.
It is a marvelous thought that all knowledge might be accessible to
all minds.

But marriage is not of minds only; and the living human community that language creates involves living human bodies. We need to
talk *together,* speaker and hearer here, now. We know that. We feel it.
We feel the absence of it.

⸮

Speech connects us so immediately and vitally because it is a physical,
bodily process, to begin with. Not a mental or spiritual one, wherever
it may end.

If you mount two clock pendulums side by side on the wall, they will gradually begin to swing together. They synchronise each other by picking up tiny vibrations they each transmit through the wall.

Any two things that oscillate at about the same interval, if they're physically near each other, will gradually tend to lock in and pulse at exactly the same interval. Things are lazy. It takes less energy to pulse cooperatively than to pulse in opposition. Physicists call this beautiful, economical laziness mutual phase locking, or entrainment.

All living beings are oscillators. We vibrate. Amoeba or human, we pulse, move rhythmically, change rhythmically; we keep time. You can see it in the amoeba under the microscope, vibrating in frequencies on the atomic, the molecular, the subcellular, and the cellular levels. That constant, delicate, complex throbbing is the process of life itself made visible.

We huge many-celled creatures have to coordinate millions of different oscillation frequencies, and interactions among frequencies, in our bodies and our environment. Most of the coordination is effected by synchronising the pulses, by getting the beats into a master rhythm, by entrainment.

Internally, a sterling example is the muscle cells of the heart, every single one of them going *lub-dub, lub-dub,* together with all the others, for a lifetime.

Then there are the longer body rhythms, circadian cycles, that take a day to happen: hunger, eating, digesting, excreting; sleeping and waking. Such rhythms entrain all the organs and functions of body and mind.

And the really long bodily rhythms, which we may not even recognise, are connected with our environment, length of daylight, season, the moon.

Being in sync—internally and with your environment—makes life easy. Getting out of sync is always uncomfortable or disastrous.

Then there are the rhythms of other human beings. Like the two pendulums, though through more complex processes, two people together can mutually phase-lock. Successful human relationship involves entrainment—getting in sync. If it doesn't, the relationship is either uncomfortable or disastrous.

Consider deliberately sychronised actions like singing, chanting, rowing, marching, dancing, playing music; consider sexual rhythms (courtship and foreplay are devices for getting into sync). Consider how the infant and the mother are linked: the milk comes before the baby cries. Consider the fact that women who live together tend to get onto the same menstrual cycle. We entrain one another all the time.

How does entrainment function in speech? William Condon did some lovely experiments which show, on film, that when we talk our whole body is involved in many tiny movements, establishing a master rhythm that coordinates our body movements with the speech rhythms. Without this beat, the speech becomes incomprehensible. "Rhythm," he says, is "a fundamental aspect of the organisation of behavior." To act, we have to have the beat.

Condon went on to photograph people listening to a speaker. His films show listeners making almost the same micromovements of lips and face as the speaker is making, almost simultaneously—a fiftieth of a second behind. They are locked into the same beat. "Communication," he says, "is like a dance, with everyone engaged in intricate, shared movements across many subtle dimensions."

Listening is not a reaction, it is a connection. Listening to a conversation or a story, we don't so much respond as join in—become part of the action.

We can entrain without seeing the speaker; we entrain with each other when talking on the telephone. Most people feel that telephoning is less satisfactory than being with one another, that communication through hearing alone is less fully mutual, but we do it quite well; teenagers, and people with cell phones in BMWs in heavy traffic, can keep it up indefinitely.

Researchers believe that some autism may be connected with difficulty in entraining—a delayed response, a failure to catch the rhythm.

We listen to ourselves as we speak, of course, and it's very hard to speak if we can't find the beat: this might help explain autistic silence. We can't understand other people if we can't get in sync with the rhythm of their speaking: this might explain autistic rage and loneliness.

Rhythm differences between dialects lead to failures in understanding. You need practice, you need training to entrain with a way of speech you aren't familiar with.

But when you can and do entrain, you are synchronising with the people you're talking with, physically getting in time and tune with them. No wonder speech is so strong a bond, so powerful in forming community.

I do not know to what extent people watching movies and TV entrain with speakers; since no mutual response is possible, it seems likely that the intense involvement characteristic of conversation would be much weakened.

ORAL SPACE AND ORAL TIME

Seeing is analytical, not integrative. The eye wants to distinguish objects. The eye selects. Seeing is active, outgoing. We look *at*. We focus *on*. We make distinctions easily so long as the field is clear. The visual ideal is clarity. That's why glasses are so satisfactory. Seeing is yang.

Hearing is integrative; it unifies. Being on opposite sides of the head, ears are pretty good at telling where a sound comes from, but though the mind, the attention, can focus hearing, can listen *to,* the ear essentially hears *from:* it can't focus narrowly and can select only with effort. The ear can't stop hearing; we have no earlids; only sleep can shut off our reception. While we are awake our ears accept what comes. As this is likely to be noise, the auditory ideal is harmony. That's why hearing aids, which increase noise, are so often unsatisfactory. Hearing is yin.

Light may come from vast distances, but sound, which is only vibrations in air, doesn't travel far. Starlight carries a thousand light-years; a human voice can carry a mile or so at most. What we hear is almost always quite local, quite nearby. Hearing is an immediate, intimate sense, not quite as close as touch, smell, taste, proprioception, but much more intimate than sight.

Sound signifies event. A noise means something is happening. Let's say there's a mountain out your window. You see the mountain. Your eyes report changes, snowy in winter, brown in summer, but mainly just report that it's there. It's scenery. But if you *hear* that mountain, then you know it's doing something. I see Mount St. Helens out my study window, about eighty miles north. I did not hear it explode in 1980: the sound wave was so huge that it skipped Portland entirely and touched down in Eugene, a hundred miles to the south. Those who did hear that noise knew that something had happened. That was a word worth hearing. Sound is event.

Speech, the most specifically *human* sound, and the most significant *kind* of sound, is never just scenery, it's always event.

Walter Ong says, "Sound exists only when it is going out of existence." This is a very complicated simple statement. You could say it also about life. Life exists only as it is going out of existence.

Consider the word *existence,* printed on a page of a book. There it sits, all of it at once, nine letters, black on white, maybe for years, for centuries, maybe in thousands of copies all over the world.

Now consider the word as you speak it: "existence." As soon as you say "tence," "exis" is already gone, and now the whole thing's gone. You can say it again, but that is a new event.

When you speak a word to a listener, the speaking is an act. And it is a mutual act: the listener's listening enables the speaker's speaking. It is a shared event, intersubjective: the listener and speaker entrain with each other. Both the amoebas are equally responsible, equally physically, immediately involved in sharing bits of themselves. The act of speaking happens NOW. And then is irrevocably, unrepeatably OVER.

Because speaking is an auditory event, not a visual one, it uses space and time differently from anything visual, including words read on paper or on a monitor.

"Auditory space has no point of favored focus. It is a sphere without fixed boundaries, space made by the thing itself, not space containing the thing." (Ong)

Sound, speech, creates its own, immediate, instantaneous space. If we shut our eyes and listen, we are contained within that sphere.

We read printed on a page, "She shouted." The page is durable, visible space containing the words. It is a thing not an act. But an actor shouts, and the shout is an act. It makes its own, local, momentary space.

The voice creates a sphere around it, which includes all its hearers: an intimate sphere or area, limited in both space and time.

Creation is an act. Action takes energy.

Sound is dynamic. Speech is dynamic—it is action.

To act is to take power, to have power, to be powerful.

Mutual communication between speakers and listeners is a powerful act. The power of each speaker is amplified, augmented, by the entrainment of the listeners. The strength of a community is amplified, augmented by its mutual entrainment in speech.

This is why utterance is magic. Words do have power. Names have power. Words are events, they do things, change things. They transform both speaker and hearer; they feed energy back and forth and amplify it. They feed understanding or emotion back and forth and amplify it.

ORAL PERFORMANCE

Oral performance is a particular kind of human speech. It is to an oral culture what reading is to a literate culture.

Reading is not superior to orality, and orality is not superior to reading. The two behaviors are different and have extremely different social effects. Silent reading is an implacably private activity, which while it is occurring separates the reader bodily and psychically from the people nearby. Oral performance is a powerful bonding force, which while it is occurring bonds people physically and psychically.

In our literate culture oral performance is seen as secondary, marginal. Only readings by poets of their own works and theatrical performance by actors may be perceived as having literary power comparable to written work read in silence. But oral performance in an oral culture is recognised as a powerful act, and for that reason it is always formal.

The formality is on both sides. The orator or storyteller tries to meet and fulfill certain definite expectations in the audience, gives formal cues to the audience, and may respond to formal cues from the audience. The audience will show attentiveness by certain expected behaviors: by keeping a posture of attention; in some cases, by total silence; more often, by formulaic responses—Yes, Lord! Hallelujah!—or formulaic words or affirmations: ah—hai—hah—enh. . . . In poetry readings, little quiet gasps. In comic performances, laughter.

Oral performance uses time and space in a particular way of its own. It creates its own, temporary, physical, actual spacetime, a sphere containing a speaking voice and listening ears, a sphere of entrained vibration, a community of body and mind.

This might be the sphere that holds a woman telling her children the tale of the Three Bears—a small, quiet, deeply intimate event.

It might be the smoky sphere that holds a stand-up comedian extemporising to an audience in a bar—a seemingly informal but, if successful, intensely and genuinely interactive event.

It could be the sphere holding a revivalist preacher speaking his hellfire sermon to a tent revival—a big, noisy, yet highly formalised, powerfully rhythmic event.

It could be the sphere that held Martin Luther King Jr. and the people who heard him say "I have a dream."

That formal oratorical event can be echoed, can be shadowed, can be recollected, by films and recordings. Images of it can be reproduced. But it cannot. An event does not happen twice. We do not step twice into the same river.

Oral performance is irreproducible.

It takes place in a time and place set apart: cyclic time, ritual time, or sacred time. Cyclical time is heartbeat, body-cycle time; lunar, seasonal, annual time: recurrent time, musical time, dancing time, rhythmic time. An event does not happen twice, yet regular recurrence is the essence of cyclic time. This year's spring is not last year's spring, yet spring returns always the same. A rite is performed anew, every year, at the same time, in the same way. A story is told again and again, and yet each new telling is a new event.

ᔐ

Each oral performance is as unique as a snowflake, but, like a snowflake, it will very likely be repeated; and its principle internal organisational device is repetition. Rhythm is basic to oral performance, and it is chiefly obtained by recurrence, by repetition.

From now on I am going to be repeating myself about repetition. One reason there is a lot of repetition in oral performance, as in ordinary speech, is the need for redundancy. The reading eye can turn back and reread and make certain; therefore, in writing you need only say a thing once, if you say it well. So we writers are taught to be afraid of repeating ourselves, to shun even the appearance of repetition. But in speaking, words go by very quickly and are gone; they fly away, they are wingéd words. Speakers know that they may need to bring the whole flock back round again more than once. Orators, reciters, storytellers shamelessly say the same thing several times, maybe varying the words maybe not. Redundancy is not a sin in oral performance, as it has become in writing, but a virtue.

Speakers also use repetition because it is the best device they have to organise, to shape and structure, what they are saying. Experienced listeners in an oral culture—such as a three-year-old who gets read to or told stories a lot—expect repetition. They wait for it. Repetition both raises expectations and fulfills them. Minor variation is expected, but extreme variation, though it adds surprise, which may be welcomed, more likely will be rejected as frivolous or corrupt. Tell it the *right* way, Mama!

Repetition may be of a single word; of a phrase or sentence; of an image; of an event or action in the story; of a character's behavior; of a structural element of the piece.

Words and phrases are the most likely to be repeated verbatim. The simplest example of this is starter words, words used to begin a sentence. In the King James Bible, it's And. And the Lord smote the idolaters. And the idols were destroyed. And the people lamented in the streets. —In a Paiute story, a lot of sentences begin with Then—*yaisi* in Paiute. Then Coyote did this. Then Grey Wolf said this. Then they went in. —*And* and *Yaisi* are key sounds, cues to the listener that a new sentence, a new event, is under way; also they may provide a tiny mental resting place for the teller or reader of the story. These repeated starter words provide a beat, not a regular, metric beat, because this isn't poetry, it's narrative prose, but just the same a beat at intervals: a pulse that follows a pause, a sound that follows a silence.

In spoken narrative, silence plays a huge active part. Without silence, pauses, rests, there is no rhythm. Only noise. Noise is by definition meaningless, sound without significance. Significance is born of the rhythmic alternation of void and event—pause and act—silence and word. Repeated words are markers of this rhythm, drumbeats to which the story dances.

For centuries, those huge poems the *Iliad* and the *Odyssey* did not exist in writing but only in oral performance. The version we have is the one that happened to get written down. We know now that a tremendous proportion of the language of the epics consists of stock phrases, repeatable terms, used where they were needed to fill out the meter or to take up slack while the performer thought of what Achilles or Odysseus did next. No performer could possibly remember the whole thing verbatim. Every performance was half recital and half improvisation, using that vast stock of ready-made phrases. So the wine-dark sea and rosy-fingered dawn are little metrical bricks, fitted in wherever the hexameter fell short. They are also, of course, beautiful images. Does it lessen them that they are repeated where the meter needs them? Do we not in fact greet their repetition with pleasure, as we do the repetition of a musical phrase or motif in a sonata or symphony?

Repeated actions in oral narrative are essential structural elements. They are usually varied, partial repetitions, building up expectation towards fulfillment. The first son of the king goes out and behaves badly to a wolf and the dragon eats him. The second son of the king goes out and behaves badly to a deer and the dragon eats him. The third son of the king goes out and rescues the wolf from a trap, frees the deer from a snare, and the wolf and the deer tell him how to kill the dragon and find the princess, and he does, and they get married and live happily ever after.

As for repeated behavior of characters, contemporary novelists are likely to consider predictability to be a fault, a flaw, in their invention. Repeated or predictable behavior, however, is what constitutes a character—in life or novels. If it's highly, obviously predictable, the character is a stereotype or caricature; but the gradations are endless. Some people find all Dickens's characters mere stereotypes. I don't. When Mr. Micawber says "Something is certain to turn up," the first time, it's insignificant; the second time, it's revealing; by the third or fourth time he's said it in the teeth of total financial disaster, it's significant and funny; and by the end of the book, when all his hopes have been savagely defeated, "Something is certain to turn up" is both funny and profoundly sad.

I use an example from literature, not from oral texts, because Dickens's relationship to orality and oral performance is very close, maybe closer than any other novelist since 1800 except, possibly, Tolkien. The repetitive behavior of Dickens's characters is more characteristic of oral narrative than of the novel in general. Delicate probings into the convolutions of the private psyche in a unique situation aren't well suited to tales told aloud. Characters of oral narratives may be vivid, powerful, worthy of a great deal of thinking about: Achilles, Hector, Odysseus, Roland and Oliver, Cinderella, the Queen and Snow White, Raven, Br'er Rabbit, Coyote. They are not one-dimensional; their motivations may be profoundly complex; the moral situations they are in are of wide and deep human relevance. But as a rule, they can be summed up in a few words, as characters in novels cannot. Their name may even be exemplary of a certain kind of behavior. And they can be summoned into the hearer's imagination by the mere mention of characteristic behavior: Then said wily Odysseus, thinking how to save himself . . . Coyote was going along and he saw some girls by the river. . . . We've heard about Odysseus being wily. We've heard about Coyote seeing some girls. We know, in general, what to expect. Odysseus will get away with it, but at a cost; he will be damaged. Coyote won't get away with it, will be made a complete fool of, and will trot away perfectly unashamed. The storyteller says the name Odysseus, or the name Coyote, and we the listeners await the fulfillment of our expectations, and that waiting is one of the great pleasures life offers us.

Genre literature offers us that pleasure. That is perhaps the central reason for the obstinate popularity of the romance, the mystery, science fiction, and the western, despite decades of critical and academic ignorance and contempt. A genre novel fulfills certain generic obligations. A mystery provides some kind of puzzle and its resolution; a fantasy breaks the rules of reality in a significant way; a romance offers the frustration and fulfillment of a love story. On the lowest plane, genre offers the kind of reliability hamburger chains offer: If you pick up a Louis L'Amour western or the eighteenth mystery in a series, you know what you're going to get. But if you pick up Molly Gloss's *The Jump-Off Creek,* a western, or Tolkien's *The Lord of the Rings,* a fantasy, or Philip K. Dick's *The Man in the High Castle,* a science fiction novel, although each reliably fulfills the obligations of its genre, it is also utterly unpredictable, a novel, a work of art.

Above the level of the merely commercial, in the realm of art, whether it's called mainstream or genre fiction, we can fulfill our expectations only by learning which authors disappoint and which authors offer the true nourishment for the soul. We find out who the good writers are, and then we look or wait for their next book. Such writers—living or dead, whatever genre they write in, critically fashionable or not, academically approved or not—are those who not only meet our expectations but surpass them. That is the gift the great storytellers have. They tell the same stories over and over (how many stories are there?), but when they tell them they are new, they are news, they renew us, they show us the world made new.

It does not matter, on this level, whether the story is told and heard, or written and read.

But if it is written and read in silence by the reader, there is some awareness in many of us that a dimension of the experience of story has been lost: the aural dimension, the whole aspect of the *telling* of the story and the *hearing* of it in a certain time and space, by a certain person, now—and maybe over again in times to come. Sound recordings, popular as they have become, supply the sound of the words and sentences, the telling voice, but it is not a living voice, it is a reproduction—a photograph not a living body. So people seek the irreproducible moment, the brief, fragile community of story told among people gathered together in one place. So children gather at the library to be read to: look at the little circle of faces, blazing with intensity. So the writer on a book tour, reading in the bookstore, and her group of listeners reenact the ancient ritual of the teller at the center of the circle. The living response has enabled that voice to speak. Teller and listener, each fulfills the other's expectations. The living tongue that tells the word, the living ear that hears it, bind and bond us in the communion we long for in the silence of our inner solitude.

THE OPERATING INSTRUCTIONS

I wrote this piece in 2000 as a talk to a group of people interested in local literacy and literature.

A poet has been appointed ambassador. A playwright is elected president. Construction workers stand in line with officer managers to buy a new novel. Adults seek moral guidance and intellectual challenge in stories about warrior monkeys, one-eyed giants, and crazy knights who fight windmills. Literacy is considered a beginning, not an end.

. . . Well, maybe in some other country, but not this one. In America the imagination is generally looked on as something that might be useful when the TV is out of order. Poetry and plays have no relation to practical politics. Novels are for students, housewives, and other people who don't work. Fantasy is for children and primitive peoples. Literacy is so you can read the operating instructions.

⸼

I think the imagination is the single most useful tool humankind possesses. It beats the opposable thumb. I can imagine living without my thumbs, but not without my imagination.

I hear voices agreeing with me. "Yes, yes!" they cry—"the creative imagination is a tremendous plus in business! We value creativity, we *reward* it!" In the marketplace, the word *creativity* has come to mean the

generation of ideas applicable to practical strategies to make larger prof-
its. This reduction has gone on so long that the word *creative* can hardly
be degraded further. I don't use it any more, yielding it to capitalists and
academics to abuse as they like. But they can't have *imagination*.

Imagination is not a means of making money. It has no place in the
vocabulary of profit making It is not a weapon, though all weapons
originate from it, and the use, or nonuse, of all weapons depends on it:
as do all tools and their uses. The imagination is a fundamental way of
thinking, an essential means of becoming and remaining human. It is
a tool of the mind.

Therefore we have to learn to use it. Children have imagination to
start with, as they have body, intellect, the capacity for language: all
things essential to their humanity, things they need to learn how to use,
how to use well. Such teaching, training, and practice should begin in
infancy and go on throughout life. Young human beings need exercises
in imagination as they need exercise in all the basic skills of life, bodily and mental: for growth, for health, for competence, for joy. This
need continues as long as the mind is alive.

When children are taught to hear and learn the central literature of
their people, or, in literate cultures, to read and understand it, their
imagination is getting a very large part of the exercise it needs.

Nothing else does as well, not even the other arts. We are a wordy
species. Words are the wings both intellect and imagination fly on.
Music, dance, visual arts, crafts of all kinds, all are central to human
development and well-being, and no art or skill is ever useless learning; but to train the mind to take off from immediate reality and return
to it with new understanding and new strength, there is nothing like
poem and story.

Through story, every culture defines itself and teaches its children
how to be people and members of their people—Hmong, !Kung, Hopi,
Quechua, French, Californian. . . . We are those who arrived at the
Fourth World. . . . We are Joan's nation. . . . We are the sons of the Sun.

. . . We came from the sea. . . . We are the people who live at the center of the world.

A people that doesn't live at the center of the world, as defined and described by its poets and storytellers, is in a bad way. The center of the world is where you live. You can breathe the air there. You know how things are done there, how things are done rightly, done well.

A child who doesn't know where the center is—where home is, *what* home is—that child is in a very bad way.

Home isn't Mom and Dad and Sis and Bud. Home isn't where they have to let you in. It's not a place at all. Home is imaginary.

Home, imagined, comes to be. It is real, realer than any other place, but you can't get to it unless your people show you how to imagine it—whoever your people are. They may not be your relatives. They may never have spoken your language. They may have been dead for a thousand years. They may be nothing but words printed on paper, ghosts of voices, shadows of minds. But they can guide you home. They are your human community.

All of us have to learn how to invent our lives, make them up, imagine them. We need to be taught these skills; we need guides to show us how. If we don't, our lives get made up for us by other people.

Human beings have always joined in groups to imagine how best to live and help one another carry out the plan. The essential function of human community is to arrive at some agreement on what we need, what life ought to be, what we want our children to learn, and then collaborate in learning and teaching so that we and they can go on the way we think is the right way.

Small communities with strong traditions are usually clear about the way they want to go, and good at teaching it. But tradition may crystallise imagination to the point of fossilizing it as dogma and forbidding new ideas. Larger communities, such as cities, open up room for people to imagine alternatives, learn from people of different traditions, and invent their own ways to live.

As alternatives proliferate, however, those who take the responsibility of teaching find little social and moral consensus on what they should be teaching—what we need, what life ought to be. In our time of huge populations exposed continuously to reproduced voices, images, and words used for commercial and political profit, there are too many people who want to and can invent us, own us, shape and control us through seductive and powerful media. It's a lot to ask of a child to find a way through all that, alone.

Nobody can do anything very much, really, alone.

What a child needs, what we all need, is to find some other people who have imagined life along lines that make sense and allow some freedom, and listen to them. Not hear passively, but listen.

Listening is an act of community, which takes space, time, and silence.

Reading is a means of listening.

Reading is not as passive as hearing or viewing. It's an act: you do it. You read at your pace, your own speed, not the ceaseless, incoherent, gabbling, shouting rush of the media. You take in what you can and want to take in, not what they shove at you so fast and hard and loud that you're overwhelmed. Reading a story, you may be told something, but you're not being sold anything. And though you're usually alone when you read, you are in communion with another mind. You aren't being brainwashed or co-opted or used; you've joined in an act of the imagination.

I know no reason why the media could not create a similar community of the imagination, as theater has often done in societies of the past, but they're not doing it. They are so controlled by advertising and profiteering that the best people who work in them, the real artists, if they resist the pressure to sell out, get drowned out by the endless rush for novelty, by the greed of the entrepreneurs.

Much of literature remains free of such co-optation simply because a lot of books were written by dead people, who by definition are not greedy.

And many living poets and novelists, though their publishers may be crawling abjectly after bestsellers, continue to be motivated less by the desire for gain than by the wish to do what they'd probably do for nothing if they could afford it, that is, practice their art—make something well, get something right. Books remain comparatively, and amazingly, honest and reliable.

They may not be "books," of course, they may not be ink on wood pulp but a flicker of electronics in the palm of a hand. Incoherent and commercialised and worm-eaten with porn and hype and blather as it is, electronic publication offers those who read a strong new means of active community. The technology is not what matters. Words are what matter. The sharing of words. The activation of imagination through the reading of words.

The reason literacy is important is that literature *is* the operating instructions. The best manual we have. The most useful guide to the country we're visiting, life.

"A WAR WITHOUT END"

Some thoughts, written down at intervals, about oppression, revolution, and imagination.

SLAVERY

My country came together in one revolution and was nearly broken by another.

The first revolution was a protest against galling, stupid, but relatively mild social and economic exploitation. It was almost uniquely successful.

Many of those who made the first revolution practiced the most extreme form of economic exploitation and social oppression: they were slave owners.

The second American revolution, the Civil War, was an attempt to preserve slavery. It was partially successful. The institution was abolished, but the mind of the master and the mind of the slave still think a good many of the thoughts of America.

RESISTANCE TO OPPRESSION

Phillis Wheatley, poet and manumitted slave, wrote in 1774: "In every human Breast, God has implanted a principle, which we call Love of Freedom; it is impatient of Oppression, and pants for Deliverance."

I would no more deny the truth of that than I would deny that the sun shines. All that is good in the institutions and politics of my country rests on it.

And yet I see that though we love freedom we are mostly patient of oppression, and even refuse deliverance.

I see a danger in insisting that our love of freedom always outweighs whatever force or inertia keeps us from resisting oppression and seeking deliverance.

If I deny that strong, intelligent, capable people will and do accept oppression, I'm identifying the oppressed as weak, stupid, and inept.

If it were true that superior people refuse to be treated as inferiors, it would follow that those low in the social order are truly inferior, since, if they were superior, they'd protest; since they accept an inferior position, they are inferior. This is the comfortably tautological argument of the slave owner, the social reactionary, the racist, and the misogynist.

It is an argument that still bedevils consideration of the Hitlerian holocaust: Why did the Jews "just get into the trains," why didn't they "fight back"? A question which—as asked—is unanswerable, and so can be used by the anti-Semite to imply the inferiority of the Jews.

But the argument appeals also to the idealist. Many liberal and humanely conservative Americans cherish the conviction that all oppressed people suffer intolerably from their oppression, must be ready and eager to rebel, and are morally weak, morally wrong, if they do not rebel.

I categorically judge as wrong any person who considers himself or herself racially or socially superior to another or enforces inferior status on another. But it is a different matter to pass categorical judgment against people who accept inferior status. If I say that they are wrong, that morality demands that they rebel, it behooves me to consider what real choice they have, whether they act in ignorance or through conviction, whether they have any opportunity to lessen their ignorance or change their conviction. Having so considered, how can I say they are at fault? Is it they, and not the oppressors, who do wrong?

The ruling class is always small, the lower orders large, even in a caste society. The poor always vastly outnumber the rich. The powerful are fewer than those they hold power over. Adult men hold superior status in almost all societies, though they are always outnumbered by women and children. Governments and religions sanction and uphold inequality, social rank, gender rank, and privilege, wholly or selectively.

Most people, in most places, in most times, are of inferior status.

And most people, even now, even in "the free world," even in "the home of the free," consider this state of affairs, or certain elements of it, as natural, necessary, and unchangeable. They hold it to be the way it has always been and therefore the way it must be. This may be conviction or it may be ignorance; often it is both. Over the centuries, most people of inferior status have had no way of knowing that any other way of ordering society has existed or could exist—that change is possible. Only those of superior status have ever known enough to know that; and it is their power and privilege that would be at stake if the order of things were changed.

We cannot trust history as a moral guide in these matters, because history is written by the superior class, the educated, the empowered. But we have only history to go on, and observation of current events. On that evidence, revolt and rebellion are rare things, revolution extremely rare. In most times, in most places, most women, slaves, serfs, low-castes, outcastes, peasants, working-class people, most people defined as inferior—that is, most people—have not rebelled against being despised and exploited. They resist, yes; but their resistance is likely to be passive, or so devious, so much a part of daily behavior, as to be all but invisible.

When voices from the oppressed and the underclasses are recorded, some are cries for justice, but most are expressions of patriotism, cheers for the king, vows to defend the fatherland, all loyally supporting the system that disenfranchises them and the people who profit from it.

Slavery would not have existed all over the world if slaves often rose against their masters. Most slavemasters are not murdered. They are obeyed.

Working men watch their company's CEOs get paid three hundred times what they are paid, and grumble, but do nothing.

Women in most societies uphold the claims and institutions of male supremacy, deferring to men, obeying them (overtly), and defending the innate superiority of men as natural fact or religious dogma.

Low-status males—young men, poor men—fight and die for the system that keeps them under. Most of the countless soldiers killed in the countless wars waged to uphold the power of a society's rulers or religion have been men considered inferior by that society.

"You have nothing to lose but your chains," but we prefer to kiss them.

ↄ

Why?

Are human societies inevitably constructed as a pyramid, with the power concentrating at the top? Is a hierarchy of power a biological imperative that human society is bound to enact? The question is almost certainly wrongly phrased and so impossible to answer, but it keeps getting asked and answered, and those who ask it usually answer it in the affirmative.

If such an inborn, biological imperative exists, is it equally imperative in both sexes? We have no incontrovertible evidence of innate gender difference in social behavior. Essentialists on both sides of the argument maintain that men are innately disposed to establish a power hierarchy while women, though they do not initiate such structures, accept or imitate them. According to the essentialists, the male program is thus certain to prevail, and we should expect to find the chain of command, the "higher" commanding the "lower," with power concentrated in a few, a nearly universal pattern of human society.

Anthropology provides some exceptions to this supposed universality. Ethnologists have described societies that have no fixed chain of command; in them power, instead of being locked into a rigid system of inequality, is fluid, shared differently in different situations, operating by checks and balances tending always towards consensus. They have described societies that do not rank one gender as superior, though there is always some gendered division of labor, and male pursuits are those most likely to be celebrated.

But these are all societies that we describe as "primitive"—tautologically, since we have already established a value hierarchy: primitive = low = weak, civilised = high = powerful.

Many "primitive" and all "civilised" societies are rigidly stratified, with much power assigned to a few and little or no power to most. Is the perpetuation of institutions of social inequality in fact the engine that drives civilisation, as Lévi-Strauss suggests?

People in power are better fed, better armed, and better educated, and therefore better able to stay that way, but is that sufficient to explain the ubiquity and permanence of extreme social inequality? Certainly the fact that men are slightly larger and more muscular (though somewhat less durable) than women is not sufficient to explain the ubiquity of gender inequality and its perpetuation in societies where size and muscularity do not make much difference.

If human beings hated injustice and inequality as we say we do and think we do, would any of the Great Empires and High Civilisations have lasted fifteen minutes?

If we Americans hate injustice and inequality as passionately as we say we do, would any person in this country lack enough to eat?

We demand a rebellious spirit of those who have no chance to learn that rebellion is possible, but we the privileged hold still and see no evil.

We have good reason to be cautious, to be quiet, not to rock the boat. A lot of peace and comfort is at stake. The mental and moral shift from denial of injustice to consciousness of injustice is often made at very high cost. My contentment, stability, safety, personal affections, may become a sacrifice to the dream of the common good, to the idea of a freedom that I may not live to share, an ideal of justice that nobody may ever attain.

The last words of the *Mahabharata* are, "By no means can I attain a goal beyond my reach." It is likely that justice, a human idea, is a goal beyond human reach. We're good at inventing things that can't exist.

Maybe freedom cannot be attained through human institutions but must remain a quality of the mind or spirit not dependent on circumstances, a gift of grace. This (if I understand it) is the religious definition of freedom. My problem with it is that its devaluation of work and circumstance encourages institutional injustices which make the gift of grace inaccessible. A two-year-old child who dies of starvation or a beating or a firebombing has not been granted access to freedom, nor any gift of grace, in any sense in which I can understand the words.

We can attain by our own efforts only an imperfect justice, a limited freedom. Better than none. Let us hold fast to that principle, the love of Freedom, of which the freed slave, the poet, spoke.

THE GROUND OF HOPE

The shift from denial of injustice to recognition of injustice can't be unmade.

What your eyes have seen they have seen. Once you see the injustice, you can never again in good faith deny the oppression and defend the oppressor. What was loyalty is now betrayal. From now on, if you don't resist, you collude.

But there is a middle ground between defense and attack, a ground of flexible resistance, a space opened for change. It is not an easy place to find or live in. Peacemakers trying to get there have ended up scuttling in panic to Munich.

Even if they reach the middle ground, they may get no thanks for it. Harriet Beecher Stowe's Uncle Tom is a slave who, for his courageous effort to persuade his owner to change his heart and his steadfast refusal to beat other slaves, is beaten to death. We insist on using him as a symbol of cringing capitulation and servility.

Admiring heroically useless defiance, we sneer at patient resistance.

But the negotiating ground, where patience makes change, is where Gandhi stood. Lincoln got there, painfully. Bishop Tutu, having lived there for years in singular honor, saw his country move, however awkwardly and uncertainly, towards that ground of hope.

THE MASTER'S TOOLS

Audre Lord said you can't dismantle the master's house with the master's tools. I think about this powerful metaphor, trying to understand it.

By radicals, liberals, conservatives, and reactionaries, education in the masters' knowledge is seen as leading *inevitably* to consciousness of oppression and exploitation, and so to the subversive desire for equality and justice. Liberals support and reactionaries oppose universal free education, public schools, uncensored discussion at the universities for exactly the same reason.

Lord's metaphor seems to say that education is irrelevant to social change. If nothing the master used can be useful to the slave, then education in the masters' knowledge must be abandoned. Thus an underclass must entirely reinvent society, achieve a new knowledge, in order to achieve justice. If they don't, the revolution will fail.

This is plausible. Revolutions generally fail. But I see their failure beginning when the attempt to rebuild the house so everybody can live in it becomes an attempt to grab all the saws and hammers, barricade Ole Massa's toolroom, and keep the others out. Power not only corrupts, it addicts. Work becomes destruction. Nothing is built.

Societies change with and without violence. Reinvention is possible. Building is possible. What tools have we to build with except hammers, nails, saws—education, learning to think, learning skills?

Are there indeed tools that have not been invented, which we must invent in order to build the house we want our children to live in? Can we go on from what we know now, or does what we know now keep us from learning what we need to know? To learn what people of color, the women, the poor, have to teach, to learn the knowledge we need, must we unlearn all the knowledge of the whites, the men, the powerful? Along with the priesthood and phallocracy, must we throw away science and democracy? Will we be left trying to build without any tools but our bare hands? The metaphor is rich and dangerous. I can't answer the questions it raises.

ONLY IN UTOPIAS

In the sense that it offers a glimpse of some imagined alternative to "the way we live now," much of my fiction can be called utopian, but I continue to resist the word. Many of my invented societies strike me as an improvement in one way or another on our own, but I find Utopia far too grand and too rigid a name for them. Utopia, and Dystopia, are intellectual places. I write from passion and playfulness. My stories are neither dire warnings nor blueprints for what we ought to do. Most of them, I think, are comedies of human manners, reminders of the infinite variety of ways in which we always come back to pretty much the same place, and celebrations of that infinite variety by the invention of still more alternatives and possibilities. Even the novels *The Dispossessed* and *Always Coming Home,* in which I worked out more methodically than usual certain variations on the uses of power, which I preferred to those that obtain in our world— even these are as much efforts to subvert as to display the ideal of an attainable social plan which would end injustice and inequality once and for all.

To me the important thing is not to offer any specific hope of betterment but, by offering an imagined but persuasive alternative reality, to dislodge my mind, and so the reader's mind, from the lazy, timorous habit of thinking that the way we live now is the only way people can live. It is that inertia that allows the institutions of injustice to continue unquestioned.

Fantasy and science fiction in their very conception offer alternatives to the reader's present, actual world. Young people in general welcome this kind of story because in their vigor and eagerness for experience they welcome alternatives, possibilities, change. Having come to fear even the imagination of true change, many adults refuse all imaginative literature, priding themselves on seeing nothing beyond what they already know, or think they know.

Yet, as if it feared its own troubling powers, much science fiction and fantasy is timid and reactionary in its social invention, fantasy clinging to feudalism, science fiction to military and imperial hierarchy. Both usually reward their hero, whether a man or woman, only for doing outstandingly manly deeds. (I wrote this way for years myself. In *The Left Hand of Darkness,* my hero is genderless but his heroics are almost exclusively manly.) In science fiction particularly, one also often meets the idea I discussed above, that anyone of inferior status, if not a rebel constantly ready to seize freedom through daring and violent action, is either despicable or simply of no consequence.

In a world so morally simplified, if a slave is not Spartacus, he is nobody. This is merciless and unrealistic. Most slaves, most oppressed people, are part of a social order which, by the very terms of their oppression, they have no opportunity even to perceive as capable of being changed.

The exercise of imagination is dangerous to those who profit from the way things are because it has the power to show that the way things are is not permanent, not universal, not necessary.

Having that real though limited power to put established institutions into question, imaginative literature has also the responsibility of power. The storyteller is the truthteller.

It is sad that so many stories that might offer a true vision settle for patriotic or religious platitude, technological miracle working, or wishful thinking, the writers not trying to imagine truth. The fashionably noir dystopia merely reverses the platitudes and uses acid instead of saccharine, while still evading engagement with human suffering and with genuine possibility. The imaginative fiction I admire presents alternatives to the status quo which not only question the ubiquity and necessity of extant institutions, but enlarge the field of social possibility and moral understanding. This may be done in as naively hopeful a tone as the first three *Star Trek* television series, or through such complex, sophisticated, and ambiguous constructions of thought and technique as the novels of Philip K. Dick or Carol Emshwiller; but the movement is recognisably the same—the impulse to make change imaginable.

We will not know our own injustice if we cannot imagine justice. We will not be free if we do not imagine freedom. We cannot demand that anyone try to attain justice and freedom who has not had a chance to imagine them as attainable.

ᔕ

I want to close and crown these inconclusive meditations with the words of a writer who never spoke anything but truth, and always spoke it quietly, Primo Levi, who lived a year in Auschwitz, and knew what injustice is.

"The ascent of the privileged, not only in the Lager but in all human coexistence, is an anguishing but unfailing phenomenon: only in utopias is it absent. It is the duty of righteous men to make war on all undeserved privilege, but one must not forget that this is a war without end."

ON WRITING

A MATTER OF TRUST

A talk given to a writing workshop in Vancouver, Washington, February 2002.

In order to write a story, you have to trust yourself, you have to trust the story, and you have to trust the reader.

Before you start writing, neither the story nor the reader even exists, and the only thing you have to trust is yourself. And the only way you can come to trust in yourself as a writer is to write. To commit yourself to that craft. To be writing, to have written, to work on writing, to plan to write. To read, to write, to practice your trade, to learn your job, until you know something about it, and know you know something about it.

This can be tricky. I have an eleven-year-old pen pal who has written half a story and is now demanding that I put him in touch with my agent and a publisher. It is my very disagreeable duty to tell him that he hasn't quite earned that much trust in himself as a writer, yet.

On the other hand I know some very good writers who never finish anything, or finish it and then destroy it with overrevising to meet real or imagined criticisms, because they don't trust themselves as writers, which means they can't trust their writing.

Confidence in yourself as a writer is pretty much the same as all other kinds of confidence, the confidence of a plumber or a school-

teacher or a horseback rider: you earn it by doing, you build it up
slowly, by working at it. And sometimes, particularly when you're new
at the game, you fake it—you act like you know what you're doing,
and maybe you can get away with it. Sometimes if you act as if you
were blessed, you will be blessed. That too is part of trusting oneself.
I think it works better for writers than it does for plumbers.

꙳

So much for trusting oneself. Now, to trust the story, what does that
mean? To me, it means being willing not to have full control over the
story as you write it.

Which would explain why it takes so long to learn to write. First
you have to learn how to write English, and learn how to tell stories in
general—techniques, practice, all that: so that you are in control. And
then you have learn how to relinquish it.

Let me say here that many writers and teachers of writing would
disagree strongly with what I'm saying. They'd say, you don't learn
how to ride a horse, control the horse, make it do what you want it to
do, and then take off its bridle and ride it bareback without reins—
that's stupid. However, that is what I recommend. (Taoism is always
stupid.) For me it's not enough to be a good rider, I want to be a cen-
taur. I don't want to be the rider controlling the horse, I want to be
both the rider and the horse.

How far to trust your story? It depends on the story, and your
own judgment and experience are the only guide. The only generalisa-
tions I'm willing to make are these: Lack of control over a story, usually arising from ignorance of the craft or from self-indulgence, may
lead to slackness of pace, incoherence, sloppy writing, spoiled work.
Overcontrol, usually arising from self-consciousness or a competitive
attitude, may lead to tightness, artificiality, self-conscious language,
dead work.

Deliberate, conscious control, in the sense of knowing and keeping
to the plan, the subject, the gait, and the direction of the work, is in-

valuable in the planning stage—before writing—and in the revision stage—after the first draft. During the actual composition it seems to be best if conscious intellectual control is relaxed. An insistent consciousness of the *intention* of the writing may interfere with the *process* of writing. The writer may get in the way of the story.

This is not as mystical as it sounds. All highly skilled work, all true craft and art, is done in a state where most aspects of it have become automatic through experience, through total familiarity with the medium, whether the medium is the sculptor's stone, or the drummer's drum, or the body of the dancer, or, for the writer, word sounds, word meanings, sentence rhythm, syntax, and so on. The dancer *knows* where her left foot goes, and the writer *knows* where the comma's needed. The only decisions a skilled artisan or artist makes while working are aesthetic ones. Aesthetic decisions are not rational; they're made on a level that doesn't coincide with rational consciousness. Thus, in fact, many artists feel they're in something like a trance state while working, and that in that state they don't make the decisions. The work tells them what needs doing and they do it. Perhaps it is as mystical as it sounds.

To go back to my horse metaphor, a good cowboy on a good horse rides with a loose rein and doesn't keep telling the horse what to do, because the horse knows. The cowboy knows where they're going, but the horse knows how to get them there.

I hope I don't sound like one of those bearers of glad tidings to writers who announce that there's nothing to it, just shut down your intellect and free up your right brain and emit words. I have enormous respect for my art as an art and my craft as a craft, for skill, for experience, for hard thought, for painstaking work. I hold those things in reverence. I respect commas far more than I do congressmen. People who say that commas don't matter may be talking about therapy or self-expression or other good things, but they're not talking about writing. They may be talking about getting started, leaping over timidity, breaking through emotional logjams; but they're still not talking about writing. If you want to be a dancer, find out how to use your feet. If you want to be a writer, find out where the comma goes. Then worry about all that other stuff.

Now, let's say I want to write a story. (Speaking for myself personally, that can be taken for granted; I always want to write a story; there never is anything I'd rather do than write a story.) In order to write that story, first I have learned how to write English, and how to write stories, by doing it quite regularly.*

I have also learned that what I need, once the story gets going, is to relinquish conscious control, get my damned intentions and theories and opinions out of the way, and let the story carry me. I need to trust it.

But as a rule, I can trust the story only if there has been a previous stage of some kind, a period of approach. This may well involve conscious planning, sitting and thinking about the setting, the events, the characters, maybe making notes. Or it may involve a long semiconscious gestation, during which events and characters and moods and ideas drift around half formed, changing forms, in a kind of dreamy limbo of the mind. And I do mean long. Years, sometimes. But then at other times, with other stories, this approach stage is quite abrupt: a sudden vision or clear sense of the shape and direction of the story comes into the mind, and one is ready to write.

All these approach states or stages may occur at any time—at your desk, walking on the street, waking up in the morning, or when your mind ought to be on what Aunt Julia is saying, or the electricity bill, or the stew. You may have a whole grandiose James Joyce epiphany thing, or you may just think, *oh, yes, I see how that'll go.*

The most important thing I have to say about this preliminary period is don't rush it. Your mind is like a cat hunting; it's not even sure

---

*And, of course, by reading stories. Reading—reading stories other writers wrote, reading voraciously but judgmentally, reading the best there is and learning from it how well, and how differently, stories can be told—this is so essential to being a writer that I tend to forget to mention it; so here it is in a footnote.

yet what it's hunting. It listens. Be patient like the cat. Very, very atten-
tive, alert, but patient. Slow. Don't push the story to take shape. Let it
show itself. Let it gather impetus. Keep listening. Make notes or whatever if you're afraid you'll forget something, but don't rush to the computer. Let the story drive you to it. When it's ready to go, you'll know it.

And if—like most of us—your life isn't all your own, if you haven't
got time to write at that moment when you know the story's ready to
be written, don't panic. It's just as tough as you are. It's yours. Make
notes, think about your story, hang on to it and it will hang on to you.
When you find or make the time to sit down to it, it will be there waiting for you.

Then comes the trancelike, selfless, rather terrifying, devouring
work or play of composition, which is very difficult to talk about.

About planning and composition I want to make one observation:
that it's delightful for a writer to be sheltered and shielded while at this
intense work, given solitude and freedom from human responsibilities,
like Proust in his padded cell, or the people who keep going to writers
colonies and having their lunch brought in a basket; delightful indeed,
but dangerous, because it makes a luxury into a condition of work—a
necessity. What you need as a writer is exactly what Virginia Woolf
said: enough to live on and a room of your own. It's not up to other
people to provide either of those necessities. It's up to you, and if you
want to work, you figure how to get what you need to do it. What you
live on probably has to come from daily work, not writing. How dirty
your room gets is probably up to you. That the door of the room is
shut, and when, and for how long, is also up to you. If you have work
to do, you have to trust yourself to do it. A kind spouse is invaluable,
a fat grant, an advance on spec, a session at a retreat may be a tremendous help: but it's your work, not theirs, and it has to be done on your
terms, not theirs.

All right, so you shut the door, and you write down a first draft, at
white heat, because that energy has been growing in you all through

the prewriting stage and when released at last, is incandescent. You trust yourself and the story and you write.

So now it's written. You sit around and feel tired and good and look at the manuscript and savor all the marvelous, wonderful bits.

Then it cools down and you cool down, and arrive, probably somewhat chilled and rueful, at the next stage. Your story is full of ugly, stupid bits. You distrust it now, and that's as it should be. But you still have to trust yourself. You have to know that you can make it better. Unless you're a genius or have extremely low standards, composition is followed by critical, patient revision, with the thinking mind turned on.

I can trust myself to write my story at white heat without asking any questions of it—if I know my craft through practice—if I have a sense of where this story's going—and if when it's got there, I'm willing to turn right round and go over it and over it, word by word, idea by idea, testing and proving it till it goes right. Till all of it goes right.

Parenthetically: This is the period when it is most useful to have criticism from others—in a peer group or a class or from professional editors. Informed, supportive criticism is invaluable. I am a strong believer in the workshop as a way of gaining confidence and critical skills not only before you get published, but also for experienced professional writers. And a trustworthy editor is a pearl beyond price. To learn to trust your readers—and which readers to trust—is a very great step. Some writers never take it. I will return to that subject in a moment.

To sum up, I have to trust the story to know where it's going, and after I've written it I have to trust myself to find out where it or I got off track and how to get it all going in one direction in one piece.

And only after all that—usually long after—will I fully know and be able to say what, in fact, the story was about and why it had to go the way it went. Any work of art has its reasons which reason does not wholly understand.

When a story's finished, it's always less than your vision of it was before it was written. But it may also do more than you knew you were doing, say more than you realised you were saying. That's the best reason of all to trust it, to let it find itself.

To conceive a story or manipulate it to make it serve a purpose outside itself, such as an ambition to be famous, or an agent's opinion about what will sell, or a publisher's wish for instant profit, or even a noble end such as teaching or healing, is a failure of trust, of respect for the work. Of course almost all writers compromise here, to some extent. Writers are professionals in an age when capitalism pretends to be the arbiter of good; they have to write for the market. Only poets totally and sublimely ignore the market and therefore live on air—air and fellowships. Writers want to right wrongs, or bear witness to outrages, or convince others of what they see as truth. But in so far as they let such conscious aims control their work, they narrow its potential scope and power. That sounds like the doctrine of Art for Art's Sake. I don't offer it as a doctrine, but as a practical observation.*

Somebody asked James Clerk Maxwell in 1820 or so, What is the *use* of electricity? and Maxwell asked right back, What is the use of a baby?

What's the use of *To the Lighthouse*? What's the use of *War and Peace*? How would I dare try to define it, to limit it?

The arts function powerfully in establishing and confirming human

---

*For example, read *War and Peace*. (If you have not read *War and Peace*, what are you waiting for?) The greatest of all novels is interrupted now and then by the voice of Count Tolstoy, telling us what we ought to think about history, great men, the Russian soul, and other matters. His opinions are far more interesting, convincing, and persuasive as we unconsciously absorb them *from the story* than when they appear as lectures. Tolstoy was a supremely and deservedly self-confident writer, and much of the power and beauty of his book lies his perfect trust in his characters. They do what they must do, and all they must do: and it is enough. But the earnestness of his convictions seem to have weakened his confidence in his power to embody those ideas in his story; and those failures of trust are the only dull and unconvincing portions of the greatest of all novels.

community. Story, told or written, certainly serves to enlarge understanding of other people and of our place in the world as a whole. Such uses are intrinsic to the work of art, integral with it. But any limited, conscious, objective purpose is likely to obscure or deform that integrity.

Even if I don't feel my skill and experience are sufficient (and they are never sufficient), I must trust my gift, and therefore trust the story I write, know that its use, its meaning or beauty, may go far beyond anything I could have planned.

⸜

A story is a collaboration between teller and audience, writer and reader. Fiction is not only illusion, but collusion.

Without a reader there's no story. No matter how well written, if it isn't read it doesn't exist as a story. The reader makes it happen just as much as the writer does. Writers are likely to ignore this fact, perhaps because they resent it.

The relationship of writer and reader is popularly seen as a matter of control and consent. The writer is The Master, who compels, controls, and manipulates the reader's interest and emotion. A lot of writers love this idea.

And lazy readers want masterful writers. They want the writer to do all the work while they just watch it happen, like on TV.

Most best-sellers are written for readers who are willing to be passive consumers. The blurbs on their covers often highlight the coercive, aggressive power of the text—compulsive page-turner, gut-wrenching, jolting, mind-searing, heart-stopping—what is this, electroshock torture?

From commercial writing of this type, and from journalism, come the how-to-write clichés, "Grab your readers with the first paragraph," "Hit them with shocker scenes," "Never give them time to breathe," and so on.

Now, a good many writers, particularly those entangled in academic programs in fiction, get their intellect and ego so involved in what they're saying and how they're saying it that they forget that they're saying it to anyone. If there's any use in the grab-'em-and-wrench-their-guts-out school of advice, it's that it at least reminds the writer that there is a reader out there to be grabbed and gutted.

But just because you realise your work may be seen by somebody other than the professor of creative writing, you don't have to go into attack mode and release the Rottweilers. There's another option. You can consider the reader, not as a helpless victim or a passive consumer, but as an active, intelligent, worthy collaborator. A colluder, a co-illusionist.

Writers who choose to try to establish mutual trust believe it is possible to attract readers' attention without verbal assault and battery. Rather than grab, frighten, coerce, or manipulate a consumer, collaborative writers try to interest a reader. To induce or seduce people into moving with the story, participating in it, joining their imagination with it.

Not a rape: a dance.

Consider the story as a dance, the reader and writer as partners. The writer leads, yes; but leading isn't pushing; it's setting up a field of mutuality where two people can move in cooperation with grace. It takes two to tango.

Readers who have only been grabbed, bashed, gut-wrenched, and electroshocked may need a little practice in being interested. They may need to learn how to tango. Once they've tried it, they'll never go back among the pit bulls.

Finally, there is the difficult question of "audience": In the mind of the writer planning or composing or revising the work, what is the presence of the potential reader or readers? Should the audience for the work dominate the writer's mind and guide the writing? Or should the writer while writing be utterly free of such considerations?

I wish there were a simple sound bite answer, but actually this is a terribly complicated question, particularly on the moral level.

Being a writer, conceiving a fiction, implies a reader. Writing is communication, though that's not all it is. One communicates *to* somebody. And what people want to read influences what people want to write. Stories are drawn out of writers by the spiritual and intellectual and moral needs of the writer's people. But all that operates on a quite unconscious level.

Once again it's useful to see the writer's work as being done in three stages. In the approach stage, it may be essential to think about your potential audience: who is this story for? For instance, is it for kids? Little kids? Young adults? Any special, limited audience calls for specific kinds of subject matter and vocabulary. All genre writing, from the average formula romance to the average *New Yorker* story, is written with an audience in mind—an audience so specific it can be called a market.

Only the very riskiest kind of fiction is entirely inconsiderate of the reader/market, saying, as it were, I will be told, and somebody, somewhere, will read me! Probably 99 percent of such stories end up, in fact, unread. And probably 98 percent of them are unreadable. The other 1 or 2 percent come to be known as masterpieces, usually very slowly, after the brave author has long been silent.

Consciousness of audience is limiting, both positively and negatively. Consciousness of audience offers choices, many of which have ethical implications—puritanism or porn? shock the readers or reassure them? do something I haven't tried or do my last book over?—and so on.

The limitations imposed by aiming at a specific readership may lead to very high art; all craft is a matter of rules and limitations, after all. But if consciousness of audience *as market* is the primary factor controlling your writing, you are a hack. There are arty hacks and artless hacks. Personally I prefer the latter.

All this has been about the approach stage, the what-am-I-going-to-write stage. Now that I know, dimly or exactly, who I'm writing for—anything from my granddaughter to all posterity—I start writing. And now, at the writing stage, consciousness of audience can be absolutely fatal. It is what makes writers distrust their story, stick, block, start over and over, never finish. Writers need a room of their own, not a room full of imaginary critics all watching over their shoulders saying "Is 'The' a good way to start that sentence?" An overactive internal aesthetic censor, or the external equivalent—what my agent or my editor is going to say—is like an avalanche of boulders across the story's way. During composition I have to concentrate entirely on the work itself, trusting and aiding it to find its way, with little or no thought of what or who it's for.

But when I get to the third stage, revision and rewriting, it reverses again: awareness that somebody's going to read this story, and of who might read this story, becomes essential.

What's the goal of revision? Clarity—impact—pace—power—beauty . . . all things that imply a mind and heart *receiving* the story. Revision clears unnecessary obstacles away so the reader can receive the story. That is why the comma is important. And why the right word, not the approximately right word, is important. And why consistency is important. And why moral implications are important. And all the rest of the stuff that makes a story readable, makes it live. In revising, you must trust yourself, your judgment, to work with the receptive intelligence of your potential readers.

You also may have to trust specific actual readers—spouse, friends, workshop peers, teachers, editors, agents. You may be pulled between your judgment and theirs, and it can be tricky to arrive at the necessary arrogance, or the necessary humility, or the right compromise. I have writer friends who simply cannot hear any critical suggestions; they drown them out by going into defensive explanation mode: *Oh, yes, but see, what I was doing*—are they geniuses or just buttheaded? Time will tell. I have writer friends who accept every critical suggestion uncritically, and end up with as many different versions as they have critics. If they meet up with bullying, manipulative agents and editors, they're helpless.

What can I recommend? Trust your story; trust yourself; trust your readers—but wisely. Trust watchfully, not blindly. Trust flexibly, not rigidly. The whole thing, writing a story, is a high-wire act—there you are out in midair walking on a spiderweb line of words, and down in the darkness people are watching. What can you trust but your sense of balance?

THE WRITER AND THE
CHARACTER

Some ideas written down when I was planning a workshop in fiction, and worked up into a small essay for this book.

Whether they invent the people they write about or borrow them from people they know, fiction writers generally agree that once these people become characters in a story they have a life of their own, sometimes to the extent of escaping from the writer's control and doing and saying things quite unexpected to the author of their being.

My people, in the stories I write, are close to me and mysterious to me, like kinfolk or friends or enemies. They are in and on my mind. I made them up, I invented them, but I have to ponder their motives and try to understand their destinies. They take on their own reality, which is not my reality, and the more they do so, the less I can or wish to control what they do or say. While I'm composing, the characters are alive in my mind, and I owe them the respect due any living soul. They are not to be used, manipulated. They are not plastic toys, they are not megaphones.

But composition is a special condition. While writing, I may yield to my characters, trust them wholly to do and say what is right for the story. In planning the story and in revising it, I do better to keep some emotional distance from the characters, especially the ones I like best or loathe most. I need to look askance at them, inquire rather coldly into their motives, and take everything they say with a grain of salt—

till I'm certain that they are really and genuinely speaking for themselves, and not for my damned ego.

If I'm using the people in my story principally to fulfill the needs of my self-image, my self-love or self-hate, my needs, my opinions, they can't be themselves and they can't tell the truth. The story, as a display of needs and opinions, may be effective as such, but the characters will not be characters; they will be puppets.

As a writer I must be conscious that *I am* my characters and that they *are not me*. I am them, and am responsible for them. But they're themselves; they have no responsibility for me, or my politics, or my morals, or my editor, or my income. They're embodiments of my experience and imagination, engaged in an imagined life that is not my life, though it may serve to illuminate it. I may feel passionately with a character who embodies my experience and emotions, but I must be wary of *confusing* myself with that character.

If I fuse or confuse a fictional person with myself, my judgment of the character becomes a self-judgment. Then justice is pretty near impossible, since I've made myself witness, defendant, prosecutor, judge, and jury, using the fiction to justify or condemn what that character does and says.

Self-knowledge takes a clear mind. Clarity can be earned by tough-mindedness and it can be earned by tender-mindedness, but it has to be earned. A writer has to learn to be transparent to the story. The ego is opaque. It fills the space of the story, blocking honesty, obscuring understanding, falsifying the language.

Fiction, like all art, takes place in a space that is the maker's loving difference from the thing made. Without that space there can be no consistent truthfulness and no true respect for the human beings the story is about.

৽

Another way to come at this matter: In so far as the author's point of view exactly coincides with that of a character, the story isn't fiction. It's either a disguised memoir or a fiction-coated sermon.

I don't like the word *distancing*. If I say there should be a distance between author and character it sounds as if I'm after the "objectivity" pretended to by naive scientists and sophisticated minimalists. I'm not. I'm all for subjectivity, the artist's inalienable privilege. But there has to be a distance between the writer and the character.

The naive reader often does not take this distance into account. In-experienced readers think writers write only from experience. They believe that the writer believes what the characters believe. The idea of the unreliable narrator takes some getting used to.

David Copperfield's experiences and emotions are very close indeed to those of Charles Dickens, but David Copperfield isn't Charles Dickens. However closely Dickens "identified with" his character, as we glibly and freudianly say, there was no confusion in Dickens's mind as to who was who. The distance between them, the difference of point of view, is crucial.

David fictionally lives what Charles factually experienced, and suffers what Charles suffered; but David doesn't know what Charles knows. He can't see his life from a distance, from a vantage point of time, thought, and feeling, as Charles can. Charles learned a great deal about himself, and so let us learn a great deal about ourselves, through *taking* David's point of view, but if he had *confused* his point of view with David's, he and we would have learned nothing. We'd never have got out of the blacking factory.

Another interesting example: *Huckleberry Finn*. What Mark Twain achieves, with great skill and at tremendous risk, all the way through the book, is an invisible but immense ironic distance between his point of view and Huck's. Huck tells the story. Every word of it is in his voice, from his point of view. Mark is silent. Mark's point of view, particularly as regards slavery and the character Jim, is never stated. It is discernible

only in the *story itself* and the *characters*—Jim's character, above all.
Jim is the only real adult in the book, a kind, warm, strong, patient
man, with a delicate and powerful sense of morality. Huck might grow
up into that kind of man, given a chance. But Huck at this point is an
ignorant, prejudiced kid who doesn't know right from wrong (though
once, when it really matters, he guesses right). In the tension between
that kid's voice and Mark Twain's silence lies much of the power of the
book. We have to understand—as soon as we're old enough to read this
way—that what the book really says lies in that silence.

Tom Sawyer, on the other hand, is going to grow up to be at best
a smart entrepreneur, at worst a shyster; his imagination has no ethical ballast at all. The last chapters of *Huckleberry Finn* are tedious and
hateful whenever that manipulative, unfeeling imagination takes over,
controlling Huck and Jim and the story.

Toni Morrison has shown that the jail Tom puts Jim into, the tor-
tures he invents for him, and Huck's uncomfortable but helpless collusion, represent the betrayal of Emancipation during Reconstruction.
Freed slaves did find themselves with no freedom at all, and whites accustomed to consider blacks as inferior inevitably colluded in that perpetuation of evil. Seen thus, the long, painful ending makes sense, and
the book makes a moral whole. But it was a risk to take, both morally
and aesthetically, and it succeeds only partially, perhaps because Mark
Twain overidentified with Tom. He loved writing about smart-alecky,
go-for-broke manipulators (not only Tom but the King and Duke), and
so Huck, and Jim, and we the readers, all have to sit and watch them
strut their second-rate stuff. Mark Twain kept his loving distance from
Huck perfectly, never breaking the tender irony. But wanting Tom for
that final bitter plot twist, he brought him in, indulged him, lost his distance from him—and the book lost its balance.

Though the author may pretend otherwise, the author's point of
view is larger than the character's and includes knowledge the character lacks. This means that the character, existing only in the author's
knowledge, may be known as we cannot ever know any actual person;

and such insight may reveal insights and durable truths relevant to our own lives.

To fuse author and character—to limit the character's behavior to what the author approves of doing, or the character's opinions to the author's opinions, and so forth—is to lose that chance of revelation.

The author's tone may be cold or passionately concerned; it may be detached or judgmental; the difference of the author's point of view from the character's may be obvious or concealed; but the difference must exist. In the space provided by that difference, discovery, change, learning, action, tragedy, fulfillment take place—the story takes place.

⸉UNQUESTIONED ASSUMPTIONS

A piece put together for this book, from notes for workshops and talks to writers during the nineties.

"Hypocrite lecteur, mon semblable, mon frère . . ." et ma soeur . . .

This essay is the somewhat grouchy result of years of reading stories—workshop manuscripts and printed books—that include me, the reader, in a group I don't belong to and don't want to belong to.

You're just like me, you're one of us, the writer tells me. And I want to shout, I'm not! You don't know who I am!

We writers of fiction don't know who reads us. We can make some limited assumptions about our readers only if we write for a publication with a restricted readership such as a campus literary periodical or a magazine with a specific religious or commercial affiliation, or in a strictly coded genre such as the Regency romance. And even then it's unwise to assume that your readers think the way you do about anything—race, sex, religion, politics, youth, age, oysters, dogs, dirt, Mozart—*anything*.

The unquestioned assumption, the mistake of thinking we all think alike, is less often made by writers who belong to a minority or oppressed social group. They know all too clearly the difference between "us" and "them." The confusion of "us" with "everybody" is most tempting to people who are members of one or more of the privileged or dominant groups in their society or in an isolated or sheltered social environment such as a college, or a white American neighborhood, or a newspaper editorial staff.

The premise is: *everybody's like me and we all think alike.*

Its corollary is: *people who don't think like me don't matter.*

The supposed phenomenon of "political correctness"—a conspiracy by bleeding-heart liberals to keep us ordinary folks from talking the normal ordinary just-folks down-home way and calling a spade a spade—exhibits the corollary as an article of belief, invoked to defend various bigotries.

Arrogance is usually ignorant. It can be innocent. Children's ignorance of how others think and feel has to be forgiven, while it's being corrected. Many adults in communities isolated by geography or poverty have known only people like themselves, of their own community, creed, values, assumptions, and so on.

But these days, no *writer* can legitimately claim either ignorance or innocence as a defense of prejudice or bigotry in their writing.

How does anybody know anything about other people's minds and feelings? Through experience, yes, but fiction writers get and handle a great part of their experience through their imagination, and pass it on to their readers entirely through the same channel. Knowledge concerning the enormous differences among people is there for any reader, no matter how isolated and protected. And a writer who doesn't read is inexcusable.

Even on television you can see that people are different. Sometimes.

⟐

I'll talk about four common varieties of the Unquestioned Assumption and explore a fifth one in more detail.

1. We're all men.

This assumption turns up in fiction in endless ways: in the belief, borne out by the entire substance of the book, that what men do is of universal interest, while women's occupations are trivial, so that men are the proper focus of story, women peripheral to it; in women being observed only as they relate to men, and their conversation reported only as it relates to men; in vivid descriptions of the bodies and faces of sexually attractive young women, but not of men or older women; in presuming the reader will welcome misogynistic statements; in pretending the pronoun *he* includes both genders; and so on.

This assumption went almost unquestioned in literature until fairly recently. It's still fiercely upheld as legitimate by reactionary and misogynist writers and critics, and is still defended by people who feel that to question it is to question the authority of great writers who accepted it in good faith. It should by now be unnecessary to say that such defensiveness is unnecessary. But alas, the *New York Times* and many academic bastions and bulwarks are still staunchly protecting us from the rabid hordes of man-eating bra-burners out to diminish Shakespeare and demonise Melville. How long will it be, I wonder, before these brave defenders notice that feminist criticism has vastly enriched our reading of such authors, by bringing to an area of darkness and denial the mild, honest illumination of cultural relativism and historical awareness?

2. We're all white.

This assumption is implied far, far too often in fiction by the author's mentioning the skin color only of nonwhite characters. This is to imply unmistakably that white is normal, anything else is abnormal. Other. Not Us.

Like misogyny, actual racial contempt and hatred, often expressed with appalling brutality and self-righteousness, is so frequent in older fiction as to be inescapable. There the reader can only handle it with—

again—historical awareness, which asks for tolerance, though it may or may not lead to forgiveness.

3. WE'RE ALL STRAIGHT.

—"of course." All sexual attraction, any sexual activity in the story, is heterosexual—of course. This Unquestioned Assumption applies to most naive fiction, even now, whether the naivete is deliberate or not.

Straightness as dominant in-group may also be implied by the nudge-and-snigger. A negatively stereotyped fag or dyke is presented by the author with a verbal wink, an invitation to more or less hateful laughter from the reader.

4. WE'RE ALL CHRISTIAN.

Writers who have not noticed that Christianity is not the universal religion of humankind, or who believe that it is the only valid religion of humankind, are likely to take it for granted that the reader will automatically and appropriately respond to Christian imagery and vocabulary (the virgin mother, sin, salvation, and so on). Such writers take a free ride on the cross. In fifteenth-century Europe, this assumption was forgivable. In modern fiction it is, at best, unwise.

A particularly silly sub–in-group is made up of Catholic or ex-Catholic writers convinced that all readers went to parochial school and are obsessed, one way or another, with nuns.

Much more frightening than these are the writers whose description of non-Christian characters exhibits their conviction that outside Christianity there is no spirituality and no morality. Special grace extended to the occasional good Jew or honest unbeliever merely includes that individual in the Christian exclusivity. Monotheistic bigotry beats all.

〜

The fifth group that assumes itself to be universal deserves special examination because it's not often talked about in the context of fiction. The assumption that *we're all young* is a complex one. Our experience of age changes as our age changes—constantly. And age-prejudice runs both ways. Some people carry their in-group right through life: when they're young they despise anybody over thirty, when they're middle-aged they dismiss the young and the old, when they're old they hate kids. Eighty years of prejudice.

Men, whites, straights, and Christians are privileged groups in American society; they have power. Youth is not a power group. But it is a privileged or dominant one in college, in fashion, film, popular music, sports, and the advertising that sets so many norms for us. The tendency at present is to adulate youth without respecting it and sentimentalise old age while despising it.

And to segregate both. In most social situations and at work, including educational work, adults, except for a few designated as caretakers or teachers, are kept segregated from children. The interests of the young and the interests of adults are supposed to be entirely different. Nothing but "the family" is left as a meeting ground, and though politicians, preachers, and pundits prate about "the family," few seem to want to look at what it consists of. Many contemporary families consist of one adult and one child, a subminimal social group, with a single-generation age spread. Divorce and remarriage can create large semidispersed families, but even children with a slew of parents, step-parents, and step-siblings often don't know anybody over fifty. Many older people, by choice or perforce, have no contact with children at all.

I don't know why this curious skewing and segregation of society by age should induce writers to use a youthful viewpoint as if it were the only one; but a great many of them do. The unquestioned assumption is that all readers are young, or identify with the young. The young are Us. Older people are Them, outsiders.

And to be sure, every adult was a child, was an adolescent. We've been there. We shared the experience.

But we aren't there now. Most readers of adult fiction are adults.

A great many book readers are also parents or accept parental responsibility in one way or another. This means that though they may identify with the young, their identification isn't simple. It's extremely complex. It's not a belonging. Nor is it mere recollection. Adults who accept their social or personal responsibility towards children and young people, and who don't need to deny that they were themselves young, have a double or multiple point of view, not a single one.

To write from the child's or adolescent's point of view is of course natural in books written for children or young adults. In books written for adults it is a valid and often powerful literary device. It may simply fulfill nostalgic yearnings to be young again; but the innocent viewpoint is inherently ironic, and in a wise writer's hands may imply the double vision of the adult with particular subtlety. In much recent fiction written for adults, however, the child's vision is not used ironically or to increase complexity, but is, implicitly or openly, valued over the depth of vision of the adult. This is nostalgia with a vengeance.

In such books an absolute division between adult and child is made and a judgment is based on it. Adults are perceived as less fully human than children or young people, and the reader is expected to accept this perception. Parents and authority figures of any kind are presented without compassion or comprehension as automatic enemies, all-powerful wielders of arbitrary power. There may be a few saintly, all-comprehending exceptions proving the rule—powerless old folks, grandparent figures rich in the Primitive Wisdom of Another (note the word) Race. Sentimentality fawns on oversimplification.

As a dead white man of the ruling class remarked, power corrupts. To the extent that adults have more power than kids, adults are inarguably corrupt, while kids are at least relatively innocent. But

innocence is not what defines people as human. It's what we share
with the animals.

An adult indeed may have absolute power over a child and may
abuse it. But even truthful, valid descriptions of abuse are weakened
when the writer's point of view is childish or infantile. To accept the
infantile view of adulthood as omnipotent, readers must abandon their
hard-earned knowledge that most adults in fact have very little power
of any kind.

I will use the same two books as examples as I did in the previous
essay, on fictional characters: *David Copperfield* and *Huckleberry
Finn*.

We are caught in and share young David's perception of his step-
father's cruelty. But Dickens's novel is not about a child abused by jeal-
ous and hateful adults: it is about a child growing up, becoming a man,
a complete human being. All David's mistakes, in fact, are the same
mistake repeated—a childish misperception of false authority as real,
which prevents him from valuing the real help that is always at hand
for him. By the end of the book he has outgrown the infantile myths
that held him helpless.

Dickens as a child was, in many respects, David, but Dickens the
novelist does not confuse himself with that child. He keeps the complex, hard-earned vision. And so *David Copperfield,* fearfully acute in
its understanding of how children suffer, is a book for adults.

Contrast J. D. Salinger's *Catcher in the Rye*. The author adopts the
childish view of adults as inhumanly powerful and uncomprehending,
and never goes beyond it; and so his novel, published for adults, is better appreciated by ten-year-olds.

The childish point of view and the child's point of view aren't
necessarily the same thing. A good deal of *Tom Sawyer* is a rather
uneasy mixture of the two, but *Huckleberry Finn*, though narrated
in a boy's voice, has nothing childish in it. Behind Huck's limited vocabulary, perceptions, and speculations, his ignorances, misconcep-
tions, and prejudices, is the steadfast, lucid, ironic intelligence of

the author, and it is through that intelligence that we understand and feel Huck's moral dilemma, which he has such difficulty understanding himself.

When I read the book as a kid Huck's age, I understood that, as well as anybody under eighteen understands irony. So I could read with understanding even when shocked by some of the language and events—until I came to the episode where the boys, at Tom's insistence, imprison and torment Jim. There I saw the black man I had come to love powerless in the hands of the white children, his fear and grief and patience ignored and devalued, and I thought Twain himself had joined in the wicked game. I thought he approved of it. I didn't understand that he was satirising the cruel mockeries of Reconstruction. I needed that historical knowledge to understand what Twain was doing: that he was honoring me by including me in the same humanity with Jim.

Throughout *Huckleberry Finn,* the boy's unquestioned assumptions (which are those of his society) and the author's convictions and perceptions (which are frequently counter to those of his society) contradict each other deliberately and shockingly. It is a profoundly complex, dangerous book. Those who want literature to be safe will never forgive it for being dangerous.

⟲

Each Unquestioned Assumption has a possible opposite, a reverse, which if written into fiction would give us stories in which men occur only as sexual objects for women, where homosexuality is the social norm, where white skin has to be mentioned whenever it appears, where only godless anarchists act morally, or where adults rebel vainly against the bullying authority of children. Such books are, in my experience, rare. One might meet them in science fiction.

Realistic fiction that merely questions or ignores the assumptions, however, is not unusual. We do have novels that assume that women represent humanity as well as men do; that gays, or people of color, or non-Christians, represent humanity as well as heterosexuals, whites, or Christians do; or that the adult or parental point of view is as valuable as the childish one.

The stigma of "political correctness," invoked by those who see all refusal of bigotry as a liberal conspiracy, may be slapped on such books. They are often ghettoised by publishers and reviewers, segregated from fiction "of general interest." If a novel is centered on the doings of men, or its major characters are male, white, straight, and/or young, nothing is said about them as members of a group, and the story is assumed to be "of general interest." If the major characters are women, or black, or gay, or old, reviewers are likely to say that the book is "about" that group, and it is assumed, even by sympathetic reviewers, to be of interest chiefly or only to that group. Thus both the critical establishment and the publishers' publicity and distribution tactics lend immense authority to prejudice.

A writer may not want to defy both the reactionary critical establishment and the pusillanimous marketplace. "I just want to write this novel about the kind of people I know!" "I just want to sell my book!" Fair enough. But how much collusion with prejudice, disguised as unquestioned assumptions about what is normal, does it take to buy safety?

The risk is real. Look again at Mark Twain. *Huckleberry Finn* is still getting bad-mouthed, banned, and censored, because its characters use the word *nigger* and for other reasons, all having to do with race. Those who allow it to be thus abused in the name of equality include people who think teenagers are incapable of understanding historical context, people who believe education for good involves suppressing knowledge of evil, people who refuse to understand a complex moral purpose, and people who distrust or fear secular literature as a tool of moral and social education. A dangerous book will always be in danger from those it threatens with the demand that they question their assumptions. They'd rather hang on to the assumptions and ban the book.

Safety lies in catering to the in-group. We are not all brave. All I would ask of writers who find it hard to question the universal validity of their personal opinions and affiliations is that they consider this: Every group we belong to—by gender, sex, race, religion, age—is an in-group, surrounded by an immense out-group, living next door and all over the world, who will be alive as far into the future as humanity has a future. That out-group is called other people. It is for them that we write.

PRIDES

An Essay on Writing Workshops

This piece was a contribution to a volume edited by Paul M. Wrigley and Debbie Cross as a benefit for the Susan Petrey Fund and Clarion West Writers Workshop in 1989. This version is different here and there, updated, but the illustrations are the same.

Sometimes I worry about workshops. I've taught quite a few—Clarion West four times; in Australia; at Haystack on the Oregon coast and at the Malheur Field Station in the Oregon desert; at the Indiana and Bennington Writers Conferences, at the Writing Centers in D.C., and at Portland State University; and many times at the beloved and much-missed Flight of the Mind. And I still teach workshops sometimes, though sometimes I think I should stop. Not only because I am getting old and lazy, but because I'm two-minded about workshops, not single-minded. I worry, are they a good thing—yes? no?

I always come down on the Yes side—lightly, but with both feet.

A workshop can certainly do harm as well as good.

The most harmless harm it can do is waste time. This happens when people come to it expecting to teach or be taught how to write. If you think you can teach people how to write you're wasting their time and if they think you can teach them how to write they're wasting yours, and vice (as it were) versa.

People attending workshops are not learning how to write.* What they are learning or doing (as I understand it) will come up later on.

A more harmful harm that can infect the workshop is the ego trip. Classes in literary writing and writers' conferences, years ago, were mostly ego trips—the Great author and his disciples. A good deal of that still goes on at "prestigious" universities and creative writing programs featuring pickled big names. It was the system of mutual group criticism, the Clarion system, now used almost everywhere writing is taught, that freed the pedagogy of writing from hierarchical authority and authorial hierarchy.

But even in a mutual-criticism workshop the instructor can go on an ego trip. I have known an instructor who ran an amateur Esalen, playing mind games and deliberately disintegrating participants' personalities without the faintest idea of how to put them back together. I have known an instructor who ran a little Devil's Island, punishing the participants for writing by trashing their work, except for a favorite trusty or two who got smarmed over. I have known an instructor—oh, many, too many—who ran a little Paris Island, where a week of systematic misogyny was supposed to result in a "few good men." I have known instructors who seemed to be running for a popularity prize, and instructors who just ran away, leaving their students to flounder, not showing up from Monday until Friday, when they came to collect their check.

Such self-indulgence can do real and permanent damage, particularly when the instructor is famous and respected, and the participant is—and they all are more or less—insecure and vulnerable. To offer one's work for criticism is an act of trust requiring real courage. It must be respected as such. I know several people who after a brutal dismissal by a writer they admired stopped writing for years, one of them

---

* I use the verb "to write" here to mean writing literary and/or commercially salable prose. Writing in the sense of how to compose a sentence, why and how to punctuate, etc., can indeed be taught and learned—usually, or at least hopefully, in grade school and high school. It is definitely a prerequisite to writing in the other sense; yet some people come to writing workshops without these skills. They believe that art does not need craft. They are mistaken.

forever. Certainly a writing instructor has a responsibility to defend the art, and the right to set very high standards, but nobody has the right to stop a person from trying to learn. The defense of excellence has nothing whatever to do with bullying.

Ego-tripping by participants can also be destructive to the work of other individuals or of the whole group, unless the instructor is savvy enough to refuse to play games with the troublemaker, who is usually either a manipulative bully or a passive bully, a psychopathically demanding person. I was slow to learn that as the instructor I must refuse to collude with these people. I am still not good at handling them, but have found that if I ask other participants to help me they do so, often with a skill, kindness, and psychological sensitivity that never cease to amaze me.

Perhaps all workshops should have a sign on the door: Do Not Feed the Ego! But then on the other side of the door should be a sign: Do Not Feed the Altruist! Because the practice of any art is impeded by both egoism and altruism. What's needed is concentration on the work.

I shall now go out on a limb, hunch my shoulders, clack my beak, stare fiercely, and announce that I think there are two types of workshop that are to some extent intrinsically harmful. Both types tend to corrupt the work. They do it differently, but are alike in using writing not as an end but as a means. I will call them commercial and establishmentarian.

Commercially oriented workshops and conferences range from the modest kind where everybody is dying to meet the New York editor and the agent who sells in six figures and nothing is talked about but "markets," "good markets for paragraphs," "good markets for religious and uplift," and so on—to the fancy kind where everybody sneers at little old ladies who write paragraphs, but would kill to meet the same editor and the same agent, and where nothing is talked about but "markets," "meeting contacts," "finding an agent with some smarts," "series sales," and so on. All these matters of business are of legitimate, immediate, and necessary interest to a writer. Writers need to learn their trade, and how to negotiate the increasingly difficult marketplace. The trade can be taught and learned just as the craft can. But a workshop where the trade is the principal focus of interest is not a writing workshop. It is a business class.

If success in selling is my primary interest, I am not primarily a writer, but a salesperson. If I teach success in selling as the writer's primary objective, I am not teaching writing; I'm teaching, or pretending to teach, the production and marketing of a commodity.

Establishmentarian workshops and programs, on the other hand, eschew low talk of marketing. *Sell* is a four-letter word at such places. You go to them to be in the right place, where you will meet the right people. The purpose of such programs, most of which are in the eastern half of the United States, is to feed an in-group or elite, the innermost members of which go to the innermost writers colonies and get the uppermost grants by recommending one another.

If being perceived as a successful writer is my primary interest, I am not primarily a writer, but a social climber: a person using certain paraliterary ploys to attain a certain kind of prestige. If I teach these techniques in a workshop, I am not teaching writing, but methods of joining an elite.

It is to be noticed that membership in the elite may, not incidentally, improve one's chances to sell work in the marketplace. There's always a well-kept road between the marketplace and the really nice part of town.

Papa Hemingway said that writers write for money and Papa Freud said that artists work for fame, money, and the love of women. I'll leave out the love of women, though it would be much more fun to talk about. Fame and money—success and power. If you agree with the Papas, there are workshops for you, but this is not the essay for you. I think both Papas were talking through their hats. I don't think writers write for either fame or money, though they love them when they can get them. Writers don't write "for" anything, not even for art's sake. They write. Singers sing, dancers dance, writers write. The whole question of what a thing is "for" has no more to do with art than it has to do with babies, or forests, or galaxies.

In a money economy, artists must sell their work or be supported by gifts while doing it. Since our national government is hysterically suspicious of all artists, and most arts foundations are particularly stingy to writers, North American writers must be directly concerned with the skills of marketing and grant-getting. They need to learn their trade. There are many guidebooks and organisations to help them learn it. But the trade is not the art. Writers and teachers of writing who put salability before quality degrade the writer and the work. Writing workshops that put marketing and contact-making before quality degrade the art.

If you don't agree with me, that's fine. Just keep out of my workshop.

Finally, one more cause of time-wasting: workshop codependency, the policy of encouraging eternal returners, workshop junkies, people who go to retreats and groups year after year but don't write anything the rest of the year . . . and the policy of giving a grant simply because the applicant has received other grants to attend other workshops and writers colonies.

A friend who was at one of the very elite New England artist colonies told me about a woman there who *had no address*. She lived at colonies and conferences. She had published two short stories in the last ten years. She was a professional, all right, but her profession was not writing.

Junkies always bring an old manuscript to the workshop, and when it gets criticised, they tell us about the great writers at greater workshops who said how great it was. If the instructor demands new work from junkies, they are outraged—"But I've been working on this since 1950!" Bearded with moss and in garments green, indistinct in the twilight, they will be hauling out that same damned unfinished manuscript twenty years from now and whining, "But *Longfellow* said it was *tremendously sensitive!*"

But then, I am a workshop junky too: I keep doing them. Why?

So, to the positive side. Maybe nobody can teach anybody how to write, but, just as techniques for attaining profit and prestige can be taught in the commercial and establishmentarian programs, so realistic expectations, useful habits, respect for the art, and respect for oneself as a writer can be acquired in work-centered workshops.

What the instructor has to give is, I think, above all, experience—whether rationalised and verbalised or just shared by being there, being a writer, reading the work, talking about the work.

What most participants need most is to learn to think of themselves as writers.

For the young, this is all too often no problem at all. Many teenagers, college-agers, having no idea what being a fiction writer entails, assume they can write novels and screenplays and play drums in a band and pass their GREs and fifteen other things at the same time, no sweat. This blithe attitude is healthy, it is endearing, and it means they do not belong in a serious workshop (or, in my opinion, in a writing program ending in a degree of any kind). The very young cannot, except in rare cases, make the commitment that is required.

With many adults the problem is the opposite—lack of confidence. Women, particularly women with children, or in middle age and older, may find it enormously difficult to take seriously anything they do that isn't done "for other people"—the altruism trap. Men brought up to consider themselves as wage earners and ordinary joes may in the same way find it hard to take the leap to considering themselves seriously as writers. And this is why, though peer groups of amateur and semi-amateur writers are a wonderful development of the last decades, and though the functioning of the workshop is strictly egalitarian, the workshop has an instructor: a central figure who is a professional, a real, indubitable, published writer, able to share professionalism and lend reality-as-a-writer to everyone in the circle.

And thus it is important that instructors should not be writing teachers but writers teaching: people who have published professionally and actively in the field of the workshop.

And it is important that they should be women as often as they are men. (If they are Gethenians, this latter requirement is no problem; otherwise it should be a central concern of the workshop managers.)

Instructors are not only symbols and gurus. They are directly useful. Their assignments, directions, discussions, exercises, criticisms, responses, and fits of temperament allow the participants to discover that they can meet a deadline, write a short story overnight, try a new form, take a risk, discover gifts they didn't know they had. The instructor directs their practice.

Practice is an interesting word. We think of practicing as beginner's stuff, playing scales, basic exercises. But the practice of an art is the doing of that art—it *is* the art. When the participants have been practicing writing with a bunch of other practicing writers for a week, they can feel with some justification that they are, in fact, writers.

So perhaps the essence of a workshop that works is the group itself. The instructor facilitates the formation of the group, but the circle of people is the source of energy. It is, by the way, important that it be literally, in so far as possible, a circle. This is the Teepee Theory of Workshopping. A circle of units is not a hierarchy. It is one shape made of many, one whole, one thing.

Participants who participate, who write, read, criticise, and discuss, are learning a great deal. First of all, they're learning to take criticism, learning that they *can* take criticism. Negative, positive, aggressive, constructive, valuable, stupid, they can take it. Most of us can, but we don't think we can till we do; and the fear of it can be crippling. To find that you have been roundly criticised and yet have gone on writing—that frees up a lot of energy.

Participants are also learning to read other people's writing and criticise it responsibly. For a good many, this is the first real reading they've ever done: reading not as passive absorption, as in reading junk for relaxation and escape; reading not as detached intellectual analysis, as in English 102; but reading as the intensely active and only partially intellectual process of *collaboration with a text*. A workshop in which one person learned to read that way would have justified itself. But if the group forms, everybody begins reading each other's work that way; and often real reading is so exciting to those new to it that it leads to the overvaluation of texts that is one of the minor hazards of a lively workshop.

Learning to read gives people a whole new approach to writing. They have learned to read what they write. They can turn their critico-collaborative skills onto their own work and so be enabled to revise, to revise constructively, without dreading revision as a destructive process, or a never-ending one, as many inexperienced writers do.

I spoke of the psychological acuteness and sensitivity I have learned to count on and call on in workshop groups. I think it rises from the fact that the people feel that they are working hard together at hard work, and that they have experienced honesty and trust as absolutely essential to getting the work done. So they will use all their skills to achieve that honesty and trust. If the group works as a group, everyone in it, including the instructor, is strengthened by its community and exhilarated by its energy.

This is such a rare and valuable experience that it's no wonder good workshops almost always spin off into small peer groups that may go on working together for months or years.

And it's one reason why I go on teaching. I come home from a workshop and I write.

⟆

The Writer, that noble heroic figure gazing at a blank page who is such an awful bore in books and movies because he doesn't get to bash holes in marble or slash brushes over canvas or conduct gigantic orchestras or die playing Hamlet—he only gets to gaze, and drink, and mope, and crumple up sheets of paper and throw them at a wastebasket, which is just as boring as what he does in real life, which is he sits there, and he sits there, and he sits there, and if you say anything he jumps and shouts WHAT?—the Writer, I say, is not only boring, but lonely, even when, perhaps especially when her family (she has changed sex, like Orlando) is with her, asking where is my blue shirt? when is dinner? The Writer is liable to feel like a little, tiny person all alone in a desert where the sand is words. Giant figures of Best-Sellers and Great Authors loom over her like statues—Look on my works, ye puny, and despair! —This lonely, sitting-there person may find that in a work-centered workshop she can draw on the kind of group support and collaborative rivalry, the pooled energy, that actors, dancers, and musicians, all performing artists, draw on all the time.

And so long as ego-tripping is discouraged, the process of the workshop, depending on mutual aid, stimulation, emulation, honesty, and trust, can produce an unusually pure and clear form of that energy.

The participant may be able to carry some of that energy home, not having learned "how to write," but having learned what it is to write.

I think of a good workshop as a pride of lions at a waterhole. They all hunt zebras all night and then they all eat the zebra, growling a good deal, and then they all come to the waterhole to drink together. Then in the heat of the day they lie around rumbling and swatting flies and looking benevolent. It is something to have belonged, even for a week, to a pride of lions.

ALONE IN THE DESERT OF WORDS

Heading for the
Waterhole

THE QUESTION I GET ASKED
MOST OFTEN

This was a talk, first given for Portland Arts and Lectures in October 2000, then for Seattle Arts and Lectures in April 2002. I have revised it slightly for publication. It has not been published before, though bits of it can be found in my book Steering the Craft *and elsewhere in my writings about writing. As a talk, it was called "Where Do You Get Your Ideas From?"—but in my previous collection of talks and essays,* The Language of the Night, *there's a different essay with that title (there being many answers to the question). So I have retitled it.*

The question fiction writers get asked most often is: Where do you get your ideas from? Harlan Ellison has been saying for years that he gets ideas for his stories from a mail-order house in Schenectady.

When people ask "Where do you get your ideas from?" what some of them really want to know is the e-mail address of that company in Schenectady.

That is: they want to be writers, because they know writers are rich and famous; and they know that there are secrets that writers know; and they know if they can just learn those secrets, that mystical address in Schenectady, they will be Stephen King.

Writers, as I know them, are poor, they are infamous, and they couldn't keep a secret if they had one. Writers are wordy people. They talk, they blab, they yadder. They whine all the time to each other about what they're writing and how hard it is, they teach writing workshops and write writing books and give talks about writing, like this. Writers tell all. If they could tell beginners where to get ideas from, they would. In fact they do, all the time. Some of them actually get somewhat rich and famous by doing it.

What do the how-to-write writers say about getting ideas? They say stuff like: Listen to conversations, note down interesting things you hear or read about, keep a journal, describe a character, imagine a dresser drawer and describe what's in it—Yeah, yeah, but that's all *work*. Anybody can do *work*. I wanna be a writer. What's the address in Schenectady?

Well, the secret to writing is writing. It's only a secret to people who don't want to hear it. Writing is how you be a writer.

ら

So why did I want to try to answer this foolish question, Where do you get your ideas from? Because underneath the foolishness is a real question, which people really yearn to have answered—a big question.

Art is craft: all art is always and essentially a work of craft: but in the true work of art, before the craft and after it, is some essential, durable core of being, which is what the craft works on, and shows, and sets free. The statue in the stone. How does the artist find that, see it, before it's visible? That is a real question.

One of my favorite answers is this: Somebody asked Willie Nelson how he thought of his tunes, and he said, "The air is full of tunes, I just reach up and pick one."

Now that is not a secret. But it is a sweet mystery.

And a true one. A true mystery. That's what it is. For a fiction writer, a storyteller, the world is full of stories, and when a story is there, it's there, and you just reach up and pick it.

Then you have to be able to let it tell itself.

First you have to be able to wait. To wait in silence. Wait in silence, and listen. Listen for the tune, the vision, the story. Not grabbing, not pushing, just waiting, listening, being ready for it when it comes. This is an act of trust. Trust in yourself, trust in the world. The artist says, the world will give me what I need and I will be able to use it rightly.

Readiness—not grabbiness, not greed—readiness: willingness to hear, to listen, listen carefully, to see clearly, see accurately—to let the words be right. Not almost right. Right. To know how to make something out of the vision, that's the craft: that's what practice is for. Because being ready doesn't mean just sitting around, even if it looks like that's what writers mostly do. Artists practice their art continually, and writing is an art that involves a lot of sitting. Scales and finger exercises, pencil sketches, endless unfinished and rejected stories. . . . The artist who practices knows the difference between practice and performance, and the essential connection between them. The gift of those seemingly wasted hours and years is patience and readiness, a good ear, a keen eye, and a skilled hand, a rich vocabulary and grammar. The Lord knows where talent comes from, but craft comes from practice.

With those tools, those instruments, with that hard-earned mastery, that craftiness, artists do their best to let the "idea"—the tune, the vision, the story—come through clear and undistorted. Clear of ineptitude, awkwardness, amateurishness. Undistorted by convention, fashion, opinion.

This is a very radical job, this dealing with the ideas you get if you are an artist and take your job seriously, this shaping a vision into the medium of words. It's what I like best to do in the world, and craft is what I like to talk about when I talk about writing, and I could happily go on and on about it. But I'm trying to talk about where the vision, the stuff you work on, the "idea" comes from. So:

The air is full of tunes.

A piece of rock is full of statues.

The earth is full of visions.

The world is full of stories.

As an artist, you trust that. You trust that that is so. You know it is so. You know that whatever your experience, it will give you the material, the "ideas" for your work. (From here on I'll leave out music and fine arts and stick to storytelling, which is the only thing I truly know anything about, though I do think all the arts are one at the root.)

All right, these "ideas"—what does that word mean? "Idea" is a shorthand way of saying: the material, the subject, subjects, the matter of a story. What the story is about. What the story *is*.

Idea is a strange word for an imagined matter, not abstract but intensely concrete, not intellectual but embodied. However, *idea* is the word we're stuck with. And it's not wholly off center, because the imagination is a rational faculty.

"I got the idea for that story from a dream I had. . . ." "I haven't had a good story idea all year. . . ." "Here am I sitting after half the morning, crammed with ideas, and visions, and so on, and can't dislodge them, for lack of the right rhythm. . . ."

That last sentence was written in 1926 by Virginia Woolf, in a letter to a writer friend; and I will come back in the end to it, because what she says about rhythm goes deeper than anything I have ever thought or read about where art comes from. But before I can talk about rhythm I have to talk about experience and imagination.

Where do writers get their ideas from? From experience. That's obvious.

And from imagination. That's less obvious.

Fiction results from imagination working on experience. We shape experience in our minds so that it makes sense. We force the world to be coherent—to tell us a story.

Not only fiction writers do this; we all do it; we do it constantly, continually, in order to survive. People who can't make the world into a story go mad. Or, like infants or (perhaps) animals, they live in a world that has no history, no time but now.

The minds of animals are a great, sacred, present mystery. I do think animals have languages, but they are entirely truthful languages.

It seems that we are the only animals who can *lie*. We can think and say what is not so and never was so, or what has never been, yet might be. We can invent; we can suppose; we can imagine. All that gets mixed in with memory. And so we're the only animals who tell stories.

An ape can remember and extrapolate from her experience: once I stuck a stick in that ant hill and the ants crawled on it, so if I put this stick in that ant hill again, maybe the ants will crawl on it again, and I can lick them off again, yum. But only we human beings can imagine—can tell the story about the ape who stuck a stick in an anthill and it came out covered with gold dust and a prospector saw it and that was the beginning of the great gold rush of 1877 in Rhodesia.

That story is not true. It is fiction. Its only relation to reality is the fact that some apes do stick sticks in anthills and there was a place once called Rhodesia. But there was no gold rush in 1877 in Rhodesia. I made it up. I am human, therefore I lie. All human beings are liars; that is true; you must believe me.

ᔓ

Fiction: imagination working on experience. A great deal of what we consider our experience, our memory, our hard-earned knowledge, our history, is in fact fiction. But never mind that. I'm talking about real fiction—stories, novels. They all come from the writer's experience of reality worked upon, changed, filtered, distorted, clarified, transfigured, by imagination.

"Ideas" come from the world through the head.

The interesting part of this process to me is the passage through the head, the action of the imagination on the raw material. But that's the part of the process that a great many people disapprove of.

I wrote a piece years ago called "Why Are Americans Afraid of Dragons?" In it I talked about how so many Americans distrust and despise not only the obviously imaginative kind of fiction we call fantasy, but all fiction, often rationalising their fear and contempt with financial or religious arguments: reading novels is a waste of valuable time, the only true book is the Bible, and so on. I said that many Americans have been taught "to repress their imagination, to reject it as something childish or effeminate, unprofitable, and probably sinful. They have learned to fear [the imagination]. But they have never learned to discipline it at all."

I wrote that in 1974. The millennium has come and gone and we still fear dragons.

If you fear something you may try to diminish it. You infantilise it. Fantasy is for children—kiddylit—can't take it seriously. But fantasy also has shown that it can make money. Gotta take *that* seriously. So when the first Harry Potter book, which combined two very familiar conventions, the British school story and the orphan-child-of-great-gifts, hit the big time, many reviewers praised it lavishly for its originality. By which they showed their absolute ignorance of both traditions the book follows—the small one of the school story, and the great one, a tradition that descends from the *Mahabharata* and the *Ramayana,* the *Thousand and One Nights* and *Beowulf* and the Tale of Monkey and medieval romance and Renaissance epic, through Lewis Carroll and Kipling to Tolkien, to Borges and Calvino and Rushdie and the rest of us: a tradition, a form of literature which really cannot be dismissed as "entertainment," "great fun for the kiddies," or "well at least they're reading *something*."

Critics and academics have been trying for forty years to bury the greatest work of imaginative fiction in English. They ignore it, they condescend to it, they stand in large groups with their backs to it—because they're afraid of it. They're afraid of dragons. They have Smaugophobia. "Oh those awful Orcs," they bleat, flocking after Edmund Wilson. They know if they acknowledge Tolkien they'll have to admit that fantasy can be literature, and that therefore they'll have to redefine what literature is. And they're too damned lazy to do it.

What the majority of our critics and teachers call "literature" is still modernist realism. All other forms of fiction—westerns mysteries science fiction fantasy romance historical regional you name it—is dismissed as "genre." Sent to the ghetto. That the ghetto is about twelve times larger than the city, and currently a great deal livelier, so what? Magic realism, though—that bothers them; they hear Gabriel García Márquez gnawing quietly at the foundations of the ivory tower, they hear all these crazy Indians (American ones and Indian ones) dancing up in the attic of the *New York Times Book Review*. They think maybe if they just call it all postmodernism it will go away.

To think that realistic fiction is by definition superior to imaginative fiction is to think imitation is superior to invention. In mean moments I have wondered if this unstated but widely accepted, highly puritanical proposition is related to the recent popularity of the memoir and the personal essay.

But that has been a genuine popularity, a real preference, not a matter of academic canonizing: people really do want to read memoir and personal essay, and writers want to write it. I've felt rather out of step. I like history and biography, sure, but when family and personal memoir seems to be the dominant narrative form—well, I have searched my soul for prejudice, and found it. I prefer invention to imitation. I love novels. I love made-up stuff.

Our high valuation of story drawn directly from personal experience may be a logical extension of our high value for realism in fiction. If faithful imitation of actual experience is fiction's greatest virtue, then memoir is more virtuous than fiction can ever be. The memoir writer's imagination, subordinated to the hard facts, serves to connect the facts aesthetically and to draw from them a moral or intellectual lesson, but is understood to be forbidden to invent. Emotion will certainly be roused, but imagination may scarcely be called upon. Recognition, rather than discovery, is the reward.

True recognition is a true reward. The personal essay is a noble and difficult discipline. I'm not knocking it. I admire it with considerable awe. But I'm not at home in it.

I keep looking for dragons in this country, and not finding any. Or only finding them in disguise.

Some of the most praised recent memoirs have been about grow-ing up in poverty. Hopeless poverty, cruel fathers, incompetent moth-ers, abused children, misery, fear, loneliness. . . . But is this the property of nonfiction? Poverty, cruelty, incompetence, dysfunctional families, injustice, degradation—that is the very stuff of the fireside tale, the folktale, stories of ghosts and vengeance beyond the grave—and of *Jane Eyre,* and *Wuthering Heights,* and *Huckleberry Finn,* and *Cien Años de Soledad.* . . . The ground of our experience is dark, and all our inventions start in that darkness. From it, some of them leap forth in fire.

The imagination can transfigure the dark matter of life. And in many personal essays and autobiographies, that's what I begin to miss, to crave: transfiguration. To recognise our shared, familiar misery is not enough. I want to *recognise something I never saw before.* I want the vision to leap out at me, terrible and blazing—the fire of the trans-figuring imagination. I want the true dragons.

ら

Experience is where the ideas come from. But a story isn't a mirror of what happened. Fiction is experience translated by, transformed by, transfigured by the imagination. Truth includes but is not coextensive with fact. Truth in art is not imitation, but reincarnation.

In a factual history or memoir, the raw material of experience, to be valuable, has to be selected, arranged, and shaped. In a novel, the process is even more radical: the raw materials are not only selected and shaped but fused, composted, recombined, reworked, reconfig-ured, reborn, and at the same time allowed to find their own forms and shapes, which may be only indirectly related to rational thinking. The whole thing may end up looking like pure invention. A girl chained to a rock as a sacrifice to a monster. A mad captain and a white whale. A ring that confers absolute power. A dragon.

But there's no such thing as pure invention. It all starts with expe-rience. Invention is recombination. We can work only with what we have. There are monsters and leviathans and chimeras in the human mind; they are psychic facts. Dragons are one of the truths about us. We have no other way of expressing that particular truth about us. People who deny the existence of dragons are often eaten by dragons. From within.

ᔕ

Another way we have recently taken of showing our deep distrust of the imagination, our puritanical lust to control it and limit it, is in the way we tell stories electronically, on TV and in media such as electronic games and CD-ROMs.

Reading is active. To read a story is to participate actively in the story. To read is to tell the story, tell it to yourself, reliving it, rewriting it with the author, word by word, sentence by sentence, chapter by chapter. . . . If you want proof, just watch an eight-year-old reading a story she likes. She is concentratedly, tensely, fiercely alive. She is as intense as a hunting cat. She is a tiger eating.

Reading is a most mysterious act. It absolutely has not been replaced and will not be replaced by any kind of viewing. Viewing is an entirely different undertaking, with different rewards.

A reader reading *makes* the book, brings it into meaning, by translating arbitrary symbols, printed letters, into an inward, private reality. Reading is an act, a creative one. Viewing is relatively passive. A viewer watching a film does not make the film. To watch a film is to be taken into it—to participate in it—be made part of it. Absorbed by it. Readers eat books. Film eats viewers.

This can be wonderful. It's wonderful to be eaten by a good movie, to let your eyes and ears take your mind into a reality you could never otherwise know. However, passivity means vulnerability; and that's what a great deal of media storytelling exploits.

Reading is an active transaction between the text and the reader. The text is under the control of the reader—she can skip, linger, interpret, misinterpret, return, ponder, go along with the story or refuse to go along with it, make judgments, revise her judgments; she has time and room to genuinely interact. A novel is an active, ongoing collaboration between the writer and the reader.

Viewing is a different transaction. It isn't collaborative. The viewer consents to participate and hands over control to the filmmaker or programmer. Psychically there is no time or room outside an audiovisual narrative for anything but the program. For the viewer, the screen or monitor temporarily becomes the universe. There's very little leeway, and no way to control the constant stream of information and imagery—unless one refuses to accept it, detaches oneself emotionally and intellectually, in which case it appears essentially meaningless. Or one can turn the program off.

Although there's a lot of talk about transactional viewing and *interactive* is a favorite word of programmers, the electronic media are a paradise of control for programmers and a paradise of passivity for viewers. There is nothing in so-called interactive programs except what the programmer put in them; the so-called choices lead only to subprograms chosen by the programmer, no more a choice than a footnote is—do you read it or don't you? The roles in role-playing games are fixed and conventional; there are no characters in games, only personae. (That's why teenagers love them; teenagers need personae. But they have to shed those personae eventually, if they're going to become persons.) Hypertext offers the storyteller a wonderful complexity, but so far hypertext fiction seems to be like Borges's garden of forking paths that lead only to other forking paths, fascinating, like fractals, and ultimately nightmarish. Interactivity in the sense of the viewer controlling the text is also nightmarish, when interpreted to mean that the viewer can rewrite the novel. If you don't like the end of *Moby Dick* you can change it. You can make it happy. Ahab kills the whale. Ooowee.

Readers can't kill the whale. They can only reread until they understand why Ahab collaborated with the whale to kill himself. Readers don't control the text: they genuinely interact with it. Viewers are either controlled by the program or try to control it. Different ball games. Different universes.

When I was working on this talk, a 3-D animated version of *The Little Prince* came out on CD-ROM. The blurb said it "offers more than just the story of the Little Prince. You can, for example, catch an orbiting planet in the Little Prince's universe and learn all about the planet's secrets and its inhabitants."

In the book the prince visits several planets, with extremely interesting inhabitants, and his own tiny planet has an immense secret—a rose—the rose he loves. Do these CD guys think Saint-Exupéry was stingy with his planets? Or are they convinced that stuffing irrelevant information into a work of art enriches it?

Ah, but there is more: you can "enter the Fox Training Game and after you've 'tamed' the fox that the Little Prince meets, he will give you a gift."

Do you remember the fox, in *The Little Prince*? He insists that the little prince tame him. Why? the prince asks, and the fox says that if he is tamed he will always love the wheat fields, because they're the color of the little prince's hair. The little prince asks how to tame him, and the fox says he has to do it by being very patient, sitting down "at a little distance from me in the grass. I shall look at you out of the corner of my eye, and you will say nothing. Words are the source of misunderstanding. But you will sit a little closer to me every day. . . ." And it should be at the same time every day, so that the fox will "know at what hour my heart is to be ready to greet you. One must observe the proper rites."

And so the fox is tamed, and when the little prince is about to leave, "Ah," said the fox, "I shall cry." So the little prince laments, "Being tamed didn't do you any good," but the fox says, "It has done me good, because of the color of the wheat fields." And when they part, the fox says, "I will make you a present of a secret. . . . It is the time you wasted for your rose that makes your rose important. . . . You become responsible, forever, for what you have tamed."

So, then, the child viewing the CD-ROM tames the fox, that is, presses buttons until the food pellet drops into the food dish—no, sorry, that's rats—the child selects the "right" choices from the program till informed that the fox is tamed. Somehow this seems different from imagining doing what the book says: coming back every day at the same time and sitting silently while a fox looks at you from the corner of its eye. Something essential has been short-circuited. Has been falsified. What do you think the fox's "gift" is, in the CD-ROM? I don't know, but if it was a twenty-four-carat gold ring with an emerald, it wouldn't top the fox's gift in the book, which is nine words—"You become responsible, forever, for what you have tamed."

The gift *The Little Prince* gives its readers is itself. It offers them absolutely nothing but a charming story with a few charming pictures, and the chance to face fear, grief, tenderness, and loss.

Which is why that story, written in the middle of a war by a man about to die in that war, is honored by children, adults, and even literary critics. Maybe the CD-ROM isn't as ghastly as it sounds; but it's hard not to see it as an effort to exploit, to tame something that, like a real fox, must be left wild: the imagination of an artist.

༬

Antoine de Saint-Exupéry did crash-land in the desert once, in the 1930s, and nearly died. That is a fact. He did not meet a little prince from another planet there. He met terror, thirst, despair, and salvation. He wrote a splendid factual account of that experience in *Wind, Sand, and Stars*. But later, it got composted, transmuted, transfigured, into a fantastic story of a little prince. Imagination working on experience. Invention springing, like a flower, a rose, out of the desert sands of reality.

Thinking about the sources of art, about where ideas come from, we often give experience too much credit. Earnest biographers often fail to realise that novelists make things up. They seek a direct source for everything in a writer's work, as if every character in a novel were based on a person the writer knew, every plot gambit had to mirror a specific actual event. Ignoring the incredible recombinatory faculty of the imagination, this fundamentalist attitude short-circuits the long, obscure process by which experience becomes story.

Aspiring writers keep telling me they'll start writing when they've gathered experience. Usually I keep my mouth shut, but sometimes I can't control myself and ask them, ah, like Jane Austen? Like the Brontë sisters? Those women with their wild, mad lives cram full of gut-wrenching adventure working as stevedores in the Congo and shooting up drugs in Rio and hunting lions on Kilimanjaro and having sex in SoHo and all that stuff that writers have to do—well, that some writers have to do?

Very young writers usually *are* handicapped by their relative poverty of experience. Even if their experiences are the stuff of which fiction can be made—and very often it's exactly the experiences of childhood and adolescence that feed the imagination all the rest of a writer's life—they don't have *context,* they don't yet have enough to compare it with. They haven't had time to learn that other people exist, people who have had similar experiences, and different experiences, and that they themselves will have different experiences . . . a breadth of comparison, a fund of empathic knowledge, crucial to the novelist, who after all is making up a whole world.

So fiction writers are slow beginners. Few are worth much till they're thirty or so. Not because they lack life experience, but because their imagination hasn't had time to context it and compost it, to work on what they've done and felt, and realise its value is where it's common to the human condition. Autobiographical first novels, self-centered and self-pitying, often suffer from poverty of imagination.

But many fantasies, works of so-called imaginative fiction, suffer from the same thing: imaginative poverty. The writers haven't actually used their imagination, haven't made up anything—they've just moved archetypes around in a game of wish fulfillment. A salable game.

In fantasy, since the fictionality of the fiction, the inventions, the dragons, are all right out in front, it's easy to assume that the story has no relation at all to experience, that everything in a fantasy can be just the way the writer wants it. No rules, all cards wild. All the ideas in fantasy are just wishful thinking—right? Well, no. Wrong.

It may be that the further a story gets away from common experience and accepted reality, the less wishful thinking it can do, the more firmly its essential ideas must be grounded in common experience and accepted reality.

Serious fantasy goes into regions of the psyche that may be very strange territory, dangerous ground, places where wise psychologists tread cautiously: and for that reason, serious fantasy is usually both conservative and realistic about human nature. Its mode is usually comic not tragic—that is, it has a more or less happy ending—but, just as the tragic hero brings his tragedy on himself, the happy outcome in fantasy is *earned* by the behavior of the protagonist. Serious fantasy invites the reader on a wild journey of invention, through wonders and marvels, through mortal risks and dangers—all the time hanging on to a common, everyday, realistic morality. Generosity, reliability, compassion, courage: in fantasy these moral qualities are seldom questioned. They are accepted, and they are tested—often to the limit, and beyond.

The people who write the stuff on the book covers obsessively describe fantasy as "a battle between good and evil." That phrase describes serious fantasy only in the sense of Solzhenitsyn's saying: "The line between good and evil runs straight through every human heart." In serious fantasy, the real battle is moral and internal. We have met the enemy, as Pogo said, and he is us. To do good, heroes must know or learn that the "axis of evil" is within them.

In commercial fantasy the so-called battle of good and evil is a mere power struggle. Look at how they act: the so-called good wizards and the so-called bad ones are equally violent and irresponsible. This is about as far from Tolkien as you can get.

But why should moral seriousness matter, why do probability and consistency matter, when it's "all just made up"?

Well, moral seriousness is what makes a fantasy matter, because it's what's real in the story. A made-up story is inevitably trivial if nothing real is at stake, if mere winning, coming out on top, replaces moral choice. Easy wish fulfillment has a great appeal to children, who are genuinely powerless; but if it's all a story has to offer, in the end it's not enough.

In the same way, the purer the invention, the more important is its credibility, consistency, coherence. The rules of the invented realm must be followed to the letter. All magicians, including writers, are extremely careful about their spells. Every word must be the right word. A sloppy wizard is a dead wizard. Serious fantasists delight in invention, in the freedom to invent, but they know that careless invention kills the magic. Fantasy shamelessly flouts fact, but it is as deeply concerned with truth as the grimmest, greyest realism.

A related point: The job of the imagination, in making a story from experience, may be not to gussy it up, but to tone it down. The world is unbelievably strange, and human behavior is frequently so weird that no kind of narrative except farce or satire can handle it. I am thinking of a true story I heard about a man who rationed his daughters' toilet paper. He had three daughters and it infuriated him that they used so much toilet paper, so he tore all the toilet paper rolls into the little component squares, and made three piles of six squares on the bathroom counter, and each daughter was to use one pile each day. You see what I mean? In a case like this, the function of the imagination is to judge whether anything so bizarre belongs in the story without turning it into farce or mere gross-out.

The whole matter of "leaving it to the imagination"—that is, including elements of the story only by allusion and implication—is enormously important. Even journalists can't report the full event, but can only tell bits of it; both the realist and the fantasist leave out a tremendous amount, *suggesting* through imagery or metaphors just enough that the reader can imagine the event.

And the reader does just that. Story is a collaborative art. The writer's imagination works in league with the reader's imagination, calls on the reader to collaborate, to fill in, to flesh out, to bring their own experience to the work. Fiction is not a camera, and not a mirror. It's much more like a Chinese painting—a few lines, a few blobs, a whole lot of blank space. From which *we* make the travellers, in the mist, climbing the mountain towards the inn under the pines.

ᔕ

I have written fantastic stories closely based on actual experience, and realistic stories totally made up out of moonshine; some of my science fiction is full of accurate and carefully researched fact, while my stories about ordinary people doing ordinary things on the Oregon coast in 1990 contain large wetlands and quicksands of pure invention. I will refer to some of my own works in hopes of showing how fictional "ideas" arise from a combination of experience and imagination that is indissoluble and unpredictable and doesn't follow orders.

In my Earthsea books, particularly the first one, people sail around all the time on the sea in small boats. They do it quite convincingly, and many people understandably assume that I spent years sailing around on the sea in small boats.

My entire experience with sailboats was in my junior semester in Berkeley High School, when they let us take Sailing for gym credit. On a windy day in the Berkeley Marina, my friend Jean and I managed to overturn and sink a nine-foot catboat in three feet of water. We sang "Nearer My God to Thee" as she went down, and then waded a half mile back to the boathouse. The boatman was incredulous. You *sank* it? he said. *How?*

That will remain one of the secrets of the writer.

All right, so all that sailing around that Ged does in Earthsea does not reflect experience—not *my* experience. Only my imagination, using that catboat, and *other people's* experience—novels I'd read—and some research (I do know why *Lookfar* is clinkerbuilt), and asking friends questions, and some trips on ocean liners. But basically, it's a fake.

So is all the snow and ice in *The Left Hand of Darkness*. I never even saw snow till I was seventeen and I certainly never pulled a sledge across a glacier. Except with Scott, and Shackleton, and those guys. In books. Where do you get your ideas from? From books, of course, from other people's books, what are books for? If I didn't read how could I write?

We writers all stand on each other's shoulders, we all use each other's ideas and skills and plots and secrets. Literature is a communal enterprise. That "anxiety of influence" stuff is just testosterone talking. Understand me: I don't mean plagiarism: I'm not talking about imitation, or copying, or theft. If I thought I had really deliberately used any other writer's writing, I certainly wouldn't stand here congratulating myself, I'd go hide my head in a paper bag (along with several eminent historians). What I mean is that stuff from other people's books gets into us just as our own experience does, and like actual experience gets composted and transmuted and transformed by the imagination, and comes forth entirely changed, our own, growing out of our own mind's earth.

So, I acknowledge with delight my endless debt to every storyteller I have ever read, factual or fictional, my colleagues, my collaborators—I praise them and honor them, the endless givers of gifts.

In my science fiction novel set on a planet populated by people whose gender arrangements are highly imaginative, the part about two people hauling a sledge across a glacier is as factually accurate as I could make it, down to the details of their gear and harness, how much weight they haul, how far they can get in a day, what different snow surfaces are like, and so on. None of this is from my direct experience;

all of it is from the books I've read about the Antarctic ever since I was in my twenties. It is factual material woven into a pure fantasy. As a matter of fact, so is all the stuff about their gender arrangements; but that's a little too complicated to go into here.

Once I wanted to write a story from the point of view of a tree. The "idea" of the story came with the sight of an oak alongside the road to McMinnville. I was thinking as we drove by that when that oak was young, Highway 18 was a quiet country road. I wondered what the oak thought about the highway, the cars. Well, so, where do I get the experience of being a tree, on which my imagination is to work? Books don't help much here. Unlike Shackleton and Scott, oaks don't keep diaries. Personal observation is my only experiential material. I have seen a lot of oaks, been around oaks, been in some oaks, externally, climbing around; now I want to be in one internally, inside. What does it feel like to be an oak? Large, for one thing; lively, but quiet, and not very flexible, except at the tips, out there in the sunlight. And deep— very deep—roots going down in the dark. . . . To live rooted, to be two hundred years in one place, unmoving, yet traveling immensely through the seasons, the years, through time . . . Well, you know how it's done. You did it as a kid, you still do it. If you don't do it, your dreams do it for you.

In dreams begins responsibility, said a poet. In dreams, in imagination, we begin to be one another. I am thou. The barriers go down.

ꜱ

Big stories, novels, don't come from just one stimulus but a whole clumping and concatenation of ideas and images, visions and mental perceptions, all slowly drawing in around some center which is usually obscure to me until long after the book's done and I finally say Oh, *that's* what that book's about. To me, two things are essential during the drawing-together, the clumping process, before I know much of anything about the story: I have to see the place, the landscape; and I have to know the principal people. By name. And it has to be the right name. If it's the wrong name, the character won't come to me. I won't know who they are. I won't be able to be them. They won't talk. They won't *do* anything. Please don't ask me how I arrive at the name and how I know when it's the right name; I have no idea. When I hear it, I know it. And I know where the person is. And then the story can begin.

Here is an example: my recent book *The Telling*. Unlike most of my stories, it started with something you really could call an idea—a fact I had learned. I have been interested most of my life in the Chinese philosophy called Taoism. At the same time that I finally also learned a little about the religion called Taoism, an ancient popular religion of vast complexity, a major element of Chinese culture for two millennia, I learned that it had been suppressed, almost entirely wiped out, by Mao Tse-tung. In one generation, one psychopathic tyrant destroyed a tradition two thousand years old. In my lifetime. And I knew nothing about it.

The enormity of the event, and the enormity of my ignorance, left me stunned. I had to think about it. Since the way I think is fiction, eventually I had to write a story about it. But how could I write a novel about China? My poverty of experience would be fatal. A novel set on an imagined world, then, about the extinction of a religion as a deliberate political act . . . counterpointed by the suppression of political freedom by a theocracy? All right, there's my theme, my idea if you will.

I'm impatient to get started, impassioned by the theme. So I look for the people who will tell me the story, the people who are going to live this story. And I find this uppity kid, this smart girl who goes from Earth to that world. I don't remember what her name was, she had five different names and none of them was the true name. I started the book five times, it got nowhere. I had to stop.

I had to sit patiently and say nothing, at the same time every day, while the fox looked at me from the corner of its eye, and slowly let me get a little bit closer.

And finally the woman whose story it was spoke to me. I'm Sutty, she said. Follow me. So I followed her; and she led me up into the high mountains; and she gave me the book.

I had a good idea, but I did not have a story. Critics talk as if stories were all idea, but intellect does not make story any more than ideology makes art. The story had to make itself, find its center, find its voice, Sutty's voice. Then, because I was waiting for it, it could give itself to me.

Or put it this way: I had a lot of stuff in my head, good stuff, clear ideas—but I couldn't pull it together, I couldn't dance with it, because I hadn't waited to catch the beat. I didn't have the rhythm.

ꙅ

This book takes its title from a letter from Virginia Woolf to her friend Vita Sackville-West. Vita had been pontificating about finding the right word, Flaubert's *mot juste,* and agonising very Frenchly about style; and Virginia wrote back, very Englishly:

> As for the *mot juste,* you are quite wrong. Style is a very simple matter: it is all *rhythm.* Once you get that, you can't use the wrong words. But on the other hand here am I sitting after half the morning, crammed with ideas, and visions, and so on, and can't dislodge them, for lack of the right rhythm. Now this is very profound, what rhythm is, and goes far deeper than words. A sight, an emotion, creates this wave in the mind, long before it makes words to fit it; and in writing (such is my present belief) one has to recapture this, and set this working (which has nothing apparently to do with words) and then, as it breaks and tumbles in the mind, it makes words to fit it. But no doubt I shall think differently next year.

Woolf wrote that eighty years ago, and if she did think differently next year, she didn't tell anybody. She says it lightly, but she means it:

this is very profound. I have not found anything more profound, or more useful, about the source of story—where the ideas come from.

Beneath memory and experience, beneath imagination and invention—beneath *words,* as she says—there are rhythms to which memory and imagination and words all move; and the writer's job is to go down deep enough to begin to feel that rhythm, to find it, move to it, be moved by it, and let it move memory and imagination to find words.

She's full of ideas but she can't dislodge them, she says, because she can't find their rhythm—can't find the beat that will unlock them, set them moving forward into a story, get them telling themselves.

A wave in the mind, she calls it; and says that a sight or an emotion may create it—like a stone dropped into still water, and the circles go out from the center in silence, in perfect rhythm, and the mind follows those circles outward and outward till they turn to words . . . but her image is greater: her wave is a sea wave, traveling smooth and silent a thousand miles across the ocean till it strikes the shore, and crashes, breaks, and flies up in a foam of words. But the wave, the rhythmic impulse, is before words, "has nothing to do with words." So the writer's job is to recognise the wave, the silent swell, way out at sea, way out in the ocean of the mind, and follow it to shore, where it can turn or be turned into words, unload its story, throw out its imagery, pour out its secrets. And ebb back into the ocean of story.

What is it that prevents the ideas and visions from finding their necessary underlying rhythm, why couldn't Woolf "dislodge" them that morning? It could be a thousand things, distractions, worries; but very often I think what keeps a writer from finding the words is that she grasps at them too soon, hurries, grabs; she doesn't wait for the wave to come in and break. She wants to write because she's a writer; she wants to say this, and tell people that, and show people something else, things she knows, her ideas, her opinions, her beliefs, important ideas . . . but she doesn't wait for the wave to come and carry her beyond all the ideas and opinions, to where you *cannot use the wrong word*.

None of us is Virginia Woolf, but I hope every writer has had at least a moment when they rode the wave, and all the words were right.

As readers, we have all ridden that wave, and known that joy.

Prose and poetry—all art, music, dance—rise from and move with the profound rhythms of our body, our being, and the body and being of the world. Physicists read the universe as a great range of vibrations, of rhythms. Art follows and expresses those rhythms. Once we get the beat, the right beat, our ideas and our words dance to it, the round dance that everybody can join. And then I am thou, and the barriers are down. For a little while.

OLD BODY NOT WRITING

Some bits of this went into a piece called "Writer's Block" for the New York Times *Syndicate, and a small part went into* Steering the Craft. *It is a rambling meditation that I came back to on and off over several years, when I wasn't writing what I wanted to be writing.*

Just now I'm not writing. That is, I'm writing here and now that I'm not writing, because I am unhappy about not writing. But if I have nothing to write I have nothing to write. Why can't I wait in patience till I do? Why is the waiting hard?

Because I am not as good at anything else and nothing else is as good. I would rather be writing than anything else.

Not because it is a direct pleasure in the physical sense, like a good dinner or sex or sunlight. Composition is hard work, involving the body not in satisfying activity and release but only in stillness and tension. It is usually accompanied by uncertainty as to the means and the outcome, and often surrounded by a kind of driving anxiety ("I have to finish this before I die and finishing it is going to kill me"). In any case, while actually composing, I'm in a kind of trance state that isn't pleasant or anything else. It has no qualities. It is unconsciousness of self. While writing I am unconscious of my existence or any existence except in the words as they sound and make rhythms and connect and make syntax and in the story as it happens.

Aha, then writing is an escape? (Oh the Puritan overtones in that word!) An escape from dissatisfactions, incompetences, woes? Yes, no doubt. And also a compensation for lack of control over life, for powerlessness. Writing, I'm in power, I control, I choose the words and shape the story. Don't I?

Do I? Who's I? Where's I while I write? Following the beat. The words. They're in control. It's the story that has the power. I'm what follows it, records it. That's my job, and the work is in doing my job right.

We use *escape* and *compensation* negatively, and so we can't used them to define the act of making, which is positive and irreducible to anything but itself. True making is truly satisfying. It is more truly satisfying than anything I know.

So when I have nothing to write I have nothing to escape to, nothing to compensate with, nothing to give control to, no power to share in, and no satisfaction. I have to just be here being old and worried and muddling and afraid that nothing makes sense. I miss and want that thread of words that runs through day and night leading me through the labyrinth of the years. I want a story to tell. What will give me one?

Having a clear time to write, often I sit and think hard, forcefully, powerfully, and make up interesting people and interesting situations from which a story could grow. I write them down, I work at them. But nothing grows. I am trying to make something happen, not waiting till it happens. I don't have a story. I don't have the person whose story it is.

When I was young, I used to know that I had a story to write when I found in my mind and body an imaginary person whom I could embody myself in, with whom I could identify strongly, deeply, bodily. It was so much like falling in love that maybe that's what it was.

That's the physical side of storytelling, and it's still mysterious to me. Since I was in my sixties it has happened again (with Teyeo and Havzhiva in *Four Ways to Forgiveness,* for example) to my great delight, for it's an active, intense delight, to be able to live in the character night and day, have the character living in me, and their world

overlapping and interplaying with my world. But I didn't embody so
deeply with anybody in *Searoad,* nor with most of my characters in the
last ten or fifteen years. Yet writing *Tehanu* or "Sur" or "Hernes" was
as exciting as anything I ever did, and the satisfaction was solid.

I still find embodying or identifying most intense when the character is a man—when the body is absolutely not my own. That reach or
leap across gender has an inherent excitement in it (which is probably
why it is like falling in love). My identification with women characters
such as Tenar or Virginia or Dragonfly is different. There is an even
more sexual aspect to it, but not genital sexuality. Deeper. In the middle of my body, where you center from in t'ai chi, where the chi is. That
is where my women live in me.

This embodying business may be different for men and women (if
other writers do it at all—how do I know?). But I incline to believe Virginia Woolf was right in thinking that the real thing goes on way past
gender. Norman Mailer may seriously believe that you have to have
balls to be a writer. If you want to write the way he writes I suppose
you do. To me a writer's balls are irrelevant if not annoying. Balls
aren't where the action is. When I say the middle of the body I don't
mean balls, prick, cunt, or womb. Sexualist reductionism is as bad as
any other kind. If not worse.

When I had a hysterectomy, I worried about my writing, because
sexualist reductionism had scared me. But I'm sure it wasn't as bad for
me as losing his balls would be for a man like Norman Mailer. Never
having identified my sex, my sexuality, or my writing with my fertility,
I didn't have to trash myself. I was able, with some pain and fear but
not dreadful pain and fear, to think about what the loss meant to me
as a writer, a person in a body who writes.

What it felt like to me was that in losing my womb I had indeed
lost some connection, a kind of easy, bodily imagination, that had to
be replaced, if it could be replaced, by the mental imagination alone.
For a while I thought that I could not embody myself in an imagined
person as I used to. I thought I couldn't "be" anyone but me.

I don't mean that when I had a womb I believed that I carried characters around in it like fetuses. I mean that when I was young I had a complete, unthinking, bodily connection and emotional apprehension of my imagined people.

Now (perhaps because of the operation, perhaps through mere aging) I was obliged to make the connection deliberately in the mind. I had to reach out with a passion that was not simply physical. I had to "be" other people in a more radical, complete way.

This wasn't necessarily a loss. I began to see it might be a gain, forcing me to take the more risky way. The more intelligence the better, so long as the passion, the bodily emotional connection is made, is there.

Essays are in the head, they don't have bodies the way stories do: that's why essays can't satisfy me in the long run. But headwork is better than nothing, as witness me right now, making strings of words to follow through the maze of the day (a very simple maze: one or two choices, a food pellet for a reward). Any string of meaningfully connected words is better than none.

If I can find intensely felt meaning in the words or invest them with it, better yet—whether the meaning be intellectual, as now, or consist in their music, in which case I would, *¡ojalá!* be writing poetry.

Best of all is if they find bodies and begin to tell a story.

Up there I said "be" somebody, "have the person," "find the person." This is the mystery.

I use the word *have* not in the sense of "having" a baby, but in the sense of "having" a body. To have a body is to be embodied. Embodiment is the key.

My plans for stories that don't become stories all lack that key, the person or people whose story it is, the heart, the soul, the embodied inwardness of a person or several people. When I am working on a story that isn't going to work, I make people up. I could describe them the way the how-to-write books say to do. I know their function in the story. I write about them—but I haven't found them, or they haven't found me. They don't inhabit me, I don't inhabit them. I don't *have* them. They are bodiless. So I don't have a story.

But as soon as I make this inward connection with a character, I know it body and soul, I *have* that person, I am that person. To have the person (and with the person, mysteriously, comes the name) is to have the story. Then I can begin writing directly, trusting the person knows where she or he is going, what will happen, what it's all about.

This is extremely risky, but it works for me, these days, more often than it used to. And it makes for a story that is without forced or extraneous elements, all of a piece, uncontrolled by intrusions of opinion, willpower, fear (of unpopularity, censorship, the editor, the market, whatever), or other irrelevancies.

So my search for a story, when I get impatient, is not so much looking for a topic or subject or nexus or resonance or place-time (though all that is or will be involved) as casting about in my head for a stranger. I wander about the mental landscape looking for somebody, an Ancient Mariner or a Miss Bates, who will (almost certainly not when I want them, not when I invite them, not when I long for them, but at the most inconvenient and impossible time) begin telling me their story and not let me go until it's told.

The times when nobody is in the landscape are silent and lonely. They can go on and on until I think nobody will ever be there again but one stupid old woman who used to write books. But it's no use trying to populate it by willpower. These people come only when they're ready, and they do not answer to a call. They answer silence.

Many writers now call any period of silence a "block."

Would it not be better to look on it as a clearing? A way to go till you get where you need to be?

If I want to write and have nothing to write I do indeed feel blocked, or rather chocked—full of energy but nothing to spend it on, knowing my craft but nothing to use it on. It is frustrating, wearing, infuriating. But if I fill the silence with constant noise, writing anything in order to be writing something, forcing my willpower to invent situations for stories, I may be blocking myself. It's better to hold still and wait and listen to the silence. It's better to do some kind of work that keeps the body following a rhythm but doesn't fill up the mind with words.

I have called this waiting "listening for a voice." It has been that, a voice. It was that in "Hernes," all through, when I'd wait and wait, and then the voice of one of the women would come and speak through me.

But it's more than voice. It's a bodily knowledge. Body is story; voice tells it.

THE WRITER ON, AND AT, HER WORK

Written for Janet Sternburg's 1995 anthology The Writer on Her Work, *volume 2,* New Essays in New Territory.

Her work
is never done.
She has been told that
and observed it for herself.
   Her work
spins unrelated filaments
into a skein: the whorl
or wheel turns the cloudy mass
into one strong thread,
over, and over, and over.
   Her work
weaves unrelated elements
into a pattern: the shuttle
thrown across the warp
makes roses, mazes, lightning,
over, and over, and over.
   Her work
brings out of dirt and water
a whole thing, a hole where
the use of the pot is,

a container for the thing
contained, a holy thing, a holder,
a saver,
happening on the clayey wheel
between her and her clayey hands,
over, and over, and over.
      Her work
is with pots and baskets,
bags, cans, boxes, carryalls,
pans, jars, pitchers, cupboards, closets,
rooms, rooms in houses, doors,
desks in the rooms in the houses,
drawers and pigeonholes in the desks,
secret compartments
in which lie for generations
secret letters.
      Her work
is with letters,
with secret letters.
Letters that were not written
for generations.
She must write them
over, and over, and over.

      She works with her body,
a day-laborer.
She labors, she travails,
sweating and complaining,
She is her instrument,
whorl, shuttle, wheel.
She is the greasy wool and the raw clay
and the wise hands

that work by day
for the wages of the worker.
    She works within her body,
a night creature.
She runs between the walls.
She is hunted down and eaten.
She prowls, pounces, kills, devours.
She flies on soundless wings.
Her eyes comprehend the darkness.
The tracks she leaves are bloody,
and at her scream
everything holds still,
hearing that other wisdom.

    Some say any woman working
is a warrior.
I resist that definition.
A fighter in necessity, sure,
a wise fighter,
but a professional?
One of los Generales?
Seems to me she has better things
to do than be a hero.
Medals were made for flatter chests.
They sort of dangle off her tits
and look embarrassing.
The uniforms don't fit.
If she shoots from the hip,
she hears the freudians applauding—
See? See? they say,
See? See? She wants one!
(She wants mine!

She can't have it!
She can't can she Daddy?

                No, son.)

Others say she's a goddess,
The Goddess, transcendant,
knowing everything by nature,
the Archetype
at the typewriter.
I resist that definition.

    Her work, I really think her work
isn't fighting, isn't winning,
isn't being the Earth, isn't being the Moon.
Her work, I really think her work
is finding what her real work is
and doing it,
her work, her own work,
her being human,
her being in the world.

So, if I am
a writer, my work
is words. Unwritten letters.
    Words are my way of being
human, woman, me.
Word is the whorl that spins me,
the shuttle thrown though the warp of years
to weave a life, the hand
that shapes to use, to grace.
Word is my tooth,
my wing.

Word is my wisdom.

I am a bundle of letters
in a secret drawer
in an old desk.
What is in the letters?
What do they say?

I am kept here a prisoner by the evil Duke.

Georgie is much better now, and I have been canning peaches like mad.

I cannot tell my husband or even my sister, I cannot live without you, I think of you day and night, when will you come to me?

My brother Will hath gone to London and though I begg'd with all my heart to go with him nor he nor my Father would have it so, but laugh'd and said, Time the wench was married.

The ghost of a woman walks in this house. I have heard her weeping in the room that was used as a nursery.

If I only knew that my letters were reaching you, but there is no way to get information at any of the bureaus, they will not say where you have been sent.

Don't grieve for me. I know what I am doing.

Bring the kids and they can all play together and we
can sit and talk till we're blue in the face.

Did he know about her cousin Roger and the shotgun?

I don't know if it's any good but I've been working on
it since September.

How many of us will it take to hang him?

I am taking the family to America, the land of
Freedom.

I have found a bundle of old letters in a secret com-
partment in my desk.

Letters of words of stories:
they tell stories.
The writer tells stories, the stories,
over, and over, and over.

Man does, they say, and Woman is.
Doing and being. Do and be.
O.K., I be writing, Man.
I be telling.
("Je suis la où ça parle,"
says la belle Hélène.)
I be saying and parlaying.
I be being
this way. How do I do being?
Same way I be doing.

I would call it working
or else, it doesn't matter, playing.

    The writer at her work
is playing.
Not chess not poker not monopoly,
none of the war games—
Even if she plays by all their rules
and wins—wins what?
Their funny money?—
not playing hero,
not playing god—
well, but listen, making things
is a kind of godly business, isn't it?
All right, then, playing god,
Aphrodite the Maker, without whom
"nothing is born into the shining
borders of light, nor is anything lovely or lovable made,"
Spider Grandmother, spinning,
Thought Woman, making it all up,
Coyote Woman, playing—
playing it, a game,
without a winner or a loser,
a game of skill, a game of make
believe.

Sure it's a gamble,
but not for money.
Sorry Ernie this ain't stud.
The stakes
are a little higher.

The writer at her work
is odd, is peculiar, is particular,
certainly, but not, I think,
singular.
She tends to the plural.

I for example am Ursula; Miss
Ursula Kroeber;
Mrs. then Ms Le Guin;
Ursula K. Le Guin; this latter is
"the writer," but who were,
who are, the others?
She is the writer
at their work.

What are they doing,
those plurals of her?
Lying in bed.
Lazy as hound dogs.
She-Plural is lying in bed
in the morning early.
Long before light, in winter;
in summer "the morning people
are chirping on the roof."
And like the sparrows
her thoughts go hopping
and flying and trying out words.
And like the light of morning
her thought impalpably touches
shape, and reveals it,
brings seeing from dimness,
being from inexhaustible chaos.

That is the good time.
That is the time when this she-plural writer
finds what is to be written.
In the first light,
seeing with the eyes
of the child waking,
lying between sleep and the day
in the body of dream,
in the body of flesh
that has been/is
a fetus, a baby, a child, a girl, a woman, a lover, a mother,
has contained other bodies,
incipient beings, minds unawakened, not to awaken,
has been sick, been damaged, been healed,
been old, is born and dying, will die,
in the mortal, inexhaustible
body
of her work:

That is the good time.

Spinning the fleece of the sun, that cloudy mass,
weaving a glance and a gesture,
shaping the clay of emotion:
housekeeping. Patterning.
Following patterns.
Lying there
in the dreamtime
following patterns.

　　So then you have to cut it out—
take a deep breath,

the first cut, the blank page!—
and sew it together (drudgery,
toil in the sacred sweatshop),
the garment, the soul-coat,
the thing made of words,
cloth of the sunfleece,
the new clothes of the Emperor.

(Yes, and some kid comes along
and yaps, "But he hasn't any clothes on!"
Muzzle the brat
till it learns
that none of us has any clothes on,
that our souls are naked,
dressed in words only,
in charity only,
the gift of the others.
Any fool can see through it.
Only fools say so.)

    Long ago when I was Ursula
writing, but not "the writer,"
and not very plural yet,
and worked with the owls not the sparrows,
being young, scribbling at midnight:

I came to a place
I couldn't see well in the darkness,
where the road turned
and divided, it seemed like,
going different ways.
I was lost.

I didn't know which way.
It looked like one roadsign said To Town
and the other didn't say anything.

So I took the way that didn't say.
I followed
myself.
"I don't care," I said,
terrified.
"I don't care if nobody ever reads it!
I'm going *this* way."

And I found myself
in the dark forest, in silence.

You maybe have to find yourself,
yourselves,
in the dark forest.
Anyhow, I did then. And still now,
always. At the bad time.

    When you find the hidden catch
in the secret drawer
behind the false panel
inside the concealed compartment
in the desk in the attic
of the house in the dark forest,
and press the spring firmly,
a door flies open to reveal
a bundle of old letters,
and in one of them
is a map

of the forest
that you drew yourself
before you ever went there.

The Writer At Her Work:
I see her walking
on a path through a pathless forest,
or a maze, a labyrinth.
As she walks she spins,
and the fine thread falls behind her
following her way,
telling
where she is going,
where she has gone.
Telling the story.
The line, the thread of voice,
the sentences saying the way.

The Writer On Her Work:
I see her, too, I see her
lying on it.
Lying, in the morning early,
rather uncomfortable.
Trying to convince herself
that it's a bed of roses,
a bed of laurels,
or an innerspring mattress,
or anyhow a futon.
But she keeps twitching.

There's a *lump,* she says.
There's something

like a *rock*—like a *lentil*—
I can't sleep.

There's something
the size of a split pea
that I haven't written.
That I haven't written right.
I can't sleep.

She gets up
and writes it.
Her work
is never done.

CREDITS

"Introducing Myself," copyright © 1992 by Ursula K. Le Guin, first appeared in *Left Bank*.

"My Island," copyright © 1996 by Ursula K. Le Guin, first appeared in *Islands: An International Magazine*.

"On the Frontier," copyright © 2003 by Ursula K. Le Guin; an earlier version of this essay entitled "Which Side Am I On, Anyway?" appeared in *Frontiers*, 1996.

"All Happy Families," copyright © 1997 by Ursula K. Le Guin, first appeared in *Michigan Quarterly Review,* Winter 1997.

"Things Not Actually Present: On *The Book of Fantasy* and J. L. Borges," copyright © 1988 by Ursula K. Le Guin, first appeared as the introduction to the Viking edition of *The Book of Fantasy*.

"Reading Young, Reading Old: Mark Twain's *Diaries of Adam and Eve*," copyright © 1995 by Ursula K. Le Guin, first appeared as the introduction to *The Diaries of Adam and Eve* in The Oxford Mark Twain.

"Thinking about Cordwainer Smith," copyright © 1994 by Ursula K. Le Guin, first appeared in the Readercon 6 program book.

"Rhythmic Pattern in *The Lord of the Rings*," copyright © 2001 by Ursula K. Le Guin, first appeared in *Meditations on Middle Earth*.